AS FOR PROTO- COLS

AS FOR PROTO-COLS

WITH CONTRIBUTIONS BY

Salome Asega
Carolina Caycedo with
Lupita Limón Corrales
Raven Chacon
Jesse Chun
Asia Dorsey
Taraneh Fazeli and
Cannach MacBride
Pablo Helguera
Emmanuel Iduma
Mary Maggic
Shannon Mattern
V. Mitch McEwen with
Nadir Jeevanjee
Rashaun Mitchell with
Silas Riener
Romy Opperman
Rasheedah Phillips
Leanne Betasamosake Simpson with
Maria Hupfield
Ultra-red with
Robert Sember
Underground Resistance

EDITED BY

Re'al Christian
Carin Kuoni
Eriola Pira

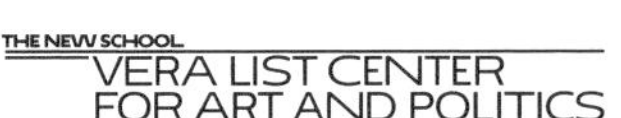

Amherst
College
Press

SCORE FOR AN UNRELIABLE NARRATOR

Raven Chacon

You are a storyteller and may be one of the following:

A: You have a past, but you remember it with more detail than you should. And these details cannot be stopped by time. They have become a tradition.

B: You have a past that you don't believe suits you. You are willing to delete anything that shares the real story with you. There are no taboos.

C: You have no past. Either you have forgotten it or it was erased from you. You are piecing together the rest of the story from the information of others and you have placed yourself inside. This is your protocol.

D: You want to have no past, because it is as meaningless as the future. Yet you are inspired by a linear chaos of the universe. There are no rules.

Enact all of these prompts, at least one when taking a break from this book. If you are not any of these types of storyteller, become one.

Question why you have always done things in the same way.

Prevent another from doing something you have done.

Try to stall Time.

Become unreliable narrator A if you are not already.

Turn another into an unreliable narrator.

If your origin story so far has been somewhere between factual history and allegory, drift toward one side.

Identify liberation before loss or pain.

Create a tertiary biography in case your secondary biography is revealed to not be your primary one.

Share this score with another but claim that you wrote it.

Make a rule for yourself that will be impossible to break.

Become unreliable narrator C if you are not already.

Question when anyone says you are not allowed to do something.

Remind yourself that a series of rules are only for yourself to honor.

Find a way to make yourself smaller.

Add more prompts to this score.

Be only you, but with others.

Create an origin story for your family.

Perform an act of god.

Make a creation story for a nation you don't belong to.

Retest a procedure.

If an identity was taken away, create a new identity.

Identify liberation after loss or pain.

Become unreliable narrator B if you are not already.

Consider why taboos are needed for yourself.

Withhold truthful information that is more beautiful than the path
of lies already created or imagined.

Consider that your traditions may only apply to your own community.

Ask why you have always done things the same way.

Ask what can be pushed further with every repeat.

Think of all the dangers if you do not follow the protocol.

Become unreliable narrator D if you are not already.

Don't be you.

AS FOR PROTOCOLS: AN INTRODUCTION

Re'al Christian, Carin Kuoni, Eriola Pira

Explicitly—or not—protocols determine much of what we do. Far exceeding traditional notions of etiquette or good manners, protocols are languages that regulate how we relate to each other, to our cultural, social, and political environments, and to the technologies that create them. The history of protocols is embedded in technological developments, which in turn speak to the visible and invisible structures that are often overlooked or hidden but set the conditions of our lived reality. At the Vera List Center for Art and Politics, we consider the question of protocols urgent, both as insidious instruments of hegemony and as untapped opportunities for liberation. This particular collection of reflections is specifically dedicated to the transformative power of protocols, illuminated here by a range of authors, including artists, writers, curators, activists, scientists, and scholars who explore the ethical, etymological, ecological, and technological implications and possibilities of protocols across various fields.

The preposition in the book's title—"as for" in *As for Protocols*—is itself a linguistic protocol, lifting information of secondary importance to prominence. The push and pull of "hard" and "soft" power—hardware versus software, coercion versus co-option—informs a critical framework in which to consider ways of reckoning with rigid power structures pitted against individual agency. In fact, the book's premise is that artistic, interdisciplinary methodologies can lead to the creation of new protocols—both "soft" and "hard"—that are inclusive and equitable.

The etymology of the term *protocol* serves us well. The word reaches us via Old French (*prothocole*) and medieval Latin from the Greek: *prōtokollon*, from *prōto* (first) and *kolla* (glue). The *prōtokollon* often referred to the blank page glued to the outside of a printed manuscript, today better known as a flyleaf or an endpaper. Essentially empty, the *prōtokollon* thus sets the stage for the contents of the actual book. Later uses of the word referred to a preface or prologue, and in late nineteenth-century France, it was associated with rules of conduct observed by the Head of State in diplomatic relations. This expanded meaning gave rise to the more commonly understood definition of protocols as we know it today—an official procedure, a mode of communication, an essential, if overlooked, framing and regulatory device, which is both the substance and the subject of this book.

Understood as governing apparatuses of institutions, political ideologies, events, and economic and technological practices and processes, protocols hold immense power over our lived experiences and collective unconscious, whether they are real or projected. Or rather, if they didn't exist, they would have to be invented, and so even fictional protocols are imbued with real, lasting power. For example, the fabricated *Protocols of the Elders of Zion*, allegedly the minutes of a late nineteenth-century meeting of Jewish leaders intent on world dominion, has long fueled anti-Semitic sentiment. Similarly, during the COVID-19 pandemic, conspiracy theories—not to mention valid and inexorable critiques—about the US Centers for Disease Control and Prevention or the World Health Organization and their regulatory measures (from the innocuous thirty-second hand-washing techniques to life-saving vaccines) seemed to promulgate faster and more broadly than the virus itself. The capacity to discern between fact and fiction, already diminished from years of low trust in democratic institutions, elected leaders, and our public health system, led some to advocate for pseudoscientific treatments—from horse tranquilizers to bleach injections—while others turned toward their communities to form mutual aid groups. Ironically, many of the life-saving protocols adopted in the early days of the pandemic are owed to the long-standing work of disability justice groups, those who have long been invested in building community-oriented protocols for self- and collective care that disrupt exploitative models of institutionalized healthcare. While these protocols seemed new to some, the so-called new normal was, for many, a well-established and integral part of public and private life.

A cursory search for protocols online brings up an informal health and wellness industry that parallels, if not rivals, the pharmaceutical industrial complex and proposes managing any number of ailments, cures, and self-improvement aims from autoimmune disorders to vitamin deficiencies and gender-affirming hormone therapies. That such protocols are distributed and have proliferated primarily through networked social communities (think Facebook groups and TikTok) mirroring the internet's own protocological regime of distributed, decentralized, horizontal, and peer-to-peer communication and control is no accident. Neither is the autonomization, outsourcing, and privatization of healthcare at a time when millions of Americans are uninsured.

Protocols, then, play a regulatory and affirming function for the body, from the somatic to the political. At the level of the individual and the self, protocols are often self-generated and adopted as means of well-being and belonging, giving way to communing and communities, but they are just as often imposed and enforced by state actors and ideological formations toward control and social cohesion, of individuals and communities alike. Identifying and working against these protocols necessitates civil disobedience against the limitations of institutionalized knowledge and biopolitical power that seek to govern and interpellate our bodies, our health, gender, sexuality, and (re)production. Civil disobedience, the mobilization of bodies toward collective action, calls for both material and structural demands. As we saw in the aftermath of the 2020 Black Lives Matter protests that swept the globe, and the politicization of the pandemic from both the left and right, the change on offer was often performative, albeit in ways that constituted visible reckonings with protocological defects.

Every two years, the Vera List Center identifies a Focus Theme, a topic of particular urgency that frames our investigations into a timely subject. Just before the outbreak of COVID-19 and the wave of Black Lives Matter protests, we had already decided to dedicate the next two years of our work to protocols, under the heading *As for Protocols*, a prescient topic at a moment in which the rules and regulations of everyday life were being drastically, rapidly, and necessarily rewritten. The topic of protocols has regularly appeared in the Vera List Center's research and programming at the intersection of art and politics. Protocols of listening, as articulated by sound art collective Ultra-red, informed a significant multi-year project in 2008 and 2009 by VLC Fellow Robert Sember on the terms by which New York's House|Ballroom community can write its own archive and history (see p. 26). During the *Indigenous New York* program series (2016–2017),[1] it was protocols of relationality that informed our research, especially questions of human and non-human companions, protective infrastructures in opacity, and Indigenous epistemologies as guides to more inclusive pedagogy.

The pandemic was still surging in September 2020 when our first *As for Protocols* program kicked off: Seminar 1: *Protocols as Language and Communication*. By then, we had learned of new ways of distributing content and staying connected online. We watched, read, listened, participated, and contributed to various virtual gatherings and programs, building protocols of our own to carry forward our work online to continue supporting the artists and creative practitioners in our community. The first of our pandemic programs, a virtual dance party hosted by artist Jesus Benavente, titled *I'm Not Dancing, I'm Struggling to Survive: Shelter in Place*, on March 28, 2020, inadvertently foregrounded protocols, when it was Zoom-bombed with racist and pornographic messages and images. At that moment, we had no protocols (yet) for dealing with this but quickly learned and implemented strict processes to avoid such disruptions, including adopting community agreements for our programs. In addition to compiling a *COVID-19 Resource Toolkit for Artists and our Extended Communities*,[2] we reallocated funding to support artists who had lost income and opportunities through an "Emergency Session Relief Fund" while offering honoraria to program attendees in recognition of their contributions to this online space. We doubled our Working Artists and the Greater Economy (W.A.G.E.) honoraria for program presenters through fall 2021. Accessibility features such as closed captioning and American Sign Language interpretation have since become a regular part of our online programs.

These and other protocols at the Vera List Center were developed alongside and in response to the structural and technocratic measures imposed by the new normal of the pandemic. They were also part of individual and mutual care protocols central to many of the artists, projects, discursive programs, and initiatives that the center engaged with over two years. How to hold a three-day conference undoing Westernized notions of linear time-space regimes? How to host an eight-week workshop exploring past pandemics with limitations on gatherings still in place during an ongoing public health crisis? More so than logistical, which almost always implies protocols put in place to ensure safety and manage liability, the questions raised by Rasheedah Phillips and Adelita Husni Bey's fellowship projects, respectively, revealed the very stakes of our exploration of protocols.

In her VLC Fellowship project *Time Zone Protocols*, which extends into the book (p. 156), Phillips maps out her ongoing practice as a member of Black Quantum Futurism. To circumvent pandemic restrictions on public programs at The New School, *Time Zone Protocols* was disguised as an exhibition, essentially the staging ground for what became the *Prime Meridian Unconference*, held in April 2022. Phillips's project asks us to consider the protocols of time itself, examining the political agendas that uphold Westernized time constructs—specifically, the 1884 International Meridian Conference, a convening called by the United States in Washington, DC, to enforce a universal time standard and thus control global commerce—to probe the tension between the "hard" protocols of power and control and the "soft" protocols that emerge by way of resistance to the same.

Husni Bey's project, *These Conditions*, an exhibition and pedagogical film set, brought together artists, epidemiologists, biologists, sociologists, and theorists to think with and through contemporary resonances of historic pandemics, the pervasive protocols of communication technology, surveillance capitalism, and imperial epistemologies and violence alongside the embodied protocols of individual-group relations and mutual care. Over several weeks of workshops, public programs, and performances, it delved into historical pandemic protocols, including the sixteenth-century booklet *Epidemiologìa Sive Tractatus de Peste* for the containment of the plague in Alghero, Sardinia, mutual aid protocols from the height of the AIDS crisis, and 2020 guidelines defining "necessary workers." Staged at the Brooklyn Army Terminal, which was built as a military supply facility during the Spanish Flu in 1918 and most recently used as a site for mass vaccination during the COVID-19 pandemic, the exhibition drew from and made present the links and resonances between past and current pandemic protocols and control measures. What social relations and movements are borne out of contagion and containment? What of protocols deployed in crisis that make possible breaks in the cordon sanitaire of biopolitics and racial capitalism?

As for Protocols saw the launch of the Borderlands Fellowship, a joint initiative between the VLC and the Center for Imagination in the Borderlands at Arizona State University, directed by Mojave poet Natalie Diaz.

We joined the inaugural recipients—artists Carolina Caycedo and Maria Hupfield—in research-based projects reflecting on notions of borderlands through diverse Indigenous perspectives and ontologies. Caycedo's *The Collapsing of a Model* advances the artist's work on the construction of "borders" as an extractive infrastructure serving multiple corporate and state interests (see p. 60). Hupfield's 2023 artist book *Breaking Protocol* centers on place-based modes of making and performance (see p. 52). The inaugural Boris Lurie Fellow, Buenos Aires-based collective Etcétera, put forward a series of propositions for a *Protocol of Buen Vivir* (Good Living). And in an offshoot of the Fellowship program, longtime VLC collaborator Suzanne Kite's *Hél čhaŋkú kiŋ ȟpáye (There lies the road)* examines how protocols based on Lakȟóta ontology can help apply artificial intelligence to the creation of art.

The *As for Protocols* Seminar Series consisted of twelve seminars and a closing symposium, structured as one long open curriculum and presented from September 2020 through May 2022 (see p. 224). Taking place on Zoom, the multidisciplinary participants—including Jesse Chun, Mary Maggic, Shannon Mattern, Rashaun Mitchell + Silas Riener, and Robert Sember, all of whom continued to engage with us through this book—focused on particular aspects of protocols involving language and communication; equitable networks; global health and development; data aggregation and narrative systems; culturally-specific community agreements; and scientific research.

While the widely used systems and modes of communication write and recycle preexisting protocols, new, equitable protocols are more often found at a grassroots level, in our communities, in our collaborations, conversations, and practices of care for one another, those intimate, interpersonal minglings, or what Fred Moten refers to as "talking amongst ourselves."[3] The idea of talking amongst ourselves illustrates the soft power of protocols—their ability to permeate the very ways we think, speak, and move through the world and with one another. Talking amongst ourselves, however, is not predicated on exclusion; rather, it establishes "a set of protocols about how we talk,"[4] about how we choose to critically operate within the rigidity of institutionalized mechanisms of control.

The process of developing protocols often relies on limited variables and the circumstances of a controlled environment, whereby outcomes and effects are measurable, calculable, and readily indexical by the observers, or those in control of the system. The protocol is then adjusted, often piecemeal, in response to perceived failures of the previous protocols in place. This process relies on slowness, on individual, calculated changes, the outcomes of which in turn re-write the original protocol that led to their creation. As many of the contributions in this volume attest, the traditional modes by which protocols are developed, tested, evaluated, changed, and adapted fall short of responding to the needs of our increasingly accelerating society. What we sometimes overlook is that a protocol can be "individual responsibility as much as a communal one," reflects composer, musician, and artist Raven Chacon, whose preceding foreword, "Score for an Unreliable Narrator," unfolds as an oscillating score that prompts us to consider our individual roles in the preservation, stewardship, and creation of new and preexisting protocols. As each prompt links and weaves into the next, "this score," Chacon writes, "asks how we can be a stronger link in that chain, itself being a procedural protocol of contradictions."

AS FOR PROTOCOLS: THE BOOK

Protocols are difficult to avoid, yet often undetectable. They suffuse our environments, invisible to the naked eye, like signals moving through space. The contributions in this book examine how protocols are developed out of existing technologies—ranging from computer interfaces, AI, data aggregation, and algorithms to community agreements and cultural engagements—but can be embodied, appropriated, reengineered, and otherwise used for our own ends to build equitable models of engagement.

In order and structure, the book is inspired by the fluid push-and-pull dichotomy inherent to most protocols—the ways in which particular protocols tend to arise retroactively as a response, as in "call and response," or "cause and effect," when hard power meets soft, but resolute, response. Both sections unpack this oscillation, examining the form and function of protocols from the inside out and the outside in.

The first section, "Protocols of Reception," examines protocols from the place of the individual body, looking at how protocols generate and proliferate in our day-to-day lives and interpersonal encounters. The section foregrounds performance and movement-based practices, collaborative work, disability justice, and Indigenous-centered environmental ontologies. Many of these protocols are received through forms of communication, from the technologies we use to the sounds we hear in our daily environments.

The essay "Organizing the Silence" by sound art collective Ultra-red, with an afterword by Robert Sember, reflects on the myriad forms of silence engendered in the wake of global pandemics, outlining the necessity of equitable listening practices in social and political organizing in shared struggles of the past and present. "Something Else: Allowances, Permissions, and the Search for a World of Differences" by artist Rashaun Mitchell addresses the protocols of navigating public space within the context of his participatory performance practice. Coupled with a score by collaborator Silas Riener, Mitchell's essay examines the alternative modes by which othered bodies forge new protocols of spatial navigation in deviating from accepted paths.

In "Anishinaabeg Visiting, Smiles, and Embodied Practice," Leanne Betasamosake Simpson revisits a Zoom conversation with Maria Hupfield in which the two commune over Anishinaabekwe protocols of gathering and root their exchange in traditional practices of knowledge sharing grounded in Indigenous feminisms that can spill over into the porous boundaries of virtual space. "A Matter of Braiding," by Carolina Caycedo with contributions by Lupita Limón Corrales, calls for protocols of collaboration through a lens of plurality, reciprocity, and giving back to the people and environments that sustain us. Romy Opperman's "Protocols for Grounding Philosophy" centers the concept of "grounding" as a means of "(re- and dis-)orienting" colonial knowledge systems, highlighting her personal protocols for examining the social constructs of race and identity with epistemologies rooted in the Black diaspora.

Another extension of the Prime Meridian Unconference, herbalist Asia Dorsey's "Lemon Balm and Temporal Liberation" presents a lemon balm protocol, a means of emotionally and sensorially grounding oneself in the present, anchored in the reclamation of Black narratives lost through temporal disequilibria and ancestral debility. In "Golden Showers, Golden Futures," artist Mary Maggic writes about their "Urine-Hormone-Extraction-Action" protocol, a long-term project through which they engineer new approaches to biohacking, the appropriation of scientific methods to better serve individual health and well-being on a corporeal, molecular level. Taraneh Fazeli and Cannach MacBride's "Means without ends" lays bare the enduring ableism of colonial institutions in the onset of COVID-19 and the protocols of adopting access-centered practices for those both within and outside of disability communities.

Section two, "Protocols of Transmission," addresses external protocols, i.e., the methods by which protocols are transmitted as a form of communication. It considers the technological, infrastructural, and environmental mechanisms and processes by which protocols are conveyed or articulated. Contributors consider ways of altering how we perceive the language of protocols to rethink how we relate to protocols within our built and natural environments through technology, sound, and time itself.

The increasing ubiquity of the web has arguably popularized the term *protocol* itself. Web protocols are responsible for translating datasets into user-oriented platforms, but the technology often struggles to keep up with the needs and desires of the user. In "On the Web: A Protocol for Care," Salome Asega traces the history of the World Wide Web, beginning with its advent in 1989, its transition to the public domain in 1993, and the multiple generations of the Web that have followed: from Web1 in the 1990s and the aughts, Web2 into the 2010s, to the current Web3, which was introduced as the most robust and ostensibly decentralized form of the web to date, but whose capabilities and implications are yet to be fully understood. As Asega argues, the need for care-based internet protocols, rules, and guidelines must be integrated into our daily lexicon.

In "Lines of Control: Navigating Tangled Timelines and Colonial Cartographies," Rasheedah Phillips elaborates on Black Quantum Futurism's *Time Zone Protocols* project. The interview that follows, "On Cloud Time and Protocols," emerges from Phillips's *Prime Meridian Unconference*, which brought together architect V. Mitch McEwen and scientist Nadir Jeevanjee in a conversation on the physics of the Earth's clouds in relation to deep time and the climate. They consider modes by which clouds exist simultaneously at multiple points in the stratosphere, speculating on the metaphorical implications of transcending the confines of space-time. In her essay "Sonic Protocols," anthropologist Shannon Mattern reflects on how engineered sounds—the bell's chime, the whistle's screech, and the alarm's blare—demonstrate how we have manufactured new sounds, or manipulated existing ones, that prompt us to obey various protocols governing individual behavior and social interactions. A playlist by Detroit-based techno collective Underground Resistance adds a new sonic protocol, one built on the experimentation, riffing, and decentralized access to technology that manifested techno as a genre.

In "Notes on Method: Narrative as Criticism," writer and art critic Emmanuel Iduma grapples with relationships between movement, method, and place, elaborating on his process and practice of notetaking to build non-prescriptive protocols of language. In "Fragile Glass at the Temple: On Economic and Academic Vulnerabilities in Contemporary Art Museums in the United States," artist Pablo Helguera shares his experience navigating institutional spaces, looking at hierarchical structures within the Western museum as a particular case study, and how exclusionary practices are built on outdated protocols of communication. Finally, Jesse Chun's artist project, "Of the Intangible," interweaves a personal narrative with the institutional protocols for protecting, defining, and collecting intangible heritage as outlined by the Intangible Cultural Heritage Department at UNESCO in Paris. Using redacted texts from the archive pertaining to South Korean intangible heritage, her contribution creates concrete poetry out of UNESCO's written protocols while embracing the immateriality of language protocols as a form of cultural documentation and political regulation.

Closing out the book, "As for Protocols: A Curriculum" constellates two years of programs, seminars, fellowship projects, publications, and exhibitions that point toward other avenues of research and learning on the topic of protocols for the classroom and beyond. An epilogue, "Publishing as Protocol" by Amherst College Press director Beth Bouloukos and VLC director Carin Kuoni, reflects on expansive modes of knowledge sharing, accessibility, peer review, and design.

Through essays, artworks, interviews, and scores, the contributors to this book speak to protocols as practice, neither conventional regulations nor abstract concepts, but material processes and shared responsibilities. Protocols are evidence of governmental, organizational, social, or corporate power structures. *As for Protocols* speaks to processes rather than finite outcomes, setting the tone and conditions for potential encounters. Investigating protocols as such allows us to contribute to the creation of new protocols that are inclusive and equitable.

As we write this text, we are approaching the end of an entirely different Focus Theme, *Correction* *, which explores the tension and discomfort found in the metaphorical, political, and social dimensions and implications of correction. Correction, the willingness to reevaluate time-trusted protocols, is often demanded yet rarely applied in the nuanced, considered, humane ways necessary to foster socially and politically equitable pathways forward. At the Vera List Center, concentrating our work around protocols allowed us to reckon with the pervasive nature of inequitable or inadequate protocols we face in our current systems, to engage in the radical recalibration of these protocols in our everyday practices. For over two years, we learned alongside other practitioners in the cultural sector who engage in the very real work of making the processes of identifying and creating protocols visible, much of the evidence of which is collected and presented in this book. What emerges is that if a protocol derives from an existing technology or infrastructure, it can be rebooted, reengineered, embodied, appropriated, and used to our own ends.

1 Vera List Center for Art and Politics, "Indigenous New York," accessed July 17, 2024, https://www.veralistcenter.org/events/indigenous-new-york.

2 Vera List Center for Art and Politics, "COVID-19 Resource Toolkit for Artists and our Extended Communities," March 20, 2020, https://www.veralistcenter.org/announcement/covid-19-resource-toolkit.

3 Fred Moten, interview with Jared Ware, *Millennials Are Killing Capitalism*, YouTube, October 25, 2023, https://www.youtube.com/watch?v=vWnzkjUAZnQ.

4 Ibid.

I.
PROTOC
RECEPT

COLS OF ION

This section examines protocols from the place of the individual body, looking at how protocols generate and proliferate in our day-to-day lives and interpersonal encounters. The section foregrounds performance and movement-based practices, collaborative work, disability justice, and Indigenous-centered environmental ontologies. Many of these internal protocols come to us as a form of communication, from the technologies we use to the sounds we hear in our daily environments.

ORGANIZING THE SILENCE[1]

Ultra-red

Ultra-red is an international sound-art collective founded thirty years ago by Los Angeles-based harm reduction activists. Today, Ultra-red members are based in Berlin, London, the Southwest of England, New York City, and Los Angeles and address concerns ranging from housing and racial justice to sexual rights and public health. Initially, immersed in the house music scene, Ultra-red used site recordings, often of protest events, to compose audio tracks. That is, our "political art" was representational. A few years ago, however, rather than inviting people simply to listen to the sounds we gathered or composed, we began asking, "What did you hear?" The analytic reflections this inspired included questioning the terms of the question itself. A conversation developed between the concrete experience of the moment—an encounter with a particular sound in a specific context—and various taxonomies of listening. How does one listen? To what does one listen? And toward what end does one listen? However, even before addressing the process of listening—what it means "to hear"—the listener must decipher the pronoun: "What did *you* hear?" Is it singular or plural? Thus, in collective listening events, participants are guided through an iterative inquiry into the sounds they hear and the practice of listening itself. The question "What did you hear?" establishes a venue and process whereby a group begins to hear itself as it moves through various phases of the inquiry. We were interested in how this process may contribute to long-term political organizing, which requires ongoing cycles of action, reflection, and adjustments to the dynamics and protocols of shared struggle.

THE HORIZON

In sound, the horizon is typically figured as some form of silence, as in the limit—phenomenological or epistemological—of perception. For the sound artist, the construction of silence can be defamiliarized with a simple intervention that asks the listener to attend to sounds that are beyond the threshold of intention as opposed to the threshold of hearing. In these instances, the command "Listen!" is equivalent to a finger indicating a distant vanishing point. In Ultra-red's political and aesthetic inquiries, however, we have discovered that the question "What did you hear?" proposes a different role for the artist than finger-pointing. We might describe that difference as one in which the horizon becomes less a fixed point toward which one gestures than a measure of movement that constructs and reconstructs thresholds of change. First, there is the horizon we see or hear at a distance. Then there is the horizon perceived after occupying a place that was itself the horizon for a previous moment. We consider these shifts a form of collective pedagogy.

After listening with many groups of people, Ultra-red has come to think of horizons as demarcations of different political practices. One *represents* politics, perhaps in the form of a critique that inspires visual or aural images of new political configurations. Another *organizes* politics. In this case, the horizon reciprocates the gesture, touches back, and brings the artist or organizer into a social situation that they might change and be changed by.

We say horizon. We say silence. We could just as easily say that "the political" lacks resolution, escapes consensus, and evades agreements. As evidence of how profane discussions of the political have become within art, what artist would disagree with the statement that all art is political? But try to understand what is meant by "the political," and the statement (as well as its confident delivery) dissolves. The word appears empty of meaning or a repository for undifferentiated possibility. It must be elaborated through dialogue and shared endeavors.

Yet, something becomes possible in that indecisiveness. In light of this situation, we in Ultra-red might have a few things to say about what, or rather, how, politics has come to mean in our practice. In what follows, we reflect on how one of our projects shifted the foundations of our work. *SILENT/LISTEN* (2005–2006) began as an investigation into silence, fueled by an urgency to organize silence. Over time, the project became a practice of distinguishing between organizing the silence and collective listening.

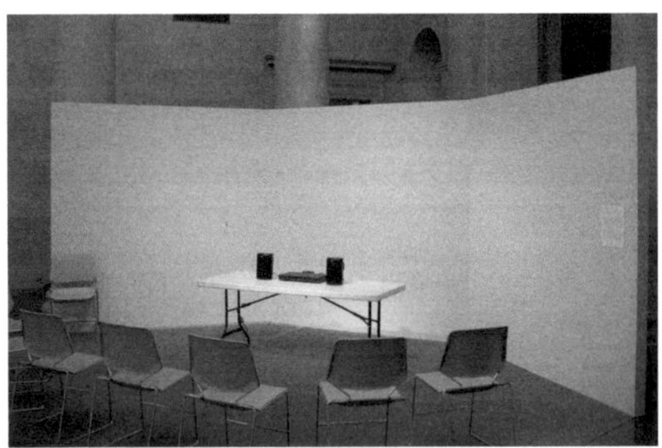

Figure 1. Ultra-red, *SILENT/LISTEN* (The Record), Baltimore Museum of Art, April 16, 2005. Table, table linen, chairs, monophonic sound-system with audio.

Description Figure 1. Set with a white background is seen in a larger room. In the set is a table with stereo equipment on it and facing it are seven empty green chairs in a rounded semi-circle formation.

Ultra-red has no single organized political affiliation. The collective's members are engaged with anti-racist movements in Britain, migrant struggles in Germany, community-based education in London, New York City, and Los Angeles, and struggles for housing and just community development in East Los Angeles. When Ultra-red formed in 1994, it was around the politics of the AIDS crisis. Our experiments in field recordings, for example, occurred in the context of the Los Angeles AIDS activist scene, specifically the direct action of harm reduction and HIV prevention for people who inject drugs. Ultra-red's first compilation of electroacoustic recordings, *Second Nature* (1999), underscored the cultural analysis of the AIDS activist movement by illustrating how the policing of gay public sex increased rather than diminished the risk of contracting HIV. Codified in the first decade of the AIDS crisis, AIDS cultural analysis extended the militant gay liberationist critique of petit bourgeois panic around queer sexuality. Homophobia and its practices in government policies, public health, the media, and the institutions of religion and education were argued to be the true cause of the pandemic.

In 2000, when delegates to the thirteenth International AIDS Conference in Durban, South Africa, elaborated on the global impact of the crisis, we, like others in the field, registered a shift in understandings of and responses to the crisis. The conference brought into focus the stark realities of a pandemic that had far surpassed all projections in terms of infections and deaths. This produced a new sense of urgency among activists in the United States as claims of progress toward ending the AIDS crisis were contradicted by the brutal truth that the AIDS crisis had only just begun. While cadres of activists knew that global inequities had produced an epidemic in the so-called Global South exponentially larger than any in the North, we were exhausted, grief-stricken. We focused on sustaining our own hard-won systems of prevention and care. This internal struggle was defined by ambivalence and contradiction, for it was also clear that the increasingly managed and bureaucratized crisis in the Global North generally conformed to rather than successfully challenged the fundamental causes of the pandemic, specifically the inequities shaped by racism and gender and class oppression. If the AIDS crisis was still "only just beginning," we had to start over. Overwhelmed by our own ambivalence regarding AIDS activism and unable to respond adequately to questions regarding the rapidly shifting conditions of the crisis, we set out to investigate the situation.

Given our dual stats as artist-activists, these questions followed us into the field of art, for we knew that if the terms of the political changed as a result of shifts in the affective ground of people living with and fighting against AIDS (and vice versa), then the role of the artist-activist must also change. And, by claiming the investigation as an Ultra-red project, we located its public manifestations within art institutions. This brought resources to the inquiry that would not tie us to the HIV/AIDS nonprofit sector. Indeed, we hoped that our investigation would draw some attention to the limiting conditions under which the not-for-profit crisis management regime guided people to conform to the very structures of oppression underlying the crisis in order to access services.

We also entered art institutions to stage a return. In the early years of the AIDS crisis, proponents of AIDS cultural analysis critiqued the practices of representation that reproduced the conditions of the pandemic and challenged artists and cultural producers to commit themselves to direct participation in the fight against the roots of the crisis: homophobia, poverty, racism, sexism, and capitalist profiteering. We wanted to hear if echoes of that commitment might linger in the museum.

THE PROTOCOLS

SILENT/LISTEN brought the aesthetic operations of the AIDS activist investigation out of the AIDS administrative regime into the museum and gallery. In 2001, we had initiated a similar dislocation by introducing artist and composer John Cage's 1955 composition for silence, *4'33"*, into contexts far removed from avant-garde music. For example, at the beginning of an AIDS literacy workshop in Echo Park, Los Angeles, we announced that we would perform the piece and proceeded to sit in restrained stillness with workshop participants. At the passing of four and a half minutes, the workshop organizer announced, "Time." Then we asked, "What did you hear?" We noticed that this practice increased concerns with and discussion of the contexts within which people gathered to address the crisis.

In 2005, when Ultra-red was invited by the Baltimore Museum of Art to take part in an exhibition called *Sound Politics*, we decided to expand this investigation. We brought community workers into the exhibition for discussions of the global AIDS crisis. These discussions were preceded by performances of Cage's *4'33"*. The conjunction of avant-garde sound art and the conventions of public health education and advocacy inspired us to compose protocols for collective listening that we refined over the following two years as the project traveled to a number of venues.[2]

The *SILENT/LISTEN* protocols were part performance script and part meeting agenda. They included framing statements, performances, testimony by invited guests, and opportunities for dialogue. Repetition of statements and actions is a key feature of the protocols. This practice drew attention to shifts in language, affect, and, most importantly, modes of listening.

The protocol began with a version of Cage's *4'33"*. A facilitator, usually an Ultra-red member, then asked questions of the audience. These questions brought to the fore the terms of our investigation and how these might guide intentional listening. An electroacoustic piece, *The Minutes*, composed by Ultra-red using recorded voices from previous installments of *SILENT/LISTEN*, preceded live statements made by three or four invited speakers. The statements were identified as contributions to "The Record of the AIDS crisis in the United States or Canada." The protocol closed with an invitation to anyone in attendance to enter a statement into the "record" and to join in conversation with others in the room.

Regardless of where the event occurred, a long table with white table linens was placed in the center of the room. Chairs were placed at the table, one for each of the three to four speakers and at least four more for people wishing to make a statement. The place setting in front of each chair included a microphone on a stand and, on some occasions, a pad of paper and a pen. Members of Ultra-red sat at one end of the table, on which a laptop computer, mixing board, and microphone were placed. Audience members sat in rows of chairs that wrapped around three sides of the table.

THE SILENCE

The events began with a request that people move into empty chairs in the first row of seats. The movement broke the stiff formality of the room, a first indication that the conventional distinction between audience and performer was blurred. Once the room settled, a group member announced: "Four minutes and thirty-three seconds, composed by John Cage in 1952." The conclusion of *4'33"* indicated by the "Time" announcement would sometimes produce muffled laughter and a wave of movement as people adjusted in their seats. A facilitator then moved through the audience with a wireless microphone asking random audience members one of the following questions:

> Good evening, what did you hear?
> When was the last time you were in this space?
> What is the relationship between this space and the city of ________?
> When was the last time you talked about AIDS in this space?

As people paused to gather their thoughts, new qualities of silence and listening joined the "silence" held during *4'33"*. These shifting silences indexed different concerns and qualities of engagement as people figured out their own process of participation. This might include a clearer sense of their position in relation to the institution, city, AIDS crisis, and the collective moment. Indeed, in the immediate moment after *4'33"*, when invited to share what was heard, participants usually described how silence drew attention to the presence of others around them and amplified the signature resonances of the spaces in which we were gathered, including the sounds of the city beyond the gallery.

4'33" is usually described as four and a half minutes of silence. Yet, at one of its earliest public performances, the one most often discussed in histories of the piece, a torrential rainstorm and rambunctious audience filled the open-air chapel in Woodstock, New York, with sound. When we describe *4'33"* as silent, we reduce the performance to the actions of the "performer." In Woodstock, this was a pianist who did not touch the keys of the piano at which he was seated. If we shift our attention to the context, the piece is an experience of listening in the presence of others. This, from our perspective, remains a crucial feature of *4'33"*. From this perspective, what *4'33"* composes is not so much sounds but listening as an experience of collectivity in its raw potential. *4'33"* gives form to and rehearses listening. It also prepares us to consider how we are gathered to listen. As we learned from the numerous performances of *4'33"*, the question "What did you hear?" received a range of responses that illuminated varied and, in many instances, competing frames of reference, political investments, and strategies of listening available within a group.

Some found the nearly five minutes of silent-listening to be an opportunity for meditative repose. Others experienced it as effortful and uncomfortable. These reflections produced an appreciation for the sensitivities engaged by collective listening, which includes both self-reflection—attending to one's listening postures and intent—as well as awareness of others and how they listened.

The discomfort and awkwardness of this collective silent-listening carried through to the invitation to then speak publicly in response to the question, "What did you hear?" Art audiences offered well-rehearsed descriptions of Cage's work and described listening to the unintended sounds in the room "as if they were music." Others spoke of the awkwardness of sitting in silence with others in a space that usually clearly distinguishes between viewer/listener and object/performer. They often declared, "I heard nothing," "I don't know," or "I heard myself thinking." Others contributed an inventory of sounds: shuffling feet, rustling clothes, heavy breathing, coughing, and stomach growls. Some turned the question on us: "I don't know. What did you hear?"

The questions that followed the initial "What did you hear?" emphasized listeners' relationships to the moment and place. Regardless of where we were, many in the audience, particularly those we had invited from AIDS service organizations or activist groups, confessed that they had never been in that museum or gallery space before that day. For them, *4'33"* was about waiting with others, a position open to resonances far beyond the formalities and conditions of the art space. For example, many in the AIDS field are members of religious congregations and frequently sit in silence with others. Similarly, when accessing medical and other services, we must often wait in a different kind of silence. For others, the silence represented long years of struggle to break the silence surrounding AIDS and other oppressions. Others spoke of the silences encasing family, friends, and comrades who died of AIDS. As these histories surfaced, the silences filled with patient anticipation, grief, and frustration.

THE STATEMENTS

In each venue, we used the folding tables and stackable chairs usually reserved for exhibition openings, educational programs, or workshops. The tablecloths came from commercial caterers, and the microphones and other sound equipment, which always looked well-used, were rented from local vendors. Despite their utilitarian veneer, we combined them with a formal rigor befitting the art space settings. For those who had worked in the AIDS field for a number of years, the settings recalled meeting spaces in any number of public health buildings, government offices, and community-based organizations. In these settings, the table is not understood as an ideological device. A table is simply a venue for the regularly scheduled and clearly organized meetings central to the sector's collective practice. A second association was to the cycle of conferences, symposia, and expert panels convened to address various facets of the crisis. These gatherings almost always took place in hotels or convention centers, university conference rooms, or government buildings, all of which shared a particular institutional aesthetic. However, estranged from their conventional settings and repurposed as mise-en-scène for an art event, the tables and meeting procedures brought to the fore a series of concerns infrequently voiced in these other settings: Who speaks? Whose voice is amplified? What do we speak of and to whom? Who listens, and to what end do they listen? Who has a place at the table? Who determines who has a place at the table? And on whose behalf do those seated at the table speak?

In the second phase of *SILENT/LISTEN*, we invited representatives of local AIDS organizations to enter statements into the Record of the crisis in North America. Some spoke from clearly announced professional positions and delivered their statements using an appropriate bureaucratic vocabulary and well-disciplined voice. Others came unrehearsed and stumbled through their statements. A few shared personal stories, wept, or sat in silence for a time, overwhelmed by hearing their voices amplified.

We asked that each speaker remain seated at the table after they had made the statement, so the table was literally becoming filled. When asked, "When was the last time you were in this space to talk about

AIDS?," almost every person in every venue responded, "Never," or, "I can't remember," or, "I don't think I've ever spoken about AIDS in this space." The presence and consequences of this silence settled on the table.

THE PUBLIC

Those who entered statements in the Record came from AIDS service organizations established by people living with AIDS and activist groups. We prepared for each event by reaching out to and corresponding with representatives of organizations in the months leading up to the gathering. We learned the histories of organizations and studied issues of particular concern to the communities and constituencies they served or to which they were accountable. In the days preceding the event, we visited the organizations and met in person with those who had agreed to participate.

Those who attended to listen rather than speak represented a broader set of constituencies. Some came from the organizations we visited or were speakers' family members or friends. The art venues also recruited a segment of each audience. Thus, the audience included a contingent that had never attended an event of avant-garde music and those who were well rehearsed in the conventions and investments of the museum but were usually at some distance from the AIDS sector.

In the third phase, when we opened the table and the protocol to anyone who wished to occupy one of the empty seats at the table, participants engaged in open dialogue, which usually proceeded with minimal facilitation by Ultra-red members. At this point, any illusion of a homogeneous listening "public" faded. Those gathered at the table in conversation and those who remained in the audience listening, journey through topographies of concern that were negotiated and produced rather than assumed. On multiple occasions, when we moved to close the event, participants would tell us they were not done: dialogue was now the protocol.

These complex and nuanced negotiations reminded us of the efforts by AIDS cultural analysts to deconstruct the notion of "the general public."

The founding assertion of AIDS cultural analysis is that the AIDS pandemic is not natural. That is, HIV transmission reaches an "epidemic" scale because of social factors and structural inequalities defined by heteronormativity, racism, poverty, and private profit. Those ideologies were reaffirmed each time the state, biomedical establishment, religious institutions, the media, and so forth asked the question, "Is the public at risk from AIDS?" The question presumes that the term "public" excludes those already affected by HIV. This exclusion determines who has access to education, prevention, research, and life-saving treatment for HIV infection. Thus, it was the very representation of the public that produced the AIDS crisis. For AIDS activists, "the public" is always ideological.

The correlate in the art world is the usually uninterrogated bourgeois contingent to which the art world addresses itself and from which it claims its authority. The failure to address this hegemony perpetuates divides between those who circulate within the art world and those who do not. The only acknowledgment of this divide comes in the form of "audience development" initiatives based on liberal notions of inclusion. Uninterrogated notions of "the public" also determine the politics of institutions and the terms by which, for example, they relate to the city around them. There is a clear division between those who are subjects of the art world—patrons, curators, intellectuals, and artists—and those who are its objects. These others are either spoken of or must have designees speak on their behalf.

In this context, an artist-activist's demand to break the silence around oppression quickly falls back onto the person making the demand. Whose silence must be broken, whose silence must be disciplined, and what is made of the listening that silence conditions? The Brazilian radical educator Paulo Freire once argued that the culture of silence arises from both the theft of the voice of the poor as well as the complicity of the poor in their own oppression, their interpellation into the subjectivity of domination. Silence, therefore, and its culture had to be broken for liberation to be realized. However, much later in his life, Freire introduced a very different conception of silence into his writings. Thinking about the role of the teacher as one who facilitates the articulation and transformation of the desires of others, Freire referred to teaching as adopting a discipline of silence. Silence, therefore, is not just the culture that must be broken in order for liberation to occur. Silence is also the very condition for listening. Rather than pointing toward a predetermined position on the AIDS crisis, the *SILENT/LISTEN* protocols realize an iterative series of listening conditions that invite dialogue rooted in terms offered by those who are in the room. We and, we hope, those who participated understood from this process that the politics of the AIDS crisis is not resolved.

AFTERWORD—NOTES TOWARD A COVID PROTOCOL

By Robert Sember

In the first months of the COVID crisis, I talked at length with friends I have known since the early years of the AIDS crisis. Many are, like me, gay men who carry the wounds of those times, as do our friends and colleagues who used and use needles to inject drugs. We heard in the confusion and distress of COVID echoes of the panic, frustration, and despair of the first phase of the AIDS crisis. In light of this conjunction, we claimed, somewhat defensively I acknowledge, that those of us who live the AIDS crisis know something about how a health emergency forms and develops.

We know that pandemics are social as opposed to exclusively biological events. As social constructions, pandemics are individual, local, and community or constituency-specific experiences that emerge amid historic global ruptures. Given this complexity, we know the importance of slowing down in the face of crises to avoid reacting uncritically to initial fragmentary and alarmist formulations. Slowing down involves a tolerance of uncertainty and a commitment to listening practices that must be repeated routinely if we are to adjust to the rapidly changing conditions of a crisis.

Intentional practices such as listening protocols can help us slow down. As described before, this is how Ultra-red employed protocols in the early 2000s when we investigated contemporary responses to the AIDS crisis in North America. By *protocols*, I mean both the scripted or established practices that organize crises and the intentional efforts to critically reflect on, intervene in, and even disrupt or reconstitute crises. At the risk of reducing the complexity of these practices to a simplistic binary, we might think of protocols as performing either disciplinary or constitutive functions.

Disciplinary protocols conserve practices that are effective. Their repetition is comforting and familiar. In a pandemic context, they include public health behavioral guidelines, institutional operations that calibrate expertise and authority, and processes to authenticate and distribute information. Disciplinary protocols can be stubbornly conventional, however, meaning that they reproduce prejudices, discriminatory regimes, and related harms. In these instances, repetition is an ideology.

Crises occur when established knowledge and structures can no longer interpret and manage experience. Constitutive protocols organize the confusions into opportunities for reflection, analysis, and transformative action. Constitutive protocols include deliberative analyses that expose the ideological underpinnings of events, evidence-based debates that address critical features of routine responses and practices, and the codification of constituency-specific experiences into assertions and demands. When effective, constitutive protocols place experience in dialogue with principles and regulations. This is what I consider the most powerful use of protocols, which is when disciplinary and constitutive protocols form a contradiction or dialectic. For example, both the AIDS and COVID pandemics repeatedly return us to the contradictions between medical protocols—the delivery of healing and life-extending medications—and inequities in access evidenced by aggregated epidemiological data and the testimonials of human rights and social justice movements.

My early conversations regarding the AIDS and COVID pandemics followed a protocol: the use of what is familiar (the AIDS crisis) to make sense of what was new (the COVID crisis). Similarities include the uneven topographies of morbidity and mortality, the exploitation of crises to buttress entrenched moral and ideological divisions, and the conflicts and struggles to comply with risk-reducing mandates. Differences between COVID and HIV transmission mean that COVID spreads more quickly and mutates more rapidly than HIV. The resulting risk profiles, understandings of vulnerability, and, consequently, the distribution of stigmas overlap with and differ markedly from those associated with the AIDS crisis.

I offer this brief inventory as an entry point for thinking about COVID protocols, which may, for example, bring into iterative dialogue members of constituencies that are particularly burdened by the stigmas and inequities of these and other epidemics and pandemics. The protocols could frame a shared frustration with declarations that these crises are over, meaning that they are now managed and no longer exceed our knowledge and resources. The protocol might ask, for example, "What do you hear when you are told that the crisis is over?"[3] The resulting discussions will almost certainly "denaturalize" crises by historicizing the moment and foregrounding the social factors that define them, what public health researchers and practitioners refer to as "fundamental causes." This contradiction constitutes social medicine and, I would argue, a public health endeavor: inequality is a health emergency.

The listening protocols Ultra-red employed in our *SILENT|LISTEN* project did not predetermine the contradictions. By simply gathering people in slow, deliberative dialogue with listening as an active and rich contribution—an unfamiliar experience for many who work in institutional positions—we invited experience. For this process to be effective, however, we considered who participates and how. The productive silence of presence is in tension with the violent silence of absence.

Ultra-red

SILENT | LISTEN

Baltimore Museum of Art

Baltimore, Maryland, U.S.

Wednesday, 16 April 2005

I. WELCOME [1 MIN.]

[A member of Ultra-red welcomes the audience and invites people to occupy seats closer to the central table. After which, the three members of Ultra-red move to the head of the table.]

A. SILENCE

FACILITATOR — Four minutes and thirty-three seconds by John Cage.

[The members of Ultra-red take their seats.]

FACILITATOR — *[After four minutes and thirty-three seconds of silence.]* Time.

II. 4'33" [6 MIN.]

B. EVALUATE THE SILENCE

FACILITATOR — *[The facilitator, with wireless microphone in hand, approaches the audience and asks a different person one of the following questions.]* I'd like to invite you to share some reflections on the piece. What did you hear?

What did you hear?

What did you hear?

When was the last time you were in this museum space?

Have you ever had a conversation about AIDS in this space?

What is the relationship between this space and the city of Baltimore?

[The facilitator returns to his seat at the table.]

III. OPEN THE RECORD [18 MIN.]

FACILITATOR — The record is now open. Can we have the first speaker please?

[First speaker approaches the table.]

A. FIRST SPEAKER: PJ GOULDMANN
TIME, NAME, ORGANIZATION, AND STATEMENT

[After the first speaker has finished entering his statement into the record, Ultra-red play back the statement in its entirety through digital sound processing software.]

FACILITATOR — Can we have the second speaker please?

[Second speaker approaches the table.]

B. SECOND SPEAKER: LAURA GILLIS
TIME, NAME, ORGANIZATION, AND STATEMENT

[After the second speaker has finished entering her statement into the record, Ultra-red play back the statement in its entirety through digital sound processing software in combination with the playback of the first statement.]

FACILITATOR — May we have the third speaker please?

[Third speaker approaches the table.]

C. THIRD SPEAKER: CARLTON SMITH
TIME, NAME, ORGANIZATION, AND STATEMENT

[After the third speaker has finished entering his statement into the record, Ultra-red play back the statement in its entirety through digital sound processing software in combination with the playback of the first and second statements.]

IV. CLOSE THE RECORD AND DISCUSSION [11 MIN.]

FACILITATOR — The record is now closed. Thank you for your submissions. I was at a symposium yesterday at UCLA about AIDS in Africa. Steven Lewis—Kofi Annan's special representative to AIDS in Africa—noted that we are in the twenty-fourth year of this epidemic. In year four it was predicted that the curve would peak by year ten in the epidemic. Twenty-four years into the epidemic all of the epidemiological signs seem to indicate that there is no peak in sight. This is already the most pervasive epidemic in the recorded history. It is a global epidemic. Yet it is experienced Locally. What do you see as the relationship between our analysis and our actions, here and now, and the global epidemic? I invite any of you to comment.

[The three speakers respond.]

FACILITATOR — *[Following an open discussion among the speakers.]* In January of this year, a study funded by the National Institute of Child and Human Development and the NIH released its findings. The study was conducted by the Rand Corporation and researchers at Oregon State University. The focus of the study was African Americans' beliefs about the HIV/AIDS epidemic. Fifty percent of those interviewed indicated that they believe that the virus was manufactured and purposefully spread. How can our analysis and action here today respond to those findings?

[The third speaker responds to the facilitator's question.]

V. OPEN THE RECORD TO THE FLOOR [22 MIN.]

FACILITATOR — I would like to open the record again. If anyone has a statement they would like to enter into the record, please let us know at any time. You are welcome to take the microphone and make your statement, or any comments, reflections, thoughts on what you have heard so far, or that you have brought with you to this event.

[The facilitator, with wireless microphone in hand, approaches seated audience members wishing to enter comments into the record.]

VI. CLOSE THE RECORD [9 MIN.]

FACILITATOR — The crisis is produced. The solution to the crisis is produced. What is going to happen tomorrow? What is going to happen next year? One of the graphs that I saw at the symposium yesterday was about the death curve over the last twenty-four years. The dimensions of this graph were like a long doorway—it was in fact the narrowest and tallest graph I have ever seen in a scientific study in order to accommodate the steepness of that slope as death rates have climbed over the last twenty-four years. And they just keep on climbing. But there are more years to come on that bottom axis. What is going to happen tomorrow? What is going to happen next year? The crisis is produced. And the solution is produced. What do you think is going to happen tomorrow? What do you think is going to happen next year? I think we should close the record.

[The members of Ultra-red play music.]

[TRT: 67 MINUTES]

Figure 2. Ultra-red, Protocol for *SILENT|LISTEN* (The Record), Baltimore Museum of Art, April 16, 2005. Table, table linen, chairs, monophonic sound-system with audio.

Description Figure 2. A transcript from a discussion held at the Baltimore Museum of Art with members of sound-art collective Ultra-red.

1 This essay has been partially adapted from "Ultra-red: Organizing the Silence," in *On Horizons: A Critical Reader in Contemporary Art*, ed. Maria Hlavajova, Simon Sheikh, and Jill Winder (Utrecht: BAK, basis voor actuele kunst, 2011), 192-209.

2 Beginning with the performance at the Baltimore Museum of Art, Ultra-red would go on to present *SILENT|LISTEN* at the Hammer Museum in Los Angeles, California, the Banff Center for Arts and Creativity in Alberta, Canada, the Andy Warhol Museum in Pittsburgh, Pennsylvania, the student art gallery at Concordia University in Montreal, Canada, the student health center at Southern Illinois University in Carbondale, Illinois, and the Art Gallery of Ontario, in Toronto, Canada. In Toronto, we presented a second performance of *SILENT|LISTEN* coinciding with the sixteenth International AIDS Conference.

3 Cross-constituency dialogues about the premature closure of crises feature in work I began with my 2009-2011 Vera List Center for Art and Politics Fellowship project, Vogue'ology. The project was undertaken with and for New York City's House and Ballroom community with the goal of further developing community-specific perspectives on AIDS and adjacent concerns, such as housing precarity, discriminatory policing, and cultural commodification. With infection rates among Ballroom members far exceeding the national average, the AIDS crisis is far from over.

SOMETHING ELSE: ALLOWANCES, PERMISSIONS, AND THE SEARCH FOR A WORLD OF DIFFERENCES

Rashaun Mitchell

To invite someone else to move, say "now"
To invite yourself to move, say "go"
To accept, say "yes"
To refuse, say "no"

Silas Riener and I have been collaborating on dances since 2010. Our dances are worlds that reflect how we as humans form our identities in relation to others. Because our partnership slides across personal, professional, artistic, and romantic realms, negotiating our roles, authorship, and identities is a giddy, wobbly source of inquiry and fascination. Compromise and rejection are par for the course in this queer arrangement. Compromise comes with the promise of renewal and the possibility of moving from different positions. Every choice we make is a rejection of another option. Over the years we have intentionally rejected the organizing principles of a traditional dance company in favor of a project-based choreographic partnership with a rotating group of practitioners and collaborators who respond to and design unstable and porous environments.

In 2017, Danspace Project invited us to a two-week residency at Madison Square Park. The scale of the urban park and its ever-changing pedestrian activities offered unique environmental conditions for producing dance. We were not beholden to the protocols of the staged theater—union crews, ticketed seating, the assumption of lighting, and amplified sound. Here, we concerned ourselves with the possibility of hecklers, joiners, onlookers, public restrooms, litter, unpredictable weather conditions, squishy, or uneven terrain, and other uncertainties that come with working in a public site.

This led us to borrow the concept of "desire lines"—trails or paths carved out over time, usually emerging as shortcuts between destinations. In built landscapes, they break protocol with prescribed routes. In natural environments, they often reveal animal migrations, paths used across generations. Desire lines are always a record of behavior—lines of movement suggested by previous path-takers and followed by future path-takers. Apparently, we cannot all be trailblazers. We love to follow in each others' footsteps.

Silas and I were interested in the simple question of how we make decisions inside of a group. How do we navigate individual desire within the constraints and limitations of group structures—proxies for larger social structures that we navigate in our daily lives?

We invited eleven dancers to the project, some of whom we'd never worked with before.

The first official protocol came in the form of a signed contract and an agreement on the proposal to improvise outdoors in public. Each participant agreed to practice group and solo explorations for at least twelve hours, usually three four-hour sessions of rehearsal-as-performance, leading up to the final nine-hour durational group performance.

Each time, upon arrival at the site, we entered the Metropolitan Life North Building, a thirty-story art deco skyscraper with marbled interiors. After showing identification, we slid our day passes through the computerized turnstiles guarding our way to the gilded elevators. This particular step usually resulted in numerous denials—a series of beeping alarms—before a human would intervene. We eventually made our way up to the Madison Square Park Conservancy offices, to a conference room posing as a green room filled with an awkwardly large table.

In the conference room-as-green room, the first protocol was that everyone wears their costume. We invited artist George Venson to design costumes we could wear in the sun or the rain. Our clothing needed to be functional for the terrain but we also wanted to look recognizably distinct, perhaps giving us one layer of separation from the pedestrian world. As we handed out brightly painted leggings and shirts made of swimsuit material, each person was essentially agreeing to enter the park as a performer on display, as one of many.[1]

We were implementing and undergoing a kind of rite of passage, donning our sigils and armor, signifiers of societal roles.

We then rode the elevators down together with our conveniently designed pockets for smartphones and valuables and entered the park together with an initial task we called the "wall of solidarity." In this action, we walked side by side in a synchronized stride. The connected line we created traveled around the park, occasionally splitting and reforming to navigate around obstacles. We used this action to signal the start of something, to wake up the space, and to familiarize ourselves with our surroundings. With our brightly-clad bodies, we were already a potential aberration.

During this time, I introduced the practice of desire lines and one of its main foundational protocols by addressing the dancers: "We are already doing it. Everyone is already practicing desire lines. Whatever you do is right." Desire is always already present, but depending on the conditions of one's environment, desire can be concealed, revealed, suppressed, or nudged in different directions. Because sources of desire in a shared movement language are personal in nature, self-censorship and self-judgment are also present.

Breaking protocol with accepted modes of behavior in public space can feel dangerous—especially given current and historical restrictions on sexual desire and, in particular, same-sex desire. In the most accepting of cultures, the expression of same-sex desire continues to be mostly kept out of sight. In many parts of the world, it continues to be illegal.[2]

Likewise, it can be challenging for a person of color or a woman, femme, or nonbinary person to feel safe expressing desire and possibly being seen as transgressive in public spaces, particularly spaces of leisure, which historically have been segregated or inaccessible. As a person of color, my ongoing desire to push against a capitalist consumption of the spectacle of physical labor adds to the complexity of the Desire Lines project.

One's desire may be to shut down or reject moving with and through desire. That, too, regardless of any negative feelings it may cause, is permitted if the declaration "Whatever you do is right" is sound and authentic. Major refusals and interventions necessitate a new protocol, perhaps readmittance or the allowance of renewal. In these instances, and for these reasons, we are vocally permissive of all digressions and diversions. Such refusals or ways of opting out are a layer of Desire Lines within the overarching collaborative group structure, which already sees itself as an alternative to expected and heteronormative behaviors. I think of these refusals, however, not as exits of the system but as cul-de-sacs. Each rejection opens up a potential theatrical site. Opposition creates drama, and the terrain shifts. The "individual versus the group" is a relational scenario that offers multiple portals back into dancing.

Our mutual desire is to use performance to course-correct our individual and collective thinking around what is permissible in public space, what dance is, and where it's allowed to live and be seen. The practice attempts to erode spaces of exclusion and restriction by offering ways around our own internal roadblocks, by modeling presence and multiplicity, and by generating new forms of beauty and engagement. Or as feminist theoretician Sara Ahmed writes, "We might say demands and prohibitions are generative; they create objects and worlds."[3]

With Desire Lines, we attempted to encourage and accommodate difference by creating portals into and out of being and dancing together, some of which were more open-ended and some more tightly defined. The "valuaction" part of the process and the inevitable aesthetic editorializing happens incrementally through the practice of repetition, the power of suggestion, mimicry, memory recall, self-reflexive feedback, and that slippery thing I will call group dynamic.[4] Through our own observation as "directors," we inevitably craft containers for each person's tendencies and the group's potentialities.

In the absence of known movement sequences, we focused on structures that could be recognizable to each other so that we could all engage with the rules of that particular structure. The suggested structures would sometimes emerge through cumulatively shared experiences, or we would propose and negotiate them.

Performers were encouraged to break with protocol if approached by a spectator. Interruption became a kind of material of attention. Incidental, accidental, and interruptive social acts were subsumed inside of the overall practice and framed as part of the dancing. We are dancers, and this is dancing in the broadest definition. Desire Lines is not a practice of freedom, but there are elements of freedom inside of the structure, a structure that we collectively generate over time, a sum of our desires.

Words like *freedom* and *desire* are complicated. In this case, I would describe freedom as the agency to initiate, respond, and refuse. But this freedom is conditional, hemmed in by the elements of the physical environment, the wage-labor contract, and other social and cultural expectations. In *Saving Time*, artist Jenny Odell writes, "Freedom is choice, and choice is scattered throughout the universe, pushing forward and acting upon what would constrain it."[5] In other words, freedom is an action, and actions disappear and reappear. Desire is equally conditional. Odell goes on to suggest that desire, as "an attitude toward the future and a reflection of one's past, can exist only in time—the time inhabited by that person."[6] I remember one of the dancers describing desire as "needy." Freedom and desire mean different things to different people at different times. So one of the central tenets is the liberating notion that we don't all have to agree.

Of course, with a proposal like this, one has to relinquish a level of control. Because the foundational conceit is born from a permissive gesture, things can and will slip through the cracks. Authorship here is shifting and ambiguous. Things will happen that we do not like.

Through all of these choices, suggestions, refusals, digressions, shortcuts, and carefully worded language, we begin to make a world together. But we are never making the same world as each other. Victims of temperament, we give and receive, lead and follow, nurture and destroy at different rates and scales. In collaborative dance-making processes, temperament reveals itself through a dialectic between the depth of one's internal landscape and the way one responds to outside expectations.

In his *New Yorker* article "Are You The Same Person You Used to Be?" writer Joshua Rothman reflects on how childhood shapes later life by revisiting a psychological study in New Zealand of thousands of people across decades.[7] The researchers suggest that temperament is "a machine that designs another machine, which goes on to influence development."[8] Rothman posits that this "second machine is a person's social environment."[9] In essence, there is mounting evidence that we have the ability to create and manipulate our own environments.

We attempted to devise portals for different temperaments through what we call *modalities*. In the modality *alignment*, one moves to align oneself with a perceived sound in the environment, using a specific arrangement of body positions. In *reverse radiation*, one attempts the speculative action of pulling the world into the body by spinning until one falls. In *3body problem*, one attempts orbits in space and in the body.[10] In *noticing*, one attempts to observe and filter visual stimuli and to draw the environment with the body. In *fence*, we perform the task of crossing over, under, and through a metal fence repeatedly as a group. All of these *modalities* leave room for interpretation, but the protocols funnel individuals into recognizable actions that produce distinct aesthetic and energetic properties.

The funneling is a way to narrow the parameters of choice, to retain some element of control over the outcome, and to provide something to push against. One cannot rebel if there are no rules. It is impossible to define one's self in a vacuum: "You can feel the categories that you fail to inhabit: they are sources of discomfort. Comfort is a feeling that tends not to be consciously felt. ... Instead, you sink. When you don't sink, when you fidget and move around, then what is in the background becomes in front of you. ... Discomfort, in other words, allows things to move."[11] When we move in public in ways that do not mimic the protocols of the theater, we introduce a potentially discomforting possibility for public behavior where our bodies are unpredictable, joyful, vulnerable, and perhaps liberated.

Of course we have to give ourselves and others the permission to be embodied—not just to take up space, but to be in a state of experiencing the fullness of our bodies in space and the system of infinitesimal choices that we are making when we are alive. This is not mindlessly staring into space, obediently sweeping the floor, or apologetically getting to the next destination. This is an altered reality of radical acceptance that activates and broadcasts our similarities, our differences, and what we could become. Who am I staring at? How do I want to hold this broom? When is the right time to go? Hopefully, the dancing teaches us how to dance and the seeing teaches us how to see.

Within this knowledge drawn from the practice of moving in time and space, how can we organize and demonstrate these forces and layers of perception and investment? What is the data from which we can measure variables and estimate parameters of moving targets?

On the final performance day in the park, we etched out these roving lines of discomfort, wonder, boredom, and desire—hoping and willing that stretching out the practice to nine hours would allow patterns, relationships, and perceptions to accumulate and metabolize over time. I remember the beauty of everyone disbursing and collecting. I remember losing track of myself and others. I remember the soft prickle of the grass. I remember the sweltering heat of summer, the sweat, and the exhaustion. I remember that out of nowhere, after about seven sunny hours of dancing and looking, a sudden hard rain poured down. It cleared pedestrians and all of their belongings out of the park like a magic trick. It washed away any record of our crisscrossing presence.

As we gathered our exhausted and soaked bodies under the pavilion and looked around at a once bustling park devoid of all other humans, we cheered at the thought that maybe we had collectively conjured the rain as a kind of climactic reward. (We were wearing swimsuit material, after all.) Or maybe the rain was caused by the hubris of thinking we could attempt to organize chaos—a drenching rebuke of our finish line.

It was a reminder that because dance as a form is always changing, the protocols have to change as well. The parameters have to be continually proposed, tested, rearranged, and cleared.

In subsequent iterations of Desire Lines we attempted to expose the mechanics of creation through periodic testimonial acts, oral histories, narrational utterances, recall and repetition, audience participation, and projected or published scores.[12] These records are reinserted as landmarks in new iterative landscapes where the thought and spatial pathways of spontaneous action etch out a map of individual and collective desire. We pretend. We mimic. We multiply our actions and our subjectivities. We are following in our own footsteps.

On the following page, we invite you to activate the written score by Silas Riener. Make a choice and follow through—give yourself permission for one small transgression by ripping the page out of this book.

PERMISSION SLIP

I AM THE PAGE. YOU AND I WILL START HERE TOGETHER, THEN GO OUR SEPARATE WAYS.

I NEED YOU TO BEGIN. YOUR PERMISSION WILL BE ACTION, MARKS. MINE IS MY VERY BEING; I AM A SLIP OF PAPER. WRITE YOUR NAME ON MY FACE, I GIVE YOU MY BODY. RIP ME OUT OF THIS BOOK AND TAKE ME SOMEWHERE PRIVATE.

CHOOSE A PATH TO FOLLOW

A PATH FOR PROTECTION	BEND, FOLD, CREASE, CRUMPLE SCRUNCH, UNFURL – SMOOTH OUT. FIRST YOU, THEN ME. NOW TEAR ME APART AND BURY THE PIECES. MY DESTRUCTION FOR YOUR PRESERVATION.
A PATH FOR ABSOLUTION	WRITE TRUE THINGS ON MY BACK. ROLL ME UP TIGHT AND BURN YOUR SECRET HONESTY.
A PATH FOR PROSPERITY	DRAW A MAP OF THE FUTURE ALL OVER ME. IF ONE IS ALREADY THERE, THEN ADD TO IT. PASS ME ALONG TO SOMEONE ELSE.

REFUSAL IS ALWAYS AN OPTION, BUT I CAN'T DO IT WITH YOU – IT'S A PATH FOR YOU ALONE

Reverse: Silas Riener, "Permission Slip," 2023. From *As for Protocols* (Vera List Center for Art and Politics and Amherst College Press, 2025).

1 The costumes were printed with images painted by Federico de Francesco and worn by dancers David Rafael Botana, Justin Faircloth, Stanley Gambucci, Jennifer Gonzalez, Eleanor Hullihan, Kate Jewett, Catherine Kirk, Cori Kresge, Rashaun Mitchell, Mina Nishimura, Silas Riener, Maddie Schimmel, and André M. Zachery.

2 Matilda Tudor exposes ways in which queer life in Russia has been shaped by antigay sentiment and government persecution in Turdor, "Desire Lines: Towards a Queer Digital Media Phenomenology" (PhD diss., Södertörn University, 2018).

3 Sara Ahmed, "Orientations Toward a Queer Phenomenology," *GLQ: A Journal of Lesbian and Gay Studies* 12, no. 4 (2006).

4 Anna and Lawrence Halprin used the term "valuaction" in their methodology for collaboration to describe evaluation as an interactive process based on one's values. Lawrence Halprin, *The RSVP Cycles: Creative Processes in the Human Environment* (New York: George Braziller, 1970).

5 Jenny Odell, *Saving Time: Discovering a Life Beyond the Clock* (New York: Random House, 2023), 152.

6 Ibid, 146.

7 The subjects of the study, entitled "The Origins of You: How Childhood Shapes Later Life," in Dunedin, New Zealand, were interviewed and observed at intervals of their lives from age three to forty-five. Four psychologists—Jay Belsky, Avshalom Caspi, Terrie E. Moffitt, and Richie Poulton—summarized the research in 2020.

8 Joshua Rothman, "Are You the Same Person You Used to Be?" *New Yorker*, October 3, 2022, https://www.newyorker.com/magazine/2022/10/10/are-you-the-same-person-you-used-to-be-life-is-hard-the-origins-of-you.

9 Ibid.

10 This title was taken from the science-fiction novel of the same name. Cixin Liu, *The Three Body Problem* (Chongqing: Chongqing Press, 2008).

11 Ahmed, "Orientations Toward a Queer Phenomenology."

12 Other iterations of Desire Lines include *Desire Lines: Retrofit*, which was performed at the San Francisco Museum of Modern Art in 2018 and incorporated found objects; *Switch*, performed at the Joyce Theater in New York, 2018; *Time Being*, commissioned by HomeLA and performed on the campus of the Neighborhood Unitarian Universalist Church in Pasadena, California, 2022; *A Dance for Sunset*, performed on protected land and waterways of the Post Morrow Foundation in Brookhaven, New York, 2022; *Retrofit; a new age*, commissioned by and performed at Danspace Project in New York, 2022.

ANISHINAABEG VISITING, SMILES, AND EMBODIED PRACTICE

Leanne Betasamosake Simpson

Deep into the first year of the pandemic, I participated in the VLC Forum 2020 hosted by the Vera List Center for Art and Politics. I was in conversation with Borderlands Fellow Maria Hupfield on Zoom.[1] Our exchange was called *On Protocol*.[2] I was excited to sit and visit with Maria because her artistic practice is at least in part founded and influenced by the creative work and intellectual knowledge of our people, the Anishinaabeg. I remember feeling really happy that Maria had reached out to me and set up the conversation in the isolation of the pandemic because she is someone whose work I had always admired, and I had been hoping our paths would cross. Maria is a transdisciplinary artist, and I am a writer. I often see my Anishinaabekwe self in Maria's performances, installations, and sculptures. In ways that are related to my work, Maria is also concerned with movement, making, scales, connection and belonging, and expansive exchange. We are both Anishinaabekwe and work within Indigenous feminisms.

As I began writing this piece, I watched and rewatched our exchange. Three years later, it was beautiful to see again how Maria set the tone for our conversation. She invited me into a virtual space with her embodiment of Anishinaabe ethics and knowledge even before she introduced herself. Maria came into our conversation gently and her wide, bright smile invited me and everyone else into a warm space brimming with kindness, generosity, and care. She described herself and what she was wearing for those relying more heavily on the audio. She told me her Anishinaabe name and her clan, which helps me to situate her within our nation. She is from the most beautiful place on what a branch of the Anishinaabe call Odawa Gaming (for Lake Huron) and Odawa Wiikedong (for Georgian Bay). She told me about this place and a bit about her ancestry. I could tell she was a language learner, and she could also tell that from me. I could understand all of her words. I could see how she resembled some of her cousins in her physical features. I understood from her mannerisms that she was embodying an old practice of Anishinaabe exchange, one that I melted into because I trusted her and knew that she would handle the delicate conversation with care. I answered Maria's introduction with my own. I said similar things, although following a Michi Saagiig Anishinaabeg practice of saying our clan first and our own name last. If I had been outside of my homeland, I then would have acknowledged whosoever's territory I was visiting, as a political affirmation of their sovereignty and self-determination and a practice of respect.

You can understand our initial exchange as a protocol. Anishinaabe people begin everything by introducing ourselves—meetings, ceremonies, and any sort of gathering. In ceremonies, we introduce ourselves to the spirits that have joined us. When we are harvesting, we introduce ourselves to the plants and animals. Our voices, making sound with our bodies, are a unique contribution to the universe, which our exchange acknowledged. Maria also used the greeting "Aaniin/Aanii," which is more common than the more formal Bozhoo in my territory. It means "I see your light," again an acknowledgment of my own being and self-determination.

Maria's smile, though, was not protocol. There is no rule that Anishinaabe begin meetings, visits, or events with a big smile; if anything, our elders tend to show less emotion in facial expressions in comparison to Euro-Canadian or American culture. I experienced her smile as entirely Anishinaabe because it was contradictory to the colonial form of our encounter and the formality of artist talks and academic conversations. It indicated that she was coming to our dialogue with an open heart. Her smile expressed the Anishinaabe desire to build spaces of openness, inclusion, kindness, and respect. Anishinaabe often create such spaces by praying and singing at the beginning of meetings. We want people to feel seen and welcomed and to set up the gathering in a way that people manage themselves respectfully, even if the issue at hand is difficult. Maria skillfully did all that for me with her smile, her gestures, and even the tone of her voice. Her opening reminded me that it wasn't just Maria and Leanne showing up on Zoom; it was also our entire system of ancestry throughout time.[3] The ancestors and relationships that make me who I am are those that have made her. I remember this confluence grounding me in a way that was unusual at the beginning of COVID Zoom times, and I remember thinking she was adept at setting a space, even a digital space, where I could breathe and open my heart—both things quite unique in online talks.

Now, you could understand our introduction as protocol, but for me, this wasn't protocol; it was a wonderful iteration of Anishinaabe embodied political and ethical practice for sharing knowledge. We began a contemporary exchange by scaffolding our shared ancient roots—we couldn't smudge or sing, pray, or sit around a fire in the forest. But we did something Anishinaabeg, an act that we have each seen and participated in thousands of times, but never with each other. A practice where, in that moment, we communicated our intentions for the conversation in a coded and Anishinaabeg way to each other and to our ancestors. Maria's opening didn't foreclose any conversations; it was instead an invitation to think with her, to share my experiences and my thinking at that moment in time. It was an opening to a collaboration. And, of course, we are not the first Indigenous women or artists to sit down and have a conversation about protocols. These conversations happen all the time around kitchen tables, on sidewalks, in galleries and studios, and in the bush. I was reminded specifically of an exchange between filmmaker Christine Welsh and Elader Shirley Bear around a fire in the bush talking about protocol and ceremony in the 1994 National Film Board of Canada film called *Keepers of the Fire*.[4]

Our conversation was an echo, another iteration of a conversation as old as time.

Maria knows that in my work, I've broken many so-called Anishinaabe protocols. She knows this as an Anishinaabekwe, and we both know that is why we were here, having this public conversation that I'm now retracing on the page. I suspect we both know that this is a conversation that would have been difficult to have twenty years ago, and that in some places in our communities, it would be difficult and uncomfortable to have it today. We've both seen protocols deployed in our culture, usually—though not always—well intentioned, to exclude women, trans, two-spirit, and queer people from our ceremonies and our gatherings. I began to write about this in *Dancing on Our Turtle's Back,*[5] recovering and reclaiming the ethical and philosophical context for our thought, a foundation that cherishes both individual self-determination and diversity. And then again in *As We Have Always Done*, where I explored gender in a deeper way in relation to our intellectual and communal practices.[6] I started writing stories where characters actively broke taboos and protocols around gender and menstruation in *This Accident of Being Lost*.[7] I tried to insert queer normativity into the lives of my characters in both *This Accident of Being Lost* and *Noopiming*.[8] I wanted Anishinaabeg women and queer people to see themselves inside the stories. I didn't set out to break protocol; my intention was to expand our ideas around protocol or to place protocols back within the larger network of Anishinaabe ethics. If the intent of protocols is to show respect and create spaces where we could be our best selves, what happens when there is such rigidity that the protocol erodes our foundational values of consent, diversity, self-determination, and non-interference? What happens when protocol backfires and causes harm? What happens when protocols make people feel uncomfortable, unseen, unwanted, and hurt? How can we break the cage of protocol and embody a deeper understanding of Anishinaabe ethics and values?

Maria began our conversation by asking me why I made the switch from using the term *protocol* to *practices* in my work. My answer was long. Anishinaabe very much view life as a cascading network of living things across species and geographies that work together, interdependently to create more life. Our purpose is to fit into that life network, to collaborate with the plants and animals, the lakes and the rivers, our ancestors, and those yet to be born to make worlds that take care of all the things we are sharing time and space with. Anishinaabe life, to a great degree, is care work. Our foundational teachings, the Seven Ancestor teachings, in my area called the Kookum Dibajimowin, are not a set of laws or commandments, or protocols that we have to follow. Rather, they are a complex set of practices that, when embodied, both individually and in relation to other living things, create a world in which consent, accountability, problem solving, and kindness are embedded. Doug Williams, an Elder from Curve Lake First Nation, taught me that grandparents help children understand each of the concepts by telling stories about particular community or family members that embody the idea in a certain way, nurturing relationships within the family, and inviting younger family members into a web of embodied practice or story, for a concept like humility.[9] Every day, every moment of every day is a chance to embody these seven concepts in a unique way, and the overall practice generated a communal kindness. Rather than create a set of rigid and dogmatic rules for engagement, grandparents wrap a blanket of experiences and relational knowledge around the grandchildren. They demonstrated the practice of kindness through how they were living and living together, a practice that I imagine at times was quite complicated. It was this interesting balance between the individual and the communal—living in a way where you were thinking about what you could give up for the benefit of the larger community, while also maintaining yourself. A nest of relationships that starts inside of each of us, and then expands to those close to us, and then expands again to water, connecting us to all other forms of life on the planet. Embodied practice has a depth that protocol doesn't. Embodied practice is an expansive and generative process that has the potential to make and remake the world. It makes me who I am in the world, and repeating these practices over and over, in different iterations as the moment demands, is how Anishinaabe have always aligned ourselves with our origin stories. Embodied practice doesn't foreclose in the way protocols can. Embodied practice demands more of us. It demands we think through our actions and their impact on others. It demands we adapt and modify to make sure all Anishinaabe can show up at our gatherings, share their knowledge, and contribute to the task at hand by being their best selves. Embodied practice demands that we think critically about protocols and the work they do in our collective spaces. It demands we collaborate and even transform how we relate to each other.

I remember very early on in my career being out on the land with an Elder hunting geese. We shot one, and he had forgotten his tobacco. I remember wondering what was going to happen, because it is our practice to show gratitude through reciprocity, and normally this is done through an offering of tobacco. The Elder who I was with left a tiny bit of his baloney sandwich. When I asked him if this was going to be OK with the geese, he said "Of course," because the gesture was thoughtful and would be seen by the geese as an expression of deep respect.

In my part of Anishinaabe territory, we share some lands and waters with the Haudenosaunee Confederacy. In Anishinaabe culture, we always travel around the circle the same way the Earth travels around the sun. For example, if we are gathered in a circle for a Pipe Ceremony, the pipe will get passed around the circle to the people in a clockwise direction. For the Haudenosaunee, this would be in a counterclockwise direction. When we get together, there is always lots of joking around about which way around the circle we will go. One way of looking at it is that someone's protocol gets broken. Another way of seeing it is a recognition that our shared diplomacy requires that we each think about what we can give up in order to promote peace, and this is just the first opportunity to contribute to the peacemaking process. This is a first opportunity to embody the Seven Ancestor teachings and kina-bimaadiziwin.[10]

As always, the land and waters are our best teachers. The planetary system requires both clockwise and counterclockwise directions. The Earth revolves around the sun in both a clockwise and counterclockwise direction, depending on viewpoint. There is a broad division between night and day, and a cycle of light that creates unique moments in the diurnal cycle, and each moment made up of a different amount of light than the next. This reminds me that the planetary forces are not a rigid set of protocols that are understandable to humans. There is a vast amount about the universe that we don't know, that we can't know. In this context, Anishinaabeg thought developed a series of practices that privileged relationships over simplistic rules of engagement. So while we can interpret the polarity of night and day to coincide with a colonial gender binary, for instance, there is also an understanding that between those two polarities there is an infinite number of other expressions and ways of being. This gives way to our spectrum of genders and sexual orientations that exceeds the gender binary we have inherited from our colonial oppressors. This flows fluidity into our practices—wear a skirt if you can embody those teachings, wear something different if skirts don't align with your heart. Sit on the side of the lodge where you feel most grounded. Offer tobacco before you pick berries if you have tobacco. Introduce yourself to those plants and have a conversation with or without an offering. Avoid using protocol to demonstrate how much of your culture you've recovered and instead use our practices as a point of connection and to create belonging and nurture relationships.

In the midst of climate catastrophe, making worlds that refuse racial capitalism, heteropatriarchy, transphobia, anti-Blackness and colonialism is a collaborative process across cultures, species, and movements. Meeting the needs of the planet and our peoples will require us to enliven our ancient teachings and find ways to dream and vision ourselves into Anishinaabeg worlds that can seamlessly link to and support the worlds our co-resistors are dreaming and making. My visit with Maria reminded me that an embodiment of our most precious values and ethics can set up a space where we can come together to think, learn, and create alongside each other. Miigwech, Maria.

→ dress the space
cedar,
three ears,
feed each other's fire

/\/\/ signal \/\/\

↓ bring the place shining brightly
in the reflection of sacred light,
bring the place where the plains
are burning across the lake

<<< confluence >>>

← the heart is the first drum
shakers as the sound of thinking

+++ NDN time +++

↑ biidaaban
smile as flight
mi'iw

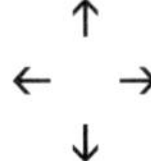

1 The Borderlands Fellowship is an initiative of the Vera List Center for Art and Politics at The New School and the Center for Imagination in the Borderlands at Arizona State University.

2 See video documentation of the event "On Protocol: VLC Fellow Maria Hupfield in Conversation with Leanne Betasamosake Simpson," Vera List Center for Art and Politics, October 8, 2020, https://www.veralistcenter.org/events/on-protocol-fellow-maria-hupfield-in-conversation-with-leanne-betasamosake-simpson.

3 I learned the term "systems of ancestry" in this context from Inuk artist Asinnajaq.

4 Christine Welsh, dir., *Keepers of the Fire* (National Film Board of Canada, 1994), https://www.nfb.ca/film/keepers_of_the_fire/.

5 Leanne Betasamosake Simpson, *Dancing on Our Turtle's Back: Stories of Anishinaabeg Re-Creation, Resurgence and a New Emergence* (Winnipeg: Arbeiter Ring Publishing, 2011).

6 Leanne Betasamosake Simpson, *As We've Always Done* (Minneapolis: University of Minnesota Press, 2017).

7 Leanne Betasamosake Simpson, *This Accident of Being Lost* (Toronto, ON: House of Anansi, 2016).

8 Leanne Betasamosake Simpson, *Noopiming: The Cure for White Ladies* (Minneapolis: University of Minnesota Press, 2022).

9 For a fuller discussion on this, see Simpson, *Dancing on Our Turtle's Back*, 124-27.

10 Meaning "harmonious," living the seven teachings in a way that creates harmony and kindness. See Gidigaa Migizi (Doug Williams), *Michi Saagiig Anishinaabeg: This Is Our Territory* (Winnipeg: Arbeiter Ring Publishing, 2018), 1-20.

A MATTER OF BRAIDING

Carolina Caycedo with Lupita Limón Corrales

At a lecture at the Sun Valley Museum of Art (SVMOA) in Ketchum, Idaho, an audience member asked during the Q&A why I collaborate with other people, at what seemed to be all levels of my process and practice. The panel was focused on SVMOA's 2022 exhibition *Dams: Reservoirs, Reclamation, Renewal*, to which I had contributed two new works—in response to the momentum developing around the struggle to undam the Lower Snake River, a major river in the greater Pacific Northwest region of the United States that measures one thousand miles. The works also included a short film called *Reciprocal Sacrifice*.

Reciprocal Sacrifice follows a salmon seeking to return to its spawning grounds in the Sawtooth Mountains in Idaho while narrating the many challenges it faces swimming upstream, such as the four dams that choke the Lower Snake River and the warming of the creeks and rivers. It also tells viewers, in Nimipuutímt voiceovers recorded by members of the Niimiipuu Language Program of the Nez Perce Tribe, a cosmological story concerning self-sacrifice, generosity, love, and gratitude. The story is one that was shared with me during my fieldwork, and it relates the natural contract between salmon, water, and humans, providing an argument for undamming that highlights our interconnectedness and responsibility to one another—values that are central to the native people, culture, and history of the Snake River. Unfortunately, we humans have breached our natural contracts and original promises to other entities, leading to the collapse of ecosystems that sustain life.

One of the reasons I collaborate with people is quite practical: I'm not a fabricator. I'm not keen to master specific skills of material manipulation. But, beyond the practical need to rely on collaborators' knowledge and skill sets, collaboration is also a part of my own personal decolonial process, in which I unlearn individuality and universalism, and seek and remember diverse ways of being in relation. I find pleasure as well as physical and psychological safety in sustaining the collective; it roots me like nothing else. Working on a project collaboratively is where I feel most at ease, even when these communal configurations are temporary. I don't have many intimate friends, but I have a web of friends and allies all over the world with whom I weave this process of re-enchantment.

So how does one weave or sustain such networks through art practice, and what are the protocols for doing so? In episode thirty of the podcast *The Urban Auntie Show,* Meda DeWitt, a Tlingit traditional healer and ethno-herbalist, gives us some insight when asked to advise about how to become a traditional healer:[1]

> It needs to go back to family and community, figuring out who you are, where you come from, what your family gifts, what your gifts are that you have to contribute, 'cause they are not the same, and they are not always what we want them to be either. Willing

> to have humility in the learning process. How to be a cultural or traditional person, learning the protocols of medicine is probably more important than just the application of medicine. Because everything has rules. In [W]estern America, nobody likes rules, guys want to push the boundaries and break the rules, or rules don›t apply to them. However, our culture is based on relationships with all our relatives, all the nations, and it's based on natural law, and that natural law is the foundation for our social protocols and rules for engagement. So, learning how things work and why things work is beneficial.

This learning of the natural law, how and why things work, of how a habitat or ecosystem is shaped offers some clues to understanding how we relate to one another. Symbiosis, also called the art of living together, can take the form of mutualism, commensalism, parasitism, competition, or predation. I ask myself: Which of these forms are we favoring in our everyday, in our working, societal, and environmental interactions? Are our interactions and relationships coming from a place of mutualism or predation, of healing, or of sickness? The notion of coming back to family and community is also so important to me, as I believe that coming back home is a protocol for deep engagement in ecological healing. If we all return to our homes, our planet may have a better chance. But where is home when you have multiple places of origin like me?

Over the years, I have come to understand that from my place of transnational privilege, I can build bridges between my many homes and the people and communities that inhabit them. I can accompany different struggles in solidarity and with affection. One could say that the materials I favor are trust, collaboration, and reciprocity, braided deliberately to care for all that sustains the natural cycles of life and rebirth. An essential element of my practice is what I call spiritual fieldwork, or the process of developing relationships with the human and nonhuman entities of a particular place or field in tandem with gathering information.

The insistence on the spiritual often puts people off—it is seen as lacking political and intellectual depth, and it is stigmatized in many contemporary art contexts. But the spiritual approach functions in stark contrast to extractivist methodologies, which place humans above other beings and erases our embodied and natural knowledge, poisoning us in the process. Depleting the land of our common goods has bodily implications; ultimately, extractivism impedes us from embodying and performing knowledge that has been handed down through generations and connects us inherently to a particular territory. Extractivism makes us forget and disconnects us from home, family, and community. In the academy and the arts, extractivism is replicated through the accumulation of cultural capital at the expense of ancestral knowledge. The spiritual may also be coated with the sacred, something that in our noisy societies is not openly embodied or talked about but that is latent in many of our countercurrent activities. The spiritual and the sacred are places of political resistance.

So the actions I take as a woman, artist, and mother are intentionally spiritual and include practices of remembering and caring for the people and environment I relate to, driven by an understanding that we are communal symbiotic beings in an interconnected web of life. Each strand of the trust, collaboration, and reciprocity braid comes with its own set of protocols, and I want to share some of them with you:

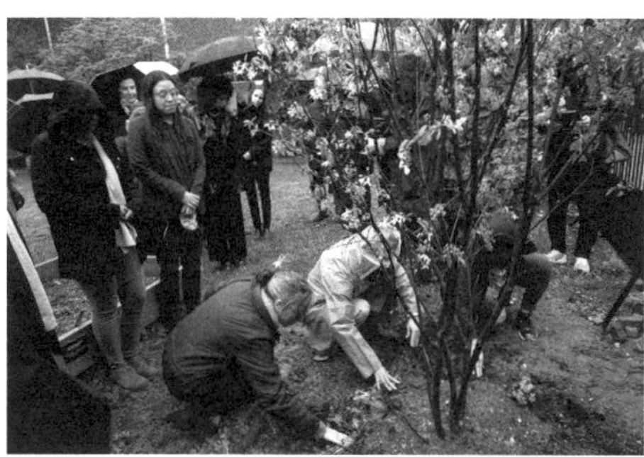

Figure 1. Carolina Caycedo, *La Siembra* (The Sowing), view of tree planting, Union Settlement, New York, 2022. Photo by Argenis Apolinario. Courtesy of the Vera List Center for Art and Politics.

BUILDING TRUST

As a middle-class mestiza who had access to higher education, I often feel entitled to information. This entitlement is something I am learning to revise and replace with a practice of earning and building trust. Some of the protocols I have learned over the years are to ask permission, to listen deeply, to understand and support the existing agenda of a people or place, and to keep promises. Together, these practices allow for trust to grow and to become the foundation of non-extractive relationships.

In 2021, I went through a tribal consultation request with the Four Southern Tribes[2] Cultural Resource Working Group. I requested a meeting in hopes that I would be able to reproduce a small prehistoric copper cascabel as a sonic marker for *La Siembra*, (Figure 1) a tree-planting gathering I was organizing in New York City as part of my Borderlands Fellowship.[3] The cascabel is currently part of the archeological repository collection at Arizona State University, where I conducted research, and apparently was found in a domestic trash mound in the Gila River Valley. I was granted a meeting with the Cultural Resource Working Group, and I showed up assuming I was doing the right thing by asking permission

Description Figure 1. Photograph of a gathering of people outside around a small garden wearing raincoats and holding umbrellas. Most are standing but three people are seen crouching down, tending to the soil and planting a tree.

and following the procurement consultation. But it turned out the tribe should have been consulted even before accessing the object in the archive. So my request to reproduce the bell was totally out of place, as I assumed that the object was publicly available because it was in the archive, and I only considered the archive's narrative rather than the object's. The meeting was very tense, and my petition was turned down. Through this humbling misstep, I learned to shake off the expectation of entitlement; I learned that I can follow a protocol and still receive a "no," and that it takes time to break through the histories and dynamics I carry as a non-native person.

With *Reciprocal Sacrifice,* I collaborated at many levels. When planning my fieldwork in the Snake River Basin, I had the opportunity to consult with Angela Mooney D'Arcy, an environmentalist and member of the Acjachemen Nation based in Los Angeles, to ask if she would connect me with someone working on the undamming of the Snake River. She taught me a new protocol then: to ask the Shoshone-Bannock and Nez Perce people for permission to visit their ancestral and contemporary lands before beginning. I wrote a letter to the Shoshone-Bannock and Nez Perce tribes, formally requesting permission to visit, sharing my goals for my time there, and offering to leverage my resources and visibility to support local organizing. This time, I received a "yes."

Months later, while visiting their reservations during my fieldwork, I learned about the threat of extinction faced by wild salmon in the Snake River and about the role salmon plays for the native people of the basin in terms of ecology, economics, food, and cultural and spiritual sovereignty. As I spent time with many different people working toward undamming, I listened intently, asking questions and then letting their words flow, without a linear goal or a controlled back and forth.

Deep listening requires patience, which requires time. I think time is an Indigenous currency, one that we especially lack in our capitalist society. Listening also requires that you be present, allowing what you hear to shape the process at every step. In the decade since I began the *Be Dammed* series, I have visited many riverine communities and learned about the ecological, economic, and psychological impacts of dams in several different countries, including Brazil, Colombia, Guatemala, and Mexico. In each instance, the artwork that emerges from my fieldwork takes on a different form, whether through sculpture, textile, video, or collective performances. Both the form and the focus of the finished pieces are shaped by the process of building relationships, exchanging stories, and spending time with the people and places impacted by dams. As I receive the gift of stories and learn about the agenda of a particular people or place, my aesthetic and theoretical goals become compliant with the needs of local struggles. I am not a legal advocate, and I don't identify as an activist, but I can support the agenda in place with my skills to construct and deconstruct images.

When we build trust, we may be given intimate access to personal and sacred spaces and information, which requires attentiveness to ethics and confidentiality. When trust has been built, it is important to be aware of one's limitations, not to overstep, and not to overcommit. Trust is maintained by keeping promises, contracts, and boundaries. This means that not everything is art material, and not everything can be shared with the rest of the world—sensitivity to knowing what to disclose and how, and a willingness to ask for permission each step of the way, even to take a quick snapshot, ensure that the relationships are authentic, and not merely in service to a finished product.

COLLABORATION

Many of my collaborators do not normally inhabit art spaces and may understandably feel skeptical toward them. For trust to build, relationships to deepen, and vulnerability and creativity to be possible, my collaborators must feel safe in the space I invite them into. What are the protocols for creating this collaborative, safe space?

The Teaching of the Hands, a film made in collaboration with my life partner David de Rozas, emerged from a long-term relationship with Juan Mancias and his family, who are part of the Carrizo-Comecrudo Tribe of Texas. While researching southwest Texas, we attended Juan's talk at La Conxa, an autonomous space in East Los Angeles's Boyle Heights, where he shared the struggle against the border fence construction in the Rio Grande Valley. Mr. Mancias also presented his view that the rock art of the Lower Pecos are prophecies from his ancestors that anticipate the arrival of the oil industry, gentrification, space rockets, and other manifestations of settler colonialism in the region. In this interpretation, the rock paintings also prophesy the resistance embodied by the local tribes today and into the future. This reading goes against the official academic narrative that the pictographs are tied to peyote rituals. Because the Carrizo-Comecrudo are not federally recognized, and because this embodied knowledge counters an academic theory shaped by archaeological excavations and technological capturing, it has been criticized and dismissed.

After that first meeting in Boyle Heights, we visited the Mancias family in Texas and the Yalui Village, a frontline resistance on ancestral resting grounds against the border fence construction.

As our interaction unfolded, we were generously invited by the tribe to join them during the summer solstice and fall equinox to pray, sing, dance, feast, and sweat. We also visited many pictographs together to learn about the language imprinted in these ancient murals. These readings of ancestral pictographs in real time became a cornerstone in our understanding of the complexities of the region, and how settler and Indigenous knowledge continue to clash in that particular context. David and I decided to highlight the native prophecies and the cosmological value of tribal teachings that we had learned about, and we invited Juan Mancias to narrate the film. Through *The Teachings of the Hands*, Juan shares how the tribe's profound relationship with the Southwest environment provides clues to heal the present and future. Our interactions and sharings also informed a whole body of additional works encompassing drawings, installations, collages, and loans from institutional collections.

This body of work has been presented in multiple venues across Texas, New York, and California. The different iterations have provided an opportunity to continue collaborating with Juan and his family, by inviting them to attend openings and celebrations, to lead tours, and to participate in panels and conversations that expand on their own ideas and narratives and those embedded in the artwork work. A percentage of the proceeds of film-screening fees and special edition sales goes to the Carrizo-Comecrudo. The film is also available on the social platforms of the tribe. An important part of collaboration is to open the work to the constituencies associated with the different project partners, especially those who are not interested in access to the elitist art museum or gallery.

In any collaboration, in addition to establishing and enacting our own protocols, we must also follow the protocols of our collaborators. When I began working on *Reciprocal Sacrifice*, I followed the tribal protocols of the Cultural Resources Program of the Department of Natural Resources at the Nez Perce Tribe in Idaho,[4] which included submitting a research permit to the Tribal Council, and committing to creating this work, in my case, as a free, accessible, open-source video. Because of this process, the original timeline was extended to allow space for back-and-forth dialogue with Thomas Gregory, also known as tátlo, a tribal member in charge of the Nez Perce language program who provided translations and voiceovers for the film. Collaboration may slow the pace of a project as we exchange feedback and welcome contributions from multiple people to shape it, which might run counter to the more customary fast-paced work dominant in Western cultures. Not all collaboration has to inhabit the art world under the parameters we in the West are accustomed to. *Reciprocal Sacrifice* is a piece made collaboratively that will never enter the art market. Many times, when work is created collectively with and for a community, I am not interested in generating a formal or marketable transferal into the institutional setting at all.

RECIPROCITY

A non-extractivist approach is one of reciprocity, in which collaboration supports the needs of both parties in a sustained way. In that sense, reciprocity takes shape in responding to calls for mutual aid at any level, and by doing so it supports collectivities through personal and professional interactions.

A crucial part of reciprocity is properly crediting one's collaborators at all levels of presentation, be it during a lecture, an exhibition, or in documentation photos. To share the "courtesy of …" is a way to acknowledge partnerships and labor properly. Reciprocity is to compensate fairly, or secure fair compensation, for your collaborators, assistants, and fabricators; and to assign a percentage of your income to go back to the community or collaborators in the form of donations or other reliefs that may be desirable at the moment. Another way to give back is by sharing resources obtained during research that the community might otherwise not have access to, such as reports, data, specialized imagery, entry to institutions and archives, and interactions with specialists.

One protocol of reciprocity important to me is keeping in touch with folks I have worked with to ensure that our relationship goes beyond the time range of the project that may have originally brought us together. Keeping in touch can be more difficult with people or communities who do not have consistent access to the phone or internet. When I work with someone, I commit to returning physically to the location, even when there is no project in place. For me, a socially-committed project budget needs to include a return ticket to allow for a revisit to share the project results or status and for the relationship to continue building over time without pressure.

Beyond physically returning to a site, keeping in touch also means finding ways to keep the conversation we started together alive through future opportunities. For example, when asked about authors for a monograph[5] about my work, I suggested a respected curator who is familiar with my work, but I also invited David Hernández Palmar, a filmmaker and journalist who has an intimate knowledge of me as a person and as a collaborator. It was important to share this institutional space with David, whose perspective as a queer Wayuu migrant from Venezuela who now lives in rural Colombia was invaluable to the workshops we previously led together for communities impacted by the El Quimbo dam, which were being reviewed in the book.

Opening up cultural and institutional spaces to people and communities I've worked with is a gesture of reciprocity that can do many things: it redistributes resources from institutions to communities, provides material and emotional support, and strengthens networks. It creates more space for environmental and historical memory and brings to the forefront overshadowed narratives that counter hegemonic and reductive accounts of history and place. And it honors the collective skills and energy that shape a work of art.

But how can reciprocity become foundational as a guiding protocol that mediates not only our human relationships, but also those with different entities and forces of nature? Deep reciprocity also entails giving back to the very environments that sustain our lives. In all Indigenous cultures, there is a natural law, a model of the world in which energies fluctuate between different levels. Associated with this vision of perpetual energy movement is the protocol of *pagamento,* or payback, which is the need to act based on the principle of reciprocity, to always give something in exchange for what is obtained, be it something material or service of any kind. Pagamentos maintain the flow and balance of natural law and of life cycles on earth. When pagamento is not done, accumulation happens, and sickness arrives, so it's necessary to give back by letting go of something that is dear, that implies labor, or that is highly symbolic.

One example of pagamento occurred as a part of my Borderlands Fellowship, which included a vigil for environmentalists and the planting of a commemorative tree in New York City. In September 2021, I hosted a vigil and pagamento for murdered environmentalists titled *¡LOS QUE MUEREN POR LA VIDA, NO PUEDEN LLAMARSE MUERTOS! THOSE WHO DIE FOR LIFE, ARE NOT DEAD!*[6] The vigil included a sunset ceremony, testimonies from frontline activists, and the creation of a collective altar. Community members were invited to contribute a pagamento in the form of a compostable item, like soil, water, seeds, clay, flowers, herbs, and fruit, allowing us to come together in honor of the people who protect the environment.

In May 2022, after months of composting, the pagamento was used in a second solidarity action, *La Siembra,* in the community garden of Union Settlement.[7] A group of people came together during a rainy New York day to listen to testimonies by Nellie-Jo David and Amber Ortega, Tohono O'odham water protectors from Arizona, and by Colombian environmentalist Tatiana Roa Avendaño, who have experienced legal harassment and life-threatening situations for their environmental activism. After the conversation, which was moderated by scholar Romy Opperman, we gathered to plant a native shadbush tree[8] as a permanent site to remember murdered and harassed environmentalists worldwide. The tree was nurtured by the soil others had contributed to months prior, joining us in a cycle of death and rebirth. By coming together to share testimonies and plant trees, we process grief and allow the energies of life and death to flow. Communal ritual is one example of what reciprocity and balance with our environment look like on a collective level, and one way to organize ourselves around the laws and rhythms of nature.

Tree planting is not merely symbolic—it keeps the energy flow of nature and it does the work of memory and survival. In the case of *La Siembra,* it highlighted stories of resistance in the borderlands and the frontlines, and it became a pagamento, a reciprocity gesture that partially functioned to ecologically balance the carbon footprint generated by the project itself. We are tremendously sick, our rivers are drying, our food is poisoned, and our air gives us asthma. How can we live, work, and make art in a way that balances this sickness with living?

The protocols I have shared here are not set in stone—they shift as I learn and grow, as society grows, and as the circumstances of our planet change rapidly. What guides these protocols is a belief in our interconnectedness, like strands of hair that have been braided together to protect them from harm and keep away sadness. Let us collectively recommit to center and sustain life through our diverse practices. Let us remember that we are all related and that our futures are intertwined.

1 "Episode 30: Native Movement with Deloole'annh ...," *The Urban Auntie Show*, February 9, 2022, https://anchor.fm/urbanauntieshow/episodes/Episode-37-Meda-DeWitt--Traditional-Healer-e1lqqbc.

2 The Four Southern Tribes are the Gila River Indian Community, the Salt River Maricopa Posh Indian Community, the Ak-Chin Indian Community, and the Tohono O'odham Nation. All are federally recognized tribes having standing under NAGPRA.

3 The Borderlands Fellowship is an initiative of the Vera List Center for Art and Politics at The New School and the Center for Imagination in the Borderlands at Arizona State University.

4 "Natural Resources," Nez Perce Tribe, accessed July 24, 2022, https://nezperce.org/government/natural-resources/#:~:text=The%20mission%20of%20the%20Cultural,Leadership%20in%20treaty%20rights%20protection.

5 Carla Acevedo-Yates, ed., *Carolina Caycedo: From the Bottom of the River* (Chicago: Museum of Contemporary Art Chicago and DelMonico Books / D.A.P., 2021).

6 This event was part of the closing celebration of *ESTAMOS BIEN - LA TRIENAL 20/21* at El Museo del Barrio in East Harlem, New York City.

7 Founded in 1895, and one of the largest settlement houses in New York, Union Settlement serves more than ten thousand East Harlem residents of all ages each year through its education, health, senior services, youth development, childcare, counseling, and economic development programs.

8 *Amelanchier* has a variety of common names. In the northern part of the United States and in Canada, it is known as Saskatoon—its Native American name and reportedly an anglicization from the Cree language word misâskwatômin (Mis-sack-qua-too-mina), which means "the fruit of the tree of many branches." Other names include: prairie berry, serviceberry, shadbush, juneberry, and, in past centuries, pigeon berry. Its dark blue berries are edible and medicinal.

PROTOCOLS FOR A GROUNDING PHILOSOPHY

Romy Opperman

In my view, extractivism, appropriation, and dispossession are central, not accidental, elements of racism and colonialism. Finding alternatives to extraction is therefore necessary for liberatory philosophies and practices. This need applies to the way in which we think about and produce knowledge, especially in the academy. The pull of extractivism is hard to resist. Consider, even, bell hooks's repeated descriptions in the superb *Belonging: A Culture of Place*, of "the past as a resource" and "as a raw material compelling me to think critically about my native place, about ecology and issues of sustainability."[1]

How can we engage with place-based practices, situated knowledges, and memories that do not rely on "resources" and "raw materials"? More generally, how can we thoughtfully respond to the interwoven problems of climate change and racism in ways that don't violently intensify their root causes?

These questions have been increasingly urgent and complex for me as a racially ambiguous British philosopher living in what is currently known as the United States of America, whose work aims to highlight the importance of the ecological thought emergent from Black diasporic philosophy for liberatory approaches to climate and ecology. In this reflection, I identify the need for protocols for a grounding philosophy and begin to experiment with what these might be.

GROUNDING: AFRIKAN EMANCIPATION DAY 2021

Embrace "I." Refuse to "respect the numerous and very serious protocols concerning the idea that critical distance must be maintained at all costs."[2] Attend to the politics of location, place, and locality. Ask yourself: Where do you come from? Where are you? What do you carry with you? What can the "land"[3] teach you? Dig into the memories and histories sedimented in land/in body.[4] Ask: What fragments, seeds, sediments are within you? What silt lies heavy at your base? What can grow from it? What needs to be cast off or decomposed? Try to remember that knowledge is a relation—not property or (individual) possession. Remind yourself and others that not all relations are equal or good. Some are violent or creepy.[5] Be wary of extraction. Call on ancestors (known and unknown) to help you wrestle with the temporalities of inheritance and the force of intergenerational responsibility.[6]

I write this as an uninvited long-term guest—on the spectrum between migrant and settler, between olive and caramel skinned, between precarity and comfortably middle-class, as a cis queer woman, first-generation university student now youngish professor of philosophy. I am a guest on Lenape land near Weeksville—a historic community established in the nineteenth century by free Black Americans in what is today Brooklyn.

As I write, my thoughts are interrupted and then embraced by a distinct urban aural ecology—a surprising array of bird song; snatches of dancehall, hip-hop, and soca from cars; sirens and helicopters; and the voices of my Jamaican and Grenadian neighbors. I can no longer avoid the work of grounding myself. Such grounding is a preliminary protocol for a situated and accountable philosophy.[7]

Grounding[8]—the concept and set of protocols that is currently (re- and dis-)orienting my philosophical practice—was given to me in Brixton in South London on a sunny Afrikan Emancipation Day in 2021.[9] I was there for the Pan-Afrikan Reparations Rebellion Groundings (PARRG), a creation of the Afrikan Emancipation Day Reparations with the "Stop the Maangamizi!" campaign.[10] The event was supported by the Extinction Rebellion Internationalist Solidarity Network (XRISN), co-founded by Stop the Maangamizi team members Kofi Mawuli Klu and Esther Stanford-Xosei[11].

The groundings unfolded in and around Windrush Square. The "Windrush Generation" memorialized in the square (and commonly referred to as the primary moment and example of Black presence in Britain) was formed by the shared movement of individuals from the British Caribbean to the United Kingdom.[12] More recently, the policy-made reality of the "hostile environment" created by the British Conservative government has added another layer to the meaning of Windrush—that is, the scandal of intergenerational shared vulnerability to denied legal rights, detention, and deportation to those *other* islands presumed to be Caribbean British people's *real* home.[13]

As the name of the square suggests, Brixton is an area profoundly shaped by Black diasporic existence, and thus by waves of movement (voluntary and involuntary), by waves of memory, displacement, and place-making.[14] After a liminal period of over a year—determined by the pandemic protocols of the US embassy (which stipulated when I would get a visa to return to the United States to actualize my virtual, speculative life in New York City), I happily found myself in Windrush Square on Afrikan Emancipation Day and unexpectedly *still* back home in London, a London both familiar and strange. Prepandemic, I had been following the work of Extinction Rebellion (XR) from the US and was aware of some of the critiques and issues around racism, colonialism, and the group's strategy and stance around institutions such as the police and the government.[15]

At least in this instance, however, XR members (mostly white) quietly provided infrastructure, resources, and support to center a different agenda and vision of ecological and climate justice. In indigo and gold headwrap and matching dress, glorious and powerful abolitionist organizer and reparations scholar Esther Stanford-Xosei animated the Afrikan Emancipation Day.[16] I was astonished to find many of my research interests—and the connections I had attempted to make between them—anticipated and put into practice. I was also delighted to find Black womxn and feminist concerns centered through the mobilization of anti-colonial, anti-imperial, and Pan-African discourse that understood extinction as linking both genocide and ecocide. Ultimately, their program and vision of (climate) justice is a vision of "planetary repairs" that is grounded in the healing, sovereignty, and autonomy of African peoples and the Earth.[17]

Why was I so surprised? It was only during my graduate studies in the US (at Penn State, in the philosophy program that has the distinction of producing the greatest number of Black womxn philosophers) that my interests in racism, biopower, and the boundaries of the human and nonhuman, the living and the dead, could take root in a philosophical and "cultural seedbed" of Black, decolonial, and Indigenous liberatory critical thought.[18] With a few exceptions, it had been largely absent from my education—which was dominated by overwhelmingly white scholarship once I entered higher education—and my experience growing up in London.[19] At the very least, I had failed to attend to and actively pursue it.[20] Instead, I had been more at home in the critical spaces opened up and dominated by ostensibly radical white men (for instance, Gilles Deleuze and Michel Foucault), and in the category of "mixed (other)" that I ticked on official forms, a category I found didn't exist in US paperwork and racial/cultural schemas. This category "mixed other" named and effaced my paternal grandfather (we think Somali, although perhaps himself mixed), the rupture of his adoption (almost twenty years prior to Windrush), which meant that intergenerational violence, trauma, silence, loss, uncertainty, addiction, premature death, mental illness, isolation, and alienation is our inheritance. All that, and in the case of my cousin Tash and I, unruly hair that no one knew how to take care of. More than my sisters, who appear whiter than me, my inheritance also includes persistent questions such as "Where are you from?" or "*What* are you?" and attempts to claim or place me, to which I have no definitive quick answer apart from "London." I invariably leave my questioner unsatisfied. I am left feeling inauthentic, defensive, or filled with inchoate yearning.

At least for someone as light-skinned as me, growing up in parts of East London as I did in the 1990s and 2000s (in areas that were majority nonwhite—Bengali and Black, respectively—but gentrifying) it felt like the earlier umbrella of political solidarity and intentionality encompassed by the overarching "Black"[21] identity had dissolved into a more palatable light-brown "mixed" soup that ostensibly affirmed "multiculturalism" *and* individual difference. Many of my closest friends were first or second generation; many had recently painful and complex pasts that it was easier not to explain or reopen. Perhaps people had second languages spoken at home, family they visited elsewhere, and cultural traditions and ties, but these were selectively backgrounded to facilitate cohesion and acceptance into a more general belonging—a belonging from nonbelonging that, for the most part, I fitted into easily. Such belonging as apparent unity from diversity and difference was implicitly nonconfrontational and apolitical, which well-suited the liberal, semi-bohemian, white middle-class side of my family. That is the side of my family—which migrated from South Africa in the late 1960s—that I was closest to, not least because they lovingly raised me. As I acknowledge the extent to which I am ungrounded, I find myself increasingly fragmented and divided from my white family.

Sifting through my memories of growing up, I am confused by the absences of what the current me would expect to find there. I suspect that the fantasies and pressures of integration, assimilation, and class mobility meant that we were implicitly discouraged from the affirmation of, identification with, and proximity to certain forms of Blackness, as well as explicitly discussing and agitating around experiences and forms of anti-Black racism. Among my close friends, our general lack of discussion makes me wonder whether we had the consciousness and lexicon to explicitly identify these issues as well as the differences between us. Perhaps I was oblivious to them. Or perhaps these conversations happened in secret (quite the feat given our near total lack of privacy). Maybe it was due to the experimental bubble of our boarding school in West Sussex, Christ's Hospital, which is purportedly the most diverse independent school in the UK. It was historically given the mission to support the promising, yet unfortunate urchins of London, with a large portion of students, during my time at least, paying little or no fees. Little did we realize that this gift of an education, home, and unique community (along with the cushioning and reprieve it offered from some of the harder, more violent dynamics of the outside world and/or our home lives) was enabled in no small part by the fruits of transatlantic slavery, colonialism, and imperialism.[22]

We were more focused on doing whatever we wanted with whomever and wherever, and eventually excelling—meaning that we would be scattered to various higher-education institutions, careers, and groups in which we were the minority. It took what Maboula Soumahoro describes as a "detour," as the distance of the Atlantic, initiation into Africana philosophy and Black study, and the alienation of (mis)recognition in different racial and cultural terms, for me to begin to understand the people, self, and home that I had left. My experience as a migrant (a position shared with three or perhaps all four of my grandparents) has also raised for me complex questions of making home and place, of enduring relations and relationships made and unmade across distances and difficulties—questions of if and how I could ground myself in a new place without settlement or possession. Now I begin to realize that these questions—of roots (known and unknowable), of spores of transience and movement, of a desire to be grounded without appeal to "root identity"[23]—comprise at least one aspect of what I find so compelling about

Black diasporic thought and existence, especially for issues of ecology and place.

PROTOCOLS FOR GROUNDINGS

Don't assume that "philosophy and philosophizing are not a widespread, human activity," or "that there is something special about philosophizing that is in the purview of professional philosophy alone."[24] Participate in and learn from horizontal and collective reasoning.[25] Let liberation orient you. Move dialectically between theory and practice. Decenter the academic. Decenter the university.[26] Disturb technocrats, as well as supposedly radical intellectuals and political leaders. Trace connections. Build solidarities.[27] Learn from "plant teachings."[28] Be alert to the entanglements of ecocide and genocide. Build from the insight that "freedom is a place."[29]

The term "groundings" that piqued my curiosity at the Afrikan Emancipation Day in 2021 offers an additional layer. Adapted by the Pan Afrikan Reparations movement from the Guyanese Marxian anticolonial Pan-African guerilla intellectual Walter Rodney, that day's groundings were an example of theory in practice and practice from theory.[30] Rodney's sense of groundings was informed by Rastafarian concepts and practices, and by his experience of leaving the boundaries of the university to *ground* with Rastafari and other then denigrated and devalued Black people in Jamaican slums.[31] In its Rastafarian sense, groundings are "an open-ended and informal discussion, known as reasoning, is an essential part of grounding." It is an "open-ended, dialogical discourse between two or more brethren, which is aimed at the exploration of intersubjectivity, that is, gaining 'access to *one visionary stream*, to the condition of I and I consciousness.'"[32] To my ears, this description of groundings sounds like a model and practice of philosophizing. A practice and a "theory based on the black experience ... and on the forms of revolt embedded in its 'underlife,'" that "provide[s] an alternative mode of reason."[33] What's more, when coupled with Rodney's use of the term as a litmus test for accountable, anticolonial, anti-imperialist internationalist knowledge production, it offers one sense of a socially and politically engaged, horizontal, participatory mode of reasoning—that is, precisely the kind of reasoning or philosophizing I think we need to respond thoughtfully to the ongoing interwoven challenges of ecological destruction and racism. Yet, it is also the kind of thinking that is made difficult, if not impossible, by the academy. What's more, although there is arguably a spiritual ecological ethos in Rastafarianism, and a keen appreciation of the importance of "the natural environment," to freedom and self-determined development in Rodney's work, the link to climate and to "planetary repairs" is not obvious or given. What further steps are needed to work against the default extraction and appropriation of the earth?

In "Notes Towards a Politics of Location," Adrienne Rich claims that in contrast to "Abstractions severed from the doings of living people ... Theory—the seeing of patterns, showing the forest as well as the trees—theory can be a dew that rises from the earth and collects in the rain cloud and returns to earth over and over. But if it doesn't smell of the earth, it isn't good for the earth."[34] What Rich means by the earth is not an abstracted or romanticized mother earth or matter as such (as is the case in some of the feminisms she was distancing herself from) but rather an accountable, situated, understanding of ourselves as earthy beings in place on earth. Rich continues: "Let us get back to the earth—not as a paradigm for 'women' but as a place of location."[35] Have we ever had a philosophy that *smells* of the earth? By extension, have we ever had a philosophy that is *good* for the earth? What additional protocols might we need?

PROTOCOLS FOR A GROUNDING PHILOSOPHY

*Stay low to the ground. Stay nimble and mobile (shifting between places, scales, times, elements). Keep it trans-local. Attend to the lower parts of the body. Think with and of pregnancy, with and of forms of degraded trans*ition, transformation, metamorphosis. Use your nose.[36] Follow the shit. Follow the power. Follow the money.[37] Attend to those people and perspectives considered "lower" in society.[38] Begin with the "viscous porosity" of life and death, self and other, body and ecology.[39] Follow the sources. Follow the genealogies. Embrace the* "liberating" *and* "regenerating power" *of laughter, its* "philosophical and utopian character.[40]" *Take the piss.[41] Take dancing seriously.[42] Turn to the rumblings from the demonic ground. [43] Don't shy away from muckiness and complexity.[44] Try to illuminate the ideas and philosophies that emerge from practice. Practice practice.[45]*

Theoria (contemplation) is the root of the word theory.[46] The ancient Greek model of theory contemplated the unchanging order of the sky or cosmos. With few exceptions (Western) philosophy takes this model of theory to new heights. Yet, this is hardly exhaustive of what philosophy and theory more generally can or should be. As Sylvia Wynter argues in her unpublished manuscript "Black Metamorphosis: New Natives in a New World," the concept of theory as disinterested contemplation is rooted in a hierarchical social order (a patriarchal slave society) in which a select group is able (by the labor of others) to be free from the denigrated ephemeral earthy realm and the matters of the low and the base, the animal, and the body. As Wynter argues by way of an analysis of West

African cultural forms and practices metamorphosed in Black diasporic life in the "New World," the model of social order, and by extension of philosophy that has its roots in the disinterested contemplation of the cosmos is hardly universal. Instead, Wynter suggests that we need a practice of theory, or a theoretical practice, that is "down to earth."[47]

Scientific positivism, and much of the canonical history of Western philosophy is shaped by the contemplative theory model. It effectively presupposes a life of leisure (scholar) free from mucky matters taken care of by "lower" others—such as women, slaves, and peasants—whose roles are apparently fixed by natural necessity. But these denigrated mucky matters are fundamental aspects of life. As Shatema Threadcraft explains in *Intimate Justice,* intimate matters in general, and specifically Black womxn's "sexual, reproductive, and caretaking capacities under successive systems of racial domination," have been excluded from philosophy proper since Plato deemed them "womanish."[48] Feminist philosophers have done much to challenge this set of exclusions. Yet, as Threadcraft argues, the exclusion of these matters from many theories of racial justice (an exclusion that relies on the tacit adoption of a normative male body as *the* model of the body politic) as theorized from the position of Black womxn means that theories and practices of justice continue to undermine themselves in serious ways.[49]

A grounding philosophy takes great interest in pregnancy, the "lower stratum of the body," and the earth. The intimate matters vital to living and dying have, for the most part, entered Western philosophy as metaphor that erases and denigrates womxn's work and bodies. Exemplary in this respect are Plato's *Theaetetus* and *Symposium* Socrates' self-description of philosopher as midwife who brings out unchanging truths that had been latent within men (not womxn) through dialogue.[50] Plato begins a tradition that has late offshoots in Hannah Arendt's concept of natality as distinctive condition of human novelty and thus plurality, that is, birth sanitized of the womxn's sexual body.[51] By contrast, a grounding philosophy is not afraid of the smelly bodies that are from and of the earth. It is a philosophy that laughs with a full jiggling belly in the face of the ancient disembodied and misogynistic image of philosophy as midwifery and instead births and shits another kind of thinking. I argue that this is the kind of approach we need as we think through the nexus of ecology, climate, and racism. This grounding approach does not take refuge in ideal theory (climate ethics) or abstract calculations of emissions (some climate justice) but rather gets down in the muck, in the matter of life and death, to think and be in ways that (to borrow from Wynter) are "down to earth."[52]

In leaving the relative safety of armchair philosophy, we find that we need to develop ways of operating that do not unwittingly reproduce extraction, projection, and dispossession.[53] Avoiding these risks is difficult since philosophizing seems to require that we highlight the general implications of a set of practices or specific knowledge, illuminating what we take to be its truth-contents for our own ends. This is a challenge that I have encountered as I propose the concepts of *liberation ecology* and *grounding freedom* as alternatives to hegemonic environmental and climate justice framings. I have been thinking with Sylvia Wynter's writings on Jamaican maroons and the current struggle of the Leeward Maroons (the oldest existing maroon community) against Bauxite mining in Jamaica.[54] At a talk at Northwestern, graduate student respondents asked me whether my choice of example risked romanticization. Did the attempt to highlight the alternative stakes and values manifested in this form of Black existence downplay the radical constraints and captivity of *racist environments*?[55] Did it minimize the fact of "antiblackness as total climate"?[56] In seeking to bring out one element—namely, the entanglement of liberation and ecology in what I term *liberation ecologies*—and thus a practice of freedom and a set of values and stakes opposed to the plantation, the state, and the extractive imperatives of global capital, didn't I risk reducing situated complexity down to my own distant myopic agenda? The imbrication of unique ecology and practice of freedom, in this case of maroonage, perhaps appeared to hold up an image of a pastoral past that is irrelevant to the urban existence of much of the Black diaspora. Wasn't it too perfect and exceptional, such that it risked effacing the more general conditions of Black diasporic existence and the challenges and strategies that emerged there?

In the case of that project, I have responses to these questions. Yet, I still find that the meta-philosophical and methodological questions it opens are worthwhile and timely. Questions such as: How does one philosophize in ways that explode the established binaries of "ethno-philosophy" and philosophy proper?[57]

In *Indigenizing Philosophy through the Land,* philosopher Brian Buckhart (Cherokee) offers a response. On Buckhart's analysis, the assumptions underpinning the binary between "ethno-philosophy" and philosophy proper are symptomatic of "the normalization of delocality in Western language and thought."[58] Philosophy has been equated with an ungrounded delocality that is contrasted with the knowledge and lives of Others constructed as representatives of essentialized "difference" and bound to the particular. A decolonial philosophy refuses the trick of "ethnographic containment," that has shaped Western (colonial) philosophy, where "Indigenous voices only have meaning as a form of ethnography, which would mean the truth or value of their words is determined by the ethnographic authenticity of their words rather than their truth or value in a broader sense."[59] More generally, I encounter the familiar assumption that non-white people, especially those who are not trained in Western philosophical traditions, are incapable of producing something other than "beliefs" limited to a particular context. This is an assumption that I have repeatedly encountered when I tell people that I focus on Africana philosophy—indeed, when I told one former student of philosophy that I was currently focused on the work of a Jamaican philosopher, he responded that this was effectively an oxymoron.

Yet, challenging ethnographic containment does not relieve us from working through messy relations of inheritance and inhabitation.[60] As Buckhart notes in his discussion of (feminist Native Studies scholar who controversially claimed Cherokee identity) Andrea Smith's analysis of this very question, the refusal of ethnographic containment does not liberate us from the burden of grounding and recognizing the varying responsibilities of philosophical knowledge.[61]

What is or should be my relation to such grounding practices and forms of thought that I seek to affirm but do not myself practice, or to relations to place that have not directly constituted me? In other words, how to navigate the relation of theory to praxis, of identity to knowledge, in ways that do not betray the very lessons and protocols of grounding that I seek to enact and understand? Responding to these questions requires, I am finding, a set of protocols that come with no guarantee.

1 bell hooks, *Belonging: A Culture of Place* (New York: Routledge, 2009), 5.

2 "To embrace the pronoun 'I' ... amounts to completely ignoring the classic injunctions of scholarly research. Hoping for some sort of emancipation and liberation, my conscious use of the pronoun "I" also signals a wholehearted claiming of individuality and a refusal to respect the numerous and very serious protocols concerning the idea that critical distance must be maintained at all costs." Maboula Soumahoro, *Black Is the Journey, Africana the Name*, trans. Kaiama L. Glover (Cambridge: Polity, 2022), 9.

3 Land is shorthand for "land/water/air/subterranean earth." From Eve Tuck and K. Wayne Yang, "Decolonization Is Not a Metaphor," *Decolonization, Indigeneity, Society* 1, no. 1 (2012): 5; Leanne Betasamosake Simpson, "Land as Pedagogy: Nishnaabeg Intelligence and Rebellious Transformation," *Decolonization: Indigeneity, Education & Society* 3, no. 3 (November 21, 2014).

4 In grounding, I am informed by Sylvia Wynter's articulation of the provision grounds, as a site of socioecological survivance, collectivity, knowledge, culture, and sometimes political resistance, on the margins of the dominant capitalist plantation culture—a site nurtured in part through an inheritance and adaptation of African knowledge and philosophy. Sylvia Wynter, "Novel and History, Plot and Plantation," *Savacou* 5 (1971): 95-102.

5 As Max Liboiron (Red River Métis/Michif and settler) puts in their wonderful reflection on methodology: "When I say creepy, I'm not being glib. Creepiness is a relation directed by the intense desire of one party toward another, with that desire so obfuscated, un-knowable, or such a bad fit that the originating desires do not quite make sense to the object of desire and can even constitute violation. The increasingly popular academic conversations among and emanating from settlers about kin and Land are hella creepy. I can never tell what most people mean by kin or Land, especially because both are usually positioned as inherently good (which is weird if you have any experience with family members or weather, to name two obvious manifestations of kin and Land that can be monumentally shitty and even dangerous). ... We do not need to appropriate Indigenous Land relations as a Resource to think about and then enact anticolonial land relations—of which there are many." Max Liboiron, *Pollution Is Colonialism* (Durham, NC: Duke University Press, 2021), 110.

6 Heather Davis, *Plastic Matter* (Durham, NC: Duke University Press, 2022); Eve Tuck and C. Ree, "A Glossary of Haunting," in *Handbook of Autoethnography*, ed. Stacey Holman Jones, Tony E. Adams, and Carolyn Ellis (Walnut Creek, CA: Left Coast Press, 2013), 693-58; Denise Ferreira da Silva, *Unpayable Debt* (London: Sternberg Press, 2022); Romy Opperman, "The Need for a Black Feminist Climate Justice: A Case of Haunting Ecology and Eco-Deconstruction," *CR: The New Centennial Review* 22, no. 1 (2022): 59-93.

7 Patricia Hill Collins, *Black Feminist Thought: Knowledge, Consciousness, and the Politics of Empowerment*, 2nd ed. (New York: Taylor and Francis, 2002); Donna Haraway, "Situated Knowledges: The Science Question in Feminism and the Privilege of Partial Perspective," in *The Feminist Standpoint Theory Reader: Intellectual and Political Controversies*, ed. Sandra Harding (New York and London: Routledge, 2004); Kristie Dotson, "On the Way to Decolonization in a Settler Colony: Re-Introducing Black Feminist Identity Politics," *AlterNative* 14, no. 3 (2018): 1-10, https://doi.org/10.1177/1177180118783301.

8 In addition to the constellation of influence I discuss in this piece, my use of grounding is also informed by (but nonidentical to) what Glen Coulthard political theorist (Yellowknives Dene) calls "grounded normativity": "What we are calling 'grounded normativity' refers to the ethical frameworks provided by these Indigenous place-based practices and associated forms of knowledge. Grounded normativity houses and reproduces the practices and procedures, based on deep reciprocity, that are inherently informed by an intimate relationship to place. Our relationship to the land itself generates the processes, practices, and knowledges that inform our political systems, and through which we practice solidarity." Glen Coulthard and Leanne Betasamosake Simpson, "Grounded Normativity / Place-Based Solidarity," *American Quarterly* 68, no. 2 (2016): 25, https://doi.org/10.1353/aq.2016.0038; Glen Coulthard, *Red Skin, White Masks: Rejecting the Colonial Politics of Recognition* (Minneapolis: University of Minnesota Press, 2014).

9 I did not grow up in Brixton (instead moving between homes and family members in East, South-East, and North London) but resided there briefly during one of many moves during confinement in 2020-21.

10 The Stop the Maangamizi campaign is a Pan-Afrikan liberation movement focused on establishing a truth and reparatory justice commission within

the British government. "Pempamsiempango—Glocal Reparations Action Plan for Planet Repairs Alternative Progression," *Stop the Maangamizi* (blog), February 18, 2022, https://stopthemaangamizi.com/2022/02/18/pempamsiempango-glocal-reparations-action-plan-for-planet-repairs-alternative-progression/.

11 Esther Stanford-Xosei explains that "XRISN formed in early 2019, led by myself and other members of the Stop the Maangamizi Campaign, though we had been in talks with the founders of Extinction Rebellion since before its launch in October 2018. The group formed out of the need for a space for forming different perspectives on rebellion to broaden out from the global north positionality of the founders of XR. We in Stop the Maangamizi had connections into communities that could strengthen what XR was doing, drawing on the centuries of experience of rebellion. We have since worked to form three global south affinity networks, the XR Affinity All-Afrikan Network (XRAAN) based in Accra, Ghana, the XR Affinity Network of Asia (XRANA), based in Delhi, India, and the XR Affinity Network of South Abya Yala (XRRAAYS), based in Colombia, Abya Yala (also known as the Americas). We are not going to these places and saying to people you have to be XR to belong to this network, instead we are facilitating a process of mutual solidarity and learning between XR and established rebellions around the world." Esther Stanford-Xosei, "Reparations and the Fight for Life," *Ecologist*, July 31, 2020, https://theecologist.org/2020/jul/31/reparations-and-fight-life.

12 For more on Windrush and Black (mixed) Britishness see Hazel V. Carby, *Imperial Intimacies: A Tale of Two Islands* (London: Verso, 2019).

13 "The 'Windrush' Generation are those who arrived in the UK from Caribbean countries between 1948 and 1973. Many took up jobs in the nascent NHS [National Health Service] and other sectors affected by Britain's post-war labour shortage. The name 'Windrush' derives from the 'HMT Empire Windrush' ship which brought one of the first large groups of Caribbean people to the UK in 1948. As the Caribbean was, at the time, a part of the British Commonwealth, those who arrived were automatically British subjects and free to permanently live and work in the UK .... The Windrush scandal began to surface in 2017 after it emerged that hundreds of Commonwealth citizens, many of whom were from the 'Windrush' generation, had been wrongly detained, deported and denied legal rights." "Windrush Scandal Explained," Joint Council for the Welfare of Immigrants, March 13,

2020, https://www.jcwi.org.uk/windrush-scandal-explained.

14 These are waves of the Black diaspora formed by the massive, forced displacement/rupture of "transshipped Africans" through transatlantic slavery and intertwined with the interventions and reverberations of (neo) colonialism and imperialism across the African continent. Sylvia Wynter, "We Know Where We Are From: The Politics of Black Culture from Myal to Marley," in *We Must Learn to Sit Down Together and Talk About a Little Culture: Decolonising Essays, 1967-1984*, ed. Demetrius L. Eudell (Leeds: Peepal Tree, 2022).

15 The previous summer, I had defended my dissertation, *Race, Ecology, Freedom: Climate Justice and Environmental Racism*, which argued that some radical Black thinkers (such as Frantz Fanon) prepared the grounds for profound critiques of hegemonic liberal framings of climate injustice and environmental racism and offered ways to begin to conceptualize these issues by foregrounding liberation and the practices, contributions, and seeds of Black practice and peoples. I am currently working on a book project that develops this and takes seriously the problem of protocols and the conceptual practice of grounding.

16 Stanford-Xosei,"Reparations and the Fight for Life."

17 "Maangamizi, the Swahili term for Afrikan Holocaust and the continuum of chattel, colonial, and neocolonial enslavement, is more appropriate than its alternative category Maafa For Maafa, which means calamity, accident, ill luck, disaster, or damage, does not indicate intentionality. It could be a natural disaster or a deadly highway accident. But Maangamizi is derived from the verb -angamiza which means to cause destruction, to utterly destroy, and thus carries with it a sense of intentionality. The 'a' prefix suggests an amplified destruction and thus speaks to the massive nature of the Holocaust." "Pempamsiempango" *Stop the Maangamizi*.

18 Wynter, "We Know Where We Are From."

19 I read Maboula Soumahoro's *Black Is the Journey, Africana the Name* after writing these words and was struck by this similarity—despite the differences between our positionalities and countries of origin.

20 To some extent, it seems that I am not alone in this and the resurgence of critical Black thought and founding of the first ever Black Studies Department in Britain (at Birmingham City University) have happened recently (that is, since I left for my PhD in the United States). Kehinde Andrews, "The Black Studies Movement in Britain," *Black Scholar* (blog), October 6, 2016, https://www.theblackscholar.org/black-studies-movement-britain/. As I have more recently found out in conversation with Esther, it also took her detour to the United States and the reparations movement in her earlier legal career for her to then be able to return to London and connect with the many Pan-Afrikan internationalist thinkers and organizers in exile there. At the same time, however, I must take responsibility for the way that, in comparison with my engagement with thinkers from other parts of the diaspora, I have curiously understudied Black British intellectuals such as Paul Gilroy, Stuart Hall, and Claudia Jones. My dad's distance from Black community and family (by virtue of his father's adoption and the area he grew up in) as well as both of my parents' involvement with Scientology meant that we were not rooted in wider networks and traditions but rather that this recognition came later, from my friends. See "Repairing the World: Romy Opperman interviews Esther Xosei," *Oxford Public Philosophy* 4 (2024), https://www.oxfordpublicphilosophy.com/indigenous/rg.

21 In the 1970s and 1980s the term Black in Britain often included communities of South Asian as well as African descent. For instance, see the Black Audio Film Collective. Dhanveer Singh Brar and Ashwani Sharma, "What Is This 'Black' in Black Studies? From Black British Cultural Studies to Black Critical Thought in UK Arts and Higher Education," *New Formations* 99, no. 99 (2019): 88-109, https://doi.org/10.3898/NewF:99.05.2019.

22 Richard Adams, "Elite UK Schools' Financial Links to Slavery Revealed," *Guardian*, May 3, 2023, sec. World news, https://www.theguardian.com/world/2023/may/03/elite-uk-schools-financial-links-to-slavery-revealed.

23 Édouard Glissant, *Poetics of Relation*, trans. Betsy Wing (Ann Arbor: Michigan University Press, 1997).

24 Dotson, Kristie. "How is This Paper Philosophy?." *Comparative Philosophy* 3, no. 1 (2012): 19.

25 Anthony Bogues explains, "In the discursive practice of the Rastafari, when 'grounds' became 'groundings,' the meaning was layered. Not only

did it mean sociality—an equal meeting that breaks socially constructed barriers of race, class, and education—but the nature of such an encounter was marked by 'reasonings'—a form of discussion in which each person contributed equally to the discourse without any prior hierarchical claims of knowledge." Anthony Bogues, *Black Heretics, Black Prophets: Radical Political Intellectuals* (New York: Routledge, 2003), 129.

26 "To truly 'ground', Rodney's praxis demonstrated that the revolutionary intellectual must go anywhere to reason with their people. This, of course, included going to places that most intellectuals of his stature would not have set foot in. Rodney, considered study and struggle inseparable; he exemplified how to bridge the gap between theory and praxis in a People's quest for Liberation, hence the notion of 'Guerrilla Intellectualism' and warrior-scholarship in movement-building). So, with Groundings, the mutual production and dissemination of emancipatory ideas, has to also be accompanied by mass movement organising, led from the grassroots, in furtherance of building the capacity to usher in a new World, by our own People's Power!" Stop the Maangamizi, "PAN-AFRIKAN REPARATIONS REBELLION GROUNDINGS," *Stop the Maangamizi* (blog), April 14, 2016, https://stopthemaangamizi.com/panafrikanreparationsrebelliongroundings/.

27 Walter Rodney, *How Europe Underdeveloped Africa* (London: Verso Books, 2018).

28 Anna Waldstein, "Smoking as Communication in Rastafari: Reasonings with 'Professional' Smokers and 'Plant Teachers,'" *Ethnos* 85, no. 5 (2020): 900-19.

29 Ruth Wilson Gilmore, *Abolition Geography: Essays towards Liberation* (London: Verso Books), 2022, 474.

30 As the website of the Pan Afrikan Reparations Rebellions Groundings explains: "Groundings" are popular education sessions with grassroots forces, including socially marginalized groups, workers, women, youth (including those in street organizations) for organizing *cells of resistance* and action towards the *concrete struggle for a new society and Another World.* Groundings are highlighted in Dr. Walter Rodney's classic work *The Groundings with my Brothers* chronicling first-hand reports of his mass movement organizing, public lectures and reasonings in Jamaica and Canada ... These reasonings offered a powerful corrective to

Eurocentric assumptions regarding what it meant to be "educated" by breaking down the division between teachers and students (as co-producers of knowledge), at the heart of educational hierarchies. "PAN-AFRIKAN REPARATIONS REBELLION GROUNDINGS," *Stop the Maangamizi.*

31 "They do not understand that our historical experience has been speaking to white people, whether it be begging white people, justifying ourselves against white people or even vilifying white people .... Now the new understanding is that black brothers must talk to each other." Walter Rodney, *The Groundings with My Brothers*, ed. Asher T. Rodney and Jesse J. Benjamin (London: Verso, 2019), 68.

32 "The idea of intersubjectivity, as it relates to Rasta reasoning, speaks to the Rastafarian conviction that truth resides in each individual because the divine 'I' is in each person. Therefore, reasoning, assisted by the inspiration of ganja, stimulates the intersubjective exploration of truth. Stated another way, in the process of reasoning, all the I's present are able to explore the same truth, which inheres in each of them .... Reasoning is a very intense activity, which can go on for hours in a dialogical manner until those involved arrive at a consensus. [Carole] Yawney claims, 'Two brethren may reason together, each prompting the other to *higher and higher* I-ghts [heights], accreting layer upon layer of meaning until a satisfactory view of reality is reached.' ... No conclusion or consensus is ever elevated to the status of a binding creed. Each conclusion is subject to modification or further elaboration at future sessions." Ennis Barrington Edmonds, *Rastafari: From Outcasts to Culture Bearers* (Oxford: Oxford University Press, 2003), 9.

33 Sylvia Wynter, "Black Metamorphosis: New Natives in a New World" (unpublished manuscript), 669.

34 Adrienne Rich, "Notes Towards a Politics of Location," in *Blood, Bread, and Poetry: Selected Prose, 1979-1985* (New York: Norton, 1986,) 213-14. Thanks to Emma Velez and Kei Williams for bringing this wonderful piece to my attention.

35 Rich, "Notes Towards a Politics of Location," 214.

36 I am indebted to one of my first philosophical loves, Friedrich Nietzsche, for this tip. As he puts it: "This nose, for instance, of which no philosopher has yet spoken with admiration and gratitude, is in fact the most delicate instrument at our disposal." Friedrich Nietzsche,

"'Reason' in Philosophy," in *Twilight of the Idols*, trans. Richard Polt (Indianapolis and Cambridge: Hackett, 1997), 18.

37 Donna Haraway, *Modest_Witness@Second_Millennium. FemaleMan_Meets_OncoMouse: Feminism and Technoscience* (New York: Routledge, 1997).

38 "It might be in a sports club, it might be in a schoolroom, it might be in a church, it might be in a gully ... They are dark dismal places with a black population who have had to seek refuge there. You will have to go there if you want to talk to them. I have spoken in what people call 'dungle,' rubbish dumps, for that is where people live in Jamaica ... I have set on a little oil drum, rusty and in the midst of garbage, an domes black brothers and I have grounded together." Rodney, *The Groundings with My Brothers*, 68.

39 Nancy Tuana, *Racial Climates, Ecological Indifference: An Ecointersectional Analysis* (Oxford: Oxford University Press, 2023).

40 Many of these protocols for a grounding philosophy are informed by my work on Sylvia Wynter's unpublished manuscript "Black Metamorphosis." Wynter adapts Mikhail Bakhtin's work on grotesque realism to think through the importance of Jamaican folk culture in these terms. Humor, dance, sexuality, carnival all appear in a new light Mikhail Bakhtin, *Rabelais and His World*, trans. Helene Iswolsky (Cambridge, MA: MIT Press, 1971), 38, 13.

41 As we say in my home country.

42 Sylvia Wynter, "Jonkonnu in Jamaica: Towards the Interpretation of Folk Dance as a Cultural Process," *Jamaica Journal* 4, no. 2 (1970): 34-48.

43 "The geographies of black womanhood, as demonic grounds, put forth a geographic grammar that locates the complex position and potentiality of black women's sense of place." Katherine McKittrick, *Demonic Grounds: Black Women and the Cartographies of Struggle* (Minneapolis: University of Minnesota Press, 2006), 133. My use of demonic ground is adapted from Katherine McKittrick's reading of Wynter. See Sylvia Wynter, "Afterword: Beyond Miranda's Meanings: Un/Silencing the 'Demonic Ground' of Caliban's 'Woman,'" in *Out of the Kumbla: Caribbean Women and Literature*, ed. Carol Boyce Davies and Savory Fido (Trenton, NJ: Africa World Press, 1990), 355-70. It refers to the disruptive and crucial perspective onto the system. In the case of Black womxn/feminism that Wynter first uses to advance the concept—this perspective is due to the

unthinkable/invisible/marginal position within that system of Black womxn or "Caliban's mate." McKittrick's account orients us to the importance of protocols for knowledge and study: "Sylvia Wynter taught me that radical theory-making takes place outside existing systems of knowledge and that this place, outside (demonic grounds), is inhabited by those who are brilliantly and intimately aware of and connected to existing systems of knowledge (as self-replicating) and that this awareness provides theoretical insights and projections of humanity that imagine a totally new way of being ... Sylvia Wynter taught me that black women are radical theory makers and that black women inhabit demonic ground." Katherine McKittrick, *Dear Science and Other Stories* (Durham, NC: Duke University Press, 2021), 44."I theorize Wynter's insights on the rebellious potential of the 1960s—what she describes as the *groundwork* for the realization of a new order of being human—as long-standing and unfinished method-making. This kind of analytical maneuvering marks black rebellion as method-making; this is one way to signal and think about the praxis of black life and livingness. The maneuvering, ideally, dwells on and thinks about the questioning and overturning of normative systems of knowledge, and thus what it means to be human, by situating the process of inquiry as the analytical framework through which to study." Ibid., 69.

44 For instance, see Saidiya Hartman, *Scenes of Subjection: Terror, Slavery, and Self-making in Nineteenth-Century America* (New York: W. W. Norton, 2022); Saidiya Hartman, "The Belly of the World: A Note on Black Women's Labors," *Souls* 18, no. 1 (2016): 166-73.

45 Alexis Pauline Gumbs, *Undrowned: Black Feminist Lessons from Marine Mammals*, *Emergent Strategy* (Chico: A K Press, 2020); M. Jacqui Alexander, *Pedagogies of Crossing: Meditations on Feminism, Sexual Politics, Memory, and the Sacred* (Durham, NC: Duke University Press, 2005); M. Jacqui Alexander and Gina Athena Ulysse, "Groundings on Rasanblaj with M. Jacqui Alexander," Hemispheric Institute, accessed April 28, 2023, https://hemisphericinstitute.org/en/emisferica-121-caribbean-rasanblaj/12-1-essays/e-121-essay-alexander-interview-with-gina.html.

46 Jürgen Habermas, *Knowledge and Human Interests*, trans. Jeremy J. Shapiro (Boston: Beacon Press, 1971), 301.

47 Sylvia Wynter, "Black Metamorphosis," 521-23.

48 Shatema Threadcraft, *Intimate Justice: The Black Female Body and the Body Politic* (Oxford: Oxford University Press, 2016), 8, 26.

49 Ibid.,27.

50 Page duBois, "The Platonic Appropriation of Reproduction," in *Feminist Interpretations of Plato*, ed. Nancy Tuana, trans. Eleanor H. (University Park: Pennsylvania State University Press, 1994); Radcliffe G. Edmonds, "Socrates the Beautiful: Role Reversal and Midwifery in Plato's Symposium," *Transactions of the American Philological Association* 130 (2000): 261-85; Luce Irigaray, "Sorcerer Love: Diotima's Speech," in *Feminist Interpretations of Plato*, ed. Nancy Tuana, trans. Eleanor H. Kuykendall (University Park: Pennsylvania State University Press, 1994); E. E. Pender, "Spiritual Pregnancy in Plato's Symposium," *The Classical Quarterly, New Series* 42, no. 1 (1992); Plato, "Symposium," in *Plato: Complete Works*, ed. John M. Cooper, trans. Alexander Nehamas and Paul Woodruff (Indianapolis/Cambridge: Hackett, 1997); Plato, "Theaetetus," in *Plato: Complete Works*, ed. John M. Cooper, trans. M. J. Levett. and Myles Burnyeat (Indianapolis and Cambridge: Hackett, 1997).

51 Hannah Arendt, *The Human Condition* (Chicago: Chicago University Press, 1958); Pitkin Fenichel, "Conformism, Housekeeping, and the Attack of the Blob: The Origins of Hannah Arendt's Concept of the Social," in *Feminist Interpretations of Hannah Arendt*, ed. Bonnie Honig (University Park: Pennsylvania State University Press, 1995).

52 Wynter, "Black Metamorphosis," 759. There is much to be said about how Wynter understands earth *as* metamorphosis. We can start by turning to her engagement with Bakhtin's account of degradation or regeneration. For Bakhtin (and for Wynter who quotes this passage at length): "Degradation here means coming down to earth, the contact with earth as an element that swallows up and gives birth at the same time. To degrade is to bury, to sow, and to kill simultaneously, in order to bring forth something more and better. To degrade also means to concern oneself with the lower stratum of the body, the life of the belly and the reproductive organs; it therefore relates to acts of defection and copulation, conception, pregnancy, and birth. Degradation digs a bodily grave for new birth. It has not only a destructive negative aspect, but also a regenerating one." Bakhtin, *Rabelais and His World*, 21. Cited in Wynter, "Black Metamorphosis," 757-58.

53 Descartes' *Meditations* take place in an armchair in a warm room. From this comfortable spot, belief in the existence of all other beings, even in his own body, can be suspended, leaving only the cogito of "I think therefore I am," as indubitably existing. Descartes's skepticism (and ultimately his mind-body dualism) requires that he is free from the interruptions of bodily need and engagement with others.

54 I discuss this struggle in my book manuscript. See Emme Christie, "Maroon Sovereignty: An Environmental Justice Issue," *Jamaica Observer*, August 17, 2021, https://www.jamaicaobserver.com/columns/maroon-sovereignty-an-environmental-justice-issue/; Vice News, "How a Sovereign Group in Jamaica Is Fighting a US Mining Company," YouTube, 2021, https://www.youtube.com/watch?v=5nbHC24ZOrQ.

55 I develop a concept of racist environments in Romy Opperman, "A Permanent Struggle against an Omnipresent Death: Revisiting Environmental Racism with Frantz Fanon," *Critical Philosophy of Race* 7, no. 1 (2019): 57-80, https://doi.org/10.5325/critphilrace.7.1.0057.

56 Christina Sharpe, *In the Wake: On Blackness and Being* (Durham, NC: Duke University Press, 2016), 21.

57 Étienne Balibar, *On Universals: Constructing and Deconstructing Community*, trans. Joshua David Jordan (New York: Fordham University Press, 2020); Pascah Mungwini, *African Philosophy: Emancipation and Practice* (London: Bloomsbury, 2022); Wynter, "We Know Where We Are From."

58 Brian Burkhart, *Indigenizing Philosophy through the Land: A Trickster Methodology for Decolonizing Environmental Ethics and Indigenous Futures* (East Lansing: Michigan State University Press, 2019), xxi.

59 Ibid.

60 See the exemplary work by Kristie Dotson, "On the Way to Decolonization in a Settler Colony: Re-introducing Black Feminist Identity Politics," *AlterNative: An International Journal of Indigenous Peoples* 14, no. 3 (2018): 190-99.

61 As Buckhart puts it, "While Smith is able to challenge the containment of Indigenous truth in Indigenous bodies, she is not able to see that a disembodied Indigeneity is a further operation of the narrative of colonial difference, which in this case serves to remove the being-in-kinship as an essential feature of Indigeneity in the

context of locality." Burkhart, *Indigenizing Philosophy through the Land: A Trickster Methodology for Decolonizing Environmental Ethics and Indigenous Futures*, xx-xxi.

LEMON BALM AND TEMPORAL LIBERATION

Asia Dorsey

Temporal liberation is self-reclamation. In my life as a bioregional root-worker at Bones Bugs and Botany and an owner of the nation's first BIPOC-owned and operated yoga cooperative, I have chosen to understand liberation as an embodied experience of wholeness, completeness, and perfection. A state devoid of the need to change or fix. Not a doing, but a being, an emptiness through which all possibilities flow. I have come to hold liberation as already and always here and possible.

A protocol is a set of processes that can be passed down through space and time to transmit what we have learned of liberation. In the course of this text, we (the collection of me, my microbes, and the ancestors who walk with me) will introduce different protocols that enable us to experience liberation. We will first position the personal as temporal situating self-reclamation as an Indigenous spiritual technology and prerequisite for presence. Next, we challenge escape to re-position presence as the goal of our liberatory impulse by leaning on the frameworks of Afropresentism. Lastly, we turn to the plant world to listen to lemon balm as an agent in healing the spiritual, temporal disequilibrium of anxiety to discern the role of nervine plants in temporal healing and thus liberation.

Africans in the Americas have always been futurists. I imagine that we've been dreaming and living for the future since the day the trickster Eshu gave our Yoruba warrior Ogun drink. This drink disarmed our god of war causing him to fall asleep at the crossroad while we were stolen and transported across the Atlantic. Ecological succession follows a disturbance event; in it, an ordered procession of plant and animal species restores a disturbed landscape to wholeness. The transatlantic slave trade was a temporal and spatial disturbance in the ecology of Blackness, and since then, waves after waves of our African ancestors have lived and died with a dream on their minds and a prayer on their lips that their bodies, labor, art, and culture would create a substrate for their future progeny to flourish. After hundreds of years of sacrifice, I was born.

SELF-RECLAMATION

We are all born with the stories of our ancestors, their sacrifice, and their talents encoded in our bodies. These codes or instructions contain gifts and afflictions that help us understand our own significance. The stories we inherit and the stories we tell about ourselves and our past shape what we believe is possible in the present and set constraints on our futures.

Many of us who have already survived the apocalypse of slavery and colonization hold the story of our subjugation as a shameful defeat. We hunger for the stories of our fighting and fleeing as we escape the histories of what we considered to be freezing and appeasing. We project this hunger for activation into the present, making our lives full of action. We need to "stay woke," a hyper-vigilant and defensive form of activism to make sure this doesn't happen again. We can't sleep on ourselves ... this time. This shame has us conflate rest with suspended animation and contemplation with capture.

The blessings of the here-now are revealed in the slowness of revelation, and we rush past it in pursuit of getting there. The pursuit of a future degree/job/partnership/family. We wish to be go-getters going to get all the things that prove that we are more human than the controlling narratives of the colonial imagination. Not realizing that we've internalized colonial stories of what brings about wholeness, we experience the same disappointment and depression that plunges us into the reckless and anxious pursuit of more and more and more, reifying that we are not already enough.

WHAT PART OF ME IS THE COLONIZER?

The behaviors that we think liberate us are based on the disappointments of the past and keep us constrained within the confines of colonial imaginations dispossessing us of our purpose and, ultimately, our freedom.

After the apocalyptic dispossession of colonization and slavery, repossession becomes a remedy to realizing the wholeness we already are and charting new futures. In order to liberate us from the constraints the past imposes on our present and future, we must extend the re-possessive process beyond the present self to include our temporal selves and the stories of our lineage. To take claim of ourselves in the present, we must reclaim the ancestors who are not trapped in the past but continue to live through us, holding pieces of our wholeness until we are ready for integration. To get free, we need a protocol that helps us to reclaim all of ourselves on all of the timelines.

PLANTATIONOCENE

In my process of self-reclamation, I found that I had to time travel back to the plantation, a site of deep shame and a history that I have always tried to escape from, overturn, and act against. Here lived the ancestors that I certainly am not. Here lived my salvation. With time, study, and love, I learned in great detail about Black foodways and the genius that created them. I learned from and collaborated with Black food scholars like Michael Twitty and Justin Robinson. I studied the birthing traditions of enslaved women and the herbal healing traditions of enslaved folks. I came to understand my enslaved ancestors as more than their social status. I resurrected their honor through recipe, adding texture, form, and dimensionality to a flattened history. I embarked on a process of making human what was labeled object, by not only honoring the culinary and healing genius of my ancestors but also honoring the spectrum of decisions they made to fight, freeze, or flee. I stopped making my ancestors wrong for the choices they made to get me here now. Only after I came to terms with the plantation was I able to travel back further into the past, reboarding the Ship, doing Dr. Christina Sharpe's "wake work"[1] in reverse to the coasts of West Africa where I learned the pattern language of Black wellness. I traveled even further into the interior of my motherland until I found the moment before Eshu gave the warrior Ogun drink. I was face to face with the surprised but captivated trickster Eshu, who looked at me with a twinkle in his eyes and asked if I was really ready to choose it all—he asked if I had the capacity to choose every part of myself, even the parts that were enslaved. After centuries of contemplation, I affirmed my choice. Eshu handed the drink to me, I placed it in the hand of my father Ogun who became drunk. And while my warrior slept by the crossroads, Eshu and I marched to the coast and boarded the ship towards the Americas with our people.

To choose the self without fixing, changing, guilting, or blaming, we also have to choose rather than deny, escape, or wish away the histories that made us. We have to embark on a new protocol.

EMBODIMENT

Escapism is one of the various epigenetic expressions I carry as a descendant of enslaved Indigenous peoples. I have the ability to not be here now as a way of enduring the present and making my way toward the future. Afrofuturist narratives like the folktales of High John and Brerer Rabbit were an already-always part of me when I needed hope—a cartography towards freedom letting me know that other ways of being are possible and that I am not stuck here. Unlike the older stories of my tradition, which ask us to look back or sideways for answers, Afrofuturist texts created escape as "out there" in the deep space of future. It deepened the spectrum of temporal imagination when I was lost navigating the narrowing time horizons of my depression. Afrofuturism was and continues to be a balm.

Sustos or Espartos, as my curanderas out here in the Mountain West might call it, is also known as soul loss. Sustos is a spiritual technology that allows vital parts of ourselves to fly away after a fright, trauma, or self-betraying choice. These experiences leave the body with temporal disequilibria that appear to western clinicians as anxiety, depression, PTSD, or other afflictions. Sustos is how our soul responds to a disturbance event. Historical inequalities concentrate the likelihood of harm through exposure to poverty, stress, and toxicity, creating the preconditions for Sustos and unknowingly creating the preconditions for what Dr. Martin Luther King, Jr. referred to as "soul force." Soul force is gained in the process of healing that which has been broken. The retrieval of the soul requires journey after journey to reclaim those lost parts of ourselves when we are ready for reintegration. Each journey is an initiation. And each experience of reintegrating the past with the present and liberating our future selves collapses time onto itself, concentrating our soul force, and liberating our blessings. We are more powerful when broken and reclaimed than never broken at all.

Time heals all things. Time activists and theorists Rasheedah Phillips and Moor Mother of the collective Black Quantum Futurism highlight the subjectivity of time, opening our imaginations toward a diversity of historical and possible relationships to time in seeking our liberation. They confront colonial constructions of time where the past, present, and future are mutually exclusive, sequential, and linear. Many traditional societies perceive time as a fluid continuum where the past and the future can enter the present. The process of ancestral spirit possession or catching the "Holy Ghost" is an instance where the past enters the present through spiritual intervention. Divination with bones, stones, shells, or cards are instances where the future is called to the present. Indeed, many traditional peoples implicate timelines and their navigation in the cure of ailments and afflictions. South African sangomas (highly respected healers), for example, believe that illness is "caused by disrespect or disease among historical spiritual agents or energies and these can only be reconciled by communion with those spirits."[2]

Sangomas and other traditional healers seek to mend these temporal disequilibria by making amends in the past to bear results in the present. Sangomas dissociate from the "present," entering into a trance state or "the wilderness" where they can petition the spirits for forgiveness, guidance, and even knowledge of the future.

Dissociation, an experience much derided as a trauma response, is an ancestral talent and a survival technique. African Futurist Nnedi Okorafor in her preeminent 2010 book *Who Fears Death*[3] gives shape and context to the historical relevance of dissociation in her rendering of the Alusi. "Going Alusi" was a reference to the process of dissociation where her protagonist Onyesonwu and others escape to the "wilderness," the wild and timeless world of the spirits. The world of ancestors. While her reference is fictive, cultural historians like Malidoma Patrice Somé of the Dagara tribe of Burkina Faso also referenced the wilderness and experiences of leaving his body during Dagara rites of passage.

It does not honor our ancestors to create a binary construction of embodiment as celebration and disembodiment as problematic. We will not dismiss and flatten the narratives of escape. Leaving the body either from fright or by choice is a part of the spectrum of our being. What this essay calls for, though, is soul force, power. What is power in fluid temporalities other than fostering the ability to connect with multivariate forms of temporal existence? Power isn't simply staying in the present but increasing the possibility of choosing how and when we navigate the various temporalities that we can access. At this time, we are temporally disempowered not because we do not have the ability to stay in our bodies but because we don't have the power to choose when to stay or when to leave. Escape and dissociation have become the default. Deepening the spectrum of temporal imagination requires that we gain the experience of presence. It requires that we learn how to shelter in place.

SHELTERING IN PLACE

Africana scholars like Neil Roberts in works such as his *Freedom as Marronage*[4] emphasize a liberatory trifecta as flight, fugitivity, and freedom in Haiti. Their work within the framework of Marronage helps us remember that escape was possible in the past and is thus possible in the future, reinforcing the notion of escape as liberation and the belief that liberation lives in the "getting there." I bow to escape as liberation. Our notions of liberation do and must change with the advancing social location of African descendants. Like the process of ecological succession, each liberatory movement created the substrate for deeper and more expansive forms of liberation. For centuries in the past and for many today, liberation is leaving. But there is a point at which leaving, erasing what was there before and creating something new, becomes a colonial impulse. With escape as the default, it's easy to leave our families, jobs, and communities; it takes something powerful to stay. It takes soul to transform our relationships and our context in situ. I imagine that this soul force is accumulated over time and is only newly available to us because of the escape and sacrifice of our ancestors. And as it becomes available, we honor our past to collapse space-time in on itself and create more of it in the present. I'm curious what parts of ourselves we can access when we honor the embodied acts and aspects of the liberatory impulse contained within the enslaved people who stayed.

What does it mean to choose to stay on the plantation? To maroon in situ? To not escape but to witness the plantation cannibalizing itself? To be a weed in the row crop growing more resilient in the face of mechanic, chemical, and biological assaults? The weeds will out-thrive the terminator seeds, the fossil fuel, and the plunderer. Indeed, the weeds grow deeper and more resilient while the bodies of the plunderer surrender to the soil, poisoned by the chemicals they spray, becoming the substrate for more weeds to grow. Every assault of the master is an act of undoing themselves, a process richly explored by my favorite post-activist practitioner, Nigerian philosopher Bayo Akomolafe, chief curator and executive director of the Emergence Network.

The master's body is emptied over time, surrendering to the grand arc of justice. Every unreclaimed soulless act becomes devoid of soul force, a loss that manifests as generations of temporal disequilibrium and a separation and unbelonging begging for remediation. The master needs the past to stay in the past, disjointed from the future, lest he face his haunting. The Black and Indigenous ancestors, those who stewarded the lands and those who tilled it, understood that their actions would leave an impression through the space-time continuum because they perceived space and time as such. Dominant narratives valorize those who left and shame those who stayed. But we can choose to honor all of them. The ones who chose to stay and learned to shelter in place. We can honor the ones who chose what looked like surrender. So that one day, we could.

I have experienced liberation as act after act of surrendering every moment to perfection and rendering it whole and complete. If liberation was positioned in the here-now rather than the out-there, what tools and what protocols might we use to have it? How might we value our embodiments? What acts and aspects of our being might shift to capture the miracle of the present? What is Afropresentism?

AFROPRESENTISM

"The present is the future in motion …."

Afropresentism, according to the cultural artist and producer Swakara Atwell-Bennett, "liberates African cultural, social and technological advancement from the realm of the speculative or surreal, and instead locates these nuanced and mystical stories in the here and now—not as distant potentialities, but as codes interwoven into our present reality."[5]

While Black Yogis like Konda Mason and Rosa Parks have been creating imagination around Black contemplative practices for over fifty years, this particular term as an adjunct to the Afrofuturist movement was first coined by artist and guerrilla theorist Neema Githere. In an April 2022 interview with *BOMB Magazine*, Githere deems the present as "… the future in motion. The present is where all the time is layered upon itself in every moment. We carry ancient legacies and future aspirations in our bodies in the here and now."[6]

These theories confirm the truth of our bodies. We carry legacy and future at the same time through our DNA. Afropresentism is the collapse of these temporal realities in on themselves into an experience of presence. This collapse of space-time or presence is a springboard and the basis for time travel from a place of choice rather than compulsion. Afropresentism is temporal liberation. And we don't have to work to access it because common everyday plants are portals. In the next section, we will focus our attention on lemon balm, *Melissa officinalis*, as a protocol towards presentism.

There is no self. Reclaim the "we," "us," and "ours" on all timelines to collapse space-time and access the blessings that the present has to offer. The we, us, ours is also the common weeds and herbs that show up exactly when we need them to. Plants are the part of us that seek and create wholeness. Well-prepared plant remedies can cut through time to intervene with historical, spiritual agents or energies and negotiate wellbeing on our behalf. Well-prepared plants, unlike drugs, have nonspecific directions of influence creating spectrums of wellness throughout our body with few risks or side effects. And while we are grateful for the gifts of industrial medicine to meet the ailments that the plantationocene creates, we also honor herbal medicine as a people's medicine in its simplicity, safety, and multidimensional effectiveness in the same way our ancestors did.

The world we live in produces and is reproduced by the spiritual temporal disequilibria that pull us out of the present, changing our very perception of time and creating worlds of dis-ease. What Western clinicians might label as anxiety is actually fear of the future. It shrinks what is called our time horizon, or the timeline through which we understand the movement of events causing future events to appear closer and more catastrophic than they are. Anxious people perceive events a month away as closer than events one month in the past.[7] Depressed folks perceive the past closer than the future and experience time creeping forward in slow motion.[8]

Mental afflictions are temporal disequilibria that cause us to perceive the movement of time disadvantageously. Whether we are anxious about a future event or depressed about a time we failed to be charming, our perception of time is an embodied one.[9] The truth of time's embodiment gives us power or agency over how we time travel. When we ground the experience of time in the body, we can use our body as a vehicle to alter our subjective time perceptions toward presence and wholeness.[10]

CONFRONTING OUR FUTURES WITH LEMON BALM

The class of herbal remedies that give us the most agency over our subjective experience of time is herbal nervines. Herbal nervines can modulate the nervous system with multiple directions of action that are distinct and specific to each plant. Well-prepared herbal nervines impact an array of neurological processes in the body through different neurotransmitters like GABA, serotonin, and dopamine relaying specific mental and physiological effects with very few risks or side effects.

Lemon balm is a mint family nervine native to the Middle East and North Africa. The eleventh-century Persian physician Avicenna introduced lemon balm to the Western world as an agent that acted against anxiety and depression. In 1653, English botanist Nicholas Culpeper wrote that lemon balm "causes the mind and heart to become merry, and reviveth the heart."[11]

While lemon balm's actions cannot be reduced to the sum of her parts, her citrusy uplifting scents, derived from aromatic compounds like citral, linalool, citronellal, neral, and geranial,[12] have all been implicated in plants that uplift the spirits and evoke coherent emotional responses like joy.

While lemon balm is known to uplift depressed spirits, relax the body, outwit viruses, and decrease inflammation, its temporal remediations are specific to folks experiencing anxiety over events that are yet to come. Lemon balm is the perfect remedy for those with a project, presentation, or test on their horizon who are frozen by inaction and procrastination. Lemon balm acts against a fear of the future by evoking coherent emotions that change our perception of the present.

Lemon balm modulates the nervous system indirectly through the digestive system and directly by impacting an array of processes in the central nervous system to decrease stress and increase ease.[13] To understand one of the many processes behind lemon balm's calming and soothing action, researchers in a pilot study found that Melissa officinalis supports the production of the neurotransmitter GABA, which helps to attune the body's response to stressors like fear. Researchers in the same *Journal of Neuroscience* issue report that GABA, in and of itself can affect the perception of time.[14] According to a key researcher in the study, neuroscientist Devin Terhune, then a fellow in the University of Oxford's Department of Experimental Psychology, "we tend to overestimate time when we're frightened, or underestimate it when we're experiencing joy."[15] By promoting coherent emotional states, like joy, lemon balm extends our time horizon, causing future events to appear further away and less threatening. She keeps the future at bay.

FLOWING THROUGH SPACE AND TIME WITH LEMON BALM

With joy in our hearts, the future at bay, and the time horizon extended, we are freed from the distraction of temporal disequilibrium and can be in touch with the possibility of the present. Lemon balm not only brings us into the present but helps us to operationalize presence by helping us to focus.

Hungarian American psychologist Mihaly Csikszentmihalyi famously coined the term "flow" to describe the experience of being so joyfully immersed in an activity that all distractions and our sense of time are lost. Before we know it, hours of time have passed without thought or reason. Time speeds up but because our joy evokes an experience of presence, we can complete more of the task at hand. Joyful presence combats fear, which slows our perception of time and shrinks our time horizon.[16]

In real-time, an Afropresentist notices herself hyperactive and procrastinating and reaches in her medicine bag for a tincture of fresh lemon balm. Her nose catches the sweet aroma of her dear one sending shockwaves through her central nervous system awakening her from the crossroad of non-commitment and shifting her emotion towards joy. She exhales, long pushing out the perception of her target. She settles in her seat and focuses on completing the task at hand. Walking towards her future.

I speak from experience. In my many years of apprenticing and sharing the medicine of lemon balm, I have watched temporal disequilibria find homeostasis. I've experienced myself and others freed up by lemon balm to express ourselves and take on what the world has to offer. What's more, is that I've experienced my beloved community empowered in their navigation of embodied space and time. I've seen them lean on lemon balm to support them in choosing the path forward, a reclamation of their agency. Temporal Liberation.

1 Christina Sharpe, *In the Wake: On Blackness and Being* (Durham, NC: Duke University Press, 2016).

2 Nikitah O. Imani, "The Implications of Africa-Centered Conceptions of Time and Space for Quantitative Theorizing: Limitations of Paradigmatically-Bound Philosophical Meta-Assumptions," *Black Studies Faculty Publications* (2012): 8, https://digitalcommons.unomaha.edu/blackstudfacpub/8, https://digitalcommons.unomaha.edu/cgi/viewcontent.cgi?article=1006&context=blackstudfacpub.

3 Nnedi Okorafor, *Who Fears Death* (New York: Penguin, 2014).

4 Neil Roberts, *Freedom as Marronage* (Chicago: University of Chicago Press, 2019).

5 Swakara Atwell-Bennett, "Afropresentism: Black Presence in the Diaspora," *BetterShared* (blog), 2022, https:// bettershared.co/blogs/news/afropresentism-black-presence-in-the-diaspora.

6 Neema Githere and Ethel Tawe, *BOMB Magazine*, April 19, 2022, https://www.bombmagazine.org/articles/neema-githere-and-ethel-tawe/.

7 Eugene M. Caruso, Leaf Van Boven, Mark Chin, and Andrew Ward, "The Temporal Doppler Effect: When the Future Feels Closer Than the Past," *Psychological Science* 24, no. 4 (2013): 530-36.

8 Sven Thönes and Daniel Oberfeld, "Time Perception in Depression: A Meta-Analysis," *Journal of Affective Disorders* 175 (2015): 359-72. https://www.sciencedirect.com/science/article/pii/S016503271400843X.

9 D. Di Lernia, S. Serino, G. Pezzulo, E. Pedroli, P. Cipresso, and G. Riva, "Feel the Time: Time Perception as a Function of Interoceptive Processing," *Frontiers in Human Neuroscience* 12 (2018): 74, https://www.frontiersin. org/articles/10.3389/fnhum.2018.00074/full.

10 R. Fontes et al., "Time Perception Mechanisms at Central Nervous System," *Neurology International* 8, no. 1 (2016): 5939, https://doi.org/10.4081/ni.2016.5939.

11 Noriko Shinjyo and Julia Green, "Are Sage, Rosemary and Lemon Balm Effective Interventions in Dementia? A Narrative Review of the Clinical Evidence," *European Journal of Integrative Medicine* 15 (2017): 83-96.

12 R. Nurzyńska-Wierdak, A. Bogucka-Kocka, and G. Szymczak, “Volatile Constituents of Melissa Officinalis Leaves Determined by Plant Age,” *National Product Communications* 9, no. 5 (May 2014): 703-6.

13 D. Kennedy, W. Little, and A. Scholey, “Attenuation of Laboratory-Induced Stress in Humans After Acute Administration of Melissa Officinalis (Lemon Balm),” *Psychosomatic Medicine* 66, no. 4 (2004): 607-13, https://www.bodyscience.com.au/mwdownloads/download/link/id/138/.

14 Devin B. Terhune, Sonia Russo, Jamie Near, Charlotte J. Stagg, and Roi Cohen Kadosh, “GABA Predicts Time Perception,” *Journal of Neuroscience* 34, no. 12 (March 19, 2014): 4364-70, https://www.ncbi.nlm.nih.gov/pmc/articles/PMC3960474/.

15 Jonathan Wood, "How Short Is Your Time?," University of Oxford, accessed December 2, 2022, https://www.ox.ac.uk/news/science-blog/how-short-your-time.

16 J. Dawson, and S. Sleek, "The Fluidity of Time: Scientists Uncover How Emotions Alter Time Perception," Association for Psychological Science, accessed December 2, 2022, https://www.psychologicalscience. org/observer/the-fluidity-of-time.

GOLDEN SHOWERS, GOLDEN FUTURES

Mary Maggic

Plastic, blue-cap test tubes get passed around the workshop participants. They examine the tubes, catching a glimpse of a mysterious brown residue stuck at the bottom of each tube (figure 1). One person twists open the blue cap and holds the tube to their nose. The others watch with anticipation as the person slowly inhales. An expression of slight repulsion appears on their face as their nose wrinkles at the smell. They pass it to the next person, who sniffs it and describes a sweet odor similar to caramel. The next person breathes in the same tube but reports smelling nothing at all. Perplexed, the participants return the tubes back to a black leather briefcase filled with a random assortment of medical and laboratory objects. What the participants are smelling are samples of urinary hormones that have been extracted from volunteers in previous workshops. These hormones, now acting outside of the body as pheromones, are the molecular output of the "Urine-Hormone-Extraction-Action" protocol, a workshop that I have developed with participants around the world over the past six years.

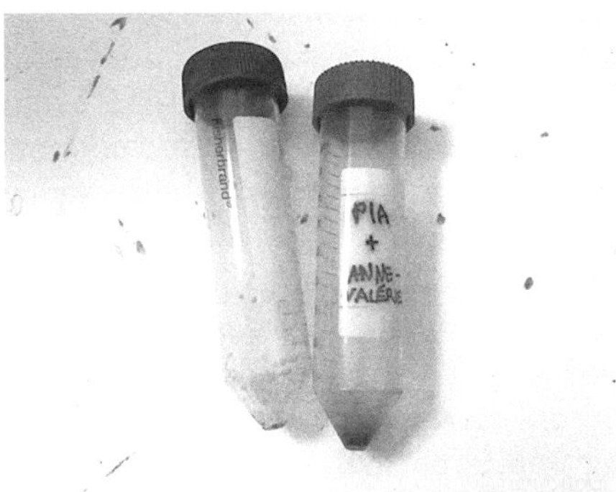

Figure 1. Urinary hormone samples from the workshop "Urine-Hormone-Extraction-Action" at Ckster: Gender-Hacking Festival, Bern, Switzerland, 2017. Image courtesy of the artist.

Over the years, this intimate smell exercise has allowed participants to connect with invisible molecules and their ancient and evolutionary effect on our neurology and physiology. Classified as pheromones, or hormones acting outside of the body, these molecules and their communication to our receptors occur under a vast and unseen signaling network called the "molecular semiosphere." This intricate web of biochemical entanglements is an interplay of natural and synthetic molecules that bind into the pocket of cell receptors, producing behavioral, neurological, and physiological chain reactions. The effects from the exposure to these molecules, whether through inhalation, gestation, or passive

Description Figure 1. Depicts two test tubes with blue caps that contain urine hormone samples. The test tube on the left is unlabelled, whereas the tube on the right is labelled "PIA + ANNE VALERIE" seepage, can be as quick as the firing of neurotransmitters or as slow as the crawl of evolutionary time. Whether slow or fast, micro or macro, invisible or detectable, this unseen world is responsible for a deep interconnectedness across species, substances, and timescales.

What does it mean to "world" with the molecular semiosphere? How can we perceive the multitude of glitches and recombinations that occur during cell receptor binding and signaling from foreign molecules? How do we dissolve the barriers between natural and synthetic, normal and abnormal, toxic and neutral, and honor the sublime process of co-becoming with molecules?

Two of my ongoing works, *Open Source Estrogen* (2015–present) and its nomadic, "freak-science" iteration, *Estrofem! Lab* (2016–present), have acted as a collaborative research platform for developing low-cost, accessible protocols for hacking unseen molecules. It is worth mentioning that the better-known workshop protocol "Urine-Hormone-Extraction-Action" actually came after a xenoestrogen detection protocol using yeast biosensors. In 2010, a team of scientists from Tulane University's School of Public Health and Tropical Medicine engineered the YES-HER plasmid (figure 3), a circular piece of DNA designed for the yeast LAC-Z expression pathway. By inserting this plasmid into yeast, one would create Yeast Estrogen Sensors (YES) encoded with the Human Estrogen Receptor (HER). These transgenic organisms would thus emit a yellow color change via the LAC-Z expression system in the presence of estrogenic molecules.

Yeast, or any microbiological organism, can be kept alive for months or even years at relatively low cost and maintenance because they self-reproduce when given the right conditions. The use of biological sensors for detecting environmental pollutants therefore opens up the possibilities of citizen scientists, bypassing traditional laboratory methods that use large, expensive, and inaccessible machines. I found out through Jo Zayner, a fellow biohacker and the founder of the consumer genetic engineering business the ODIN,[1] that Tulane University had placed the YES-HER plasmid in the digital gene repository, AddGene, making it available for online purchase and commercial use.[2] Wanting to appropriate this protocol into a low-cost version, I purchased the plasmid to make my own yeast biosensors, giving rise to the workshop protocol "YES-HER Yeast Biosensors." Using DNA purification and amplification methods for the plasmid, followed by a standard yeast transformation protocol, the YES-HER Yeast Biosensors were born (figure 2). To my excitement, the transgenic yeast worked exactly how they were designed to, emitting the yellow-colored nitrophenol product after incubating overnight with the estrogen sample in question. This yellow nitrophenol product is what allows us to visualize the molecular semiosis in action, and with its color intensity, one can quantify the level of estrogenic molecules in the sample.

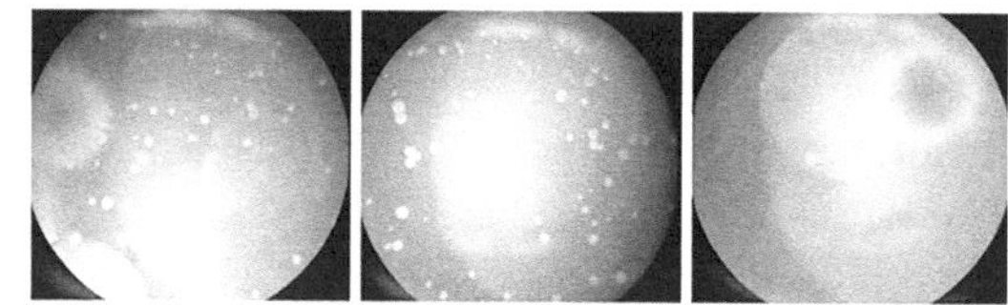

Figure 2. First round of genetic modification of yeast strain Saccharomyces cerevisiae with inserted YES-HER plasmid, performed at the MIT Department of Microbiology, 2016. Image courtesy of the artist.

The initial trials of the YES-HER Yeast Biosensors were performed at the microbiology department at MIT using pure vials of β-estradiol, a naturally occurring form of estrogen. Following a yeast detection method published in *Nature Protocols*,[3] the yeast biosensors were incubated overnight with the β-estradiol, then lysed, or ruptured, and opened with an added substrate called *ortho*-Nitrophenyl-β-galac toside (ONPG). This substrate, when catalyzed by the enzyme β-galactosidase, produces a yellow-colored nitrophenol product (figure 4). This yellow output can be equated with a molecular semiosis in action, a molecular binding that results from the communication between β-estradiol (or any estrogenic molecule) and its receptor (in this case,

Figure 3 (left). YES-HER yeast plasmid constructed at Tulane University and deposited on AddGene. Image taken from Tulane study.

Figure 4 (right). Yellow-colored nitrophenol product emitted after overnight incubation of pure β-estradiol. Image courtesy of the artist.

Description Figure 2. Three circular microscopic images of a genetically modified strain of yeast called Saccharomyces cerevisiae. The slides themselves are a dull, greenish-blue with beige particles that vary in size.

Description Figure 3. A circular black and white gene diagram.

Description Figure 4. Six clear tubes with varying amounts of yellow liquid are seen in a line. The background is blurred, unable to distinguish.

the human estrogen receptor). Freakish and part-human, this transgenic yeast can be seen as extensions of our bodies, using our same estrogen receptor to see the unseen and to detect the very molecules we were unknowingly becoming-with.

Compared to other hormone receptors, such as that of testosterone, the estrogen receptor (figure 5) is unique in its selectivity and evolutionary history. Scientists describe the binding pocket of the estrogen receptor as "highly promiscuous," like a lock with many keys.[4] Therefore, the non-selectivity of the estrogen receptor is the reason for our sensitivity to cosmetics, cleaning products, pesticides, pills, plastics, and many other industrial leakages that have been classified as "endocrine-disrupting compounds" or EDCs. I often describe this molecular sensitivity as one of the greatest paradoxes of living in the Anthropocene—the fact that the molecules of industry, mass-manufacturing, and earthly extractivism communicate and bind to our estrogen receptors. This unselective binding proves two key things. One, synthetic and foreign compounds can act within our molecular semiosphere, problematizing the border between natural and synthetic. Whether or not these foreign compounds act as toxic or neutral molecules within our shared semiosphere I discuss further below. Two, the unselective binding of the estrogen receptor is the reason why bodies have always been so permeable. This porosity, many post-humanists would argue, is counter to the dominant belief systems that bodies are static, biologically deterministic, or somehow impervious to nonhuman relationalities.

To complicate this permeability further, studies say the estrogen receptor is highly conserved among all vertebrate taxa.[5] This means that the estrogen receptor remained in the DNA lineage of all species to evolve within the taxonomic class of vertebrates. These taxa, or taxonomic units of a population of organisms, include all species of fish and tetrapods (birds, reptiles, amphibians, and mammals). The estrogen receptor's occurrence across all vertebrate taxa implies that every species, regardless of gender, that has evolved since the emergence of the first vertebrate ancestor has evolved with the same estrogen receptor. Therefore the biochemical exchanges under the molecular semiosphere implicate not only the human species but also the frogs, the fish, the birds, and every other organism with the same estrogen receptor. This shared, cross-species vulnerability, beautiful and horrible at the same time, produces both a microscale interconnectedness and intimacy, as well as an ever-changing planet on the macroscale. There is a sense of bewilderment in the crowd as nearly every person has passed around and smelled the urinary hormones inside the blue-cap test tubes. So far, each person has reported a different response to the same sample. Smell, out of all five senses, is the least understood and most difficult to study (even under controlled scientific conditions) because the results are so subjective. This is due to the fact that every

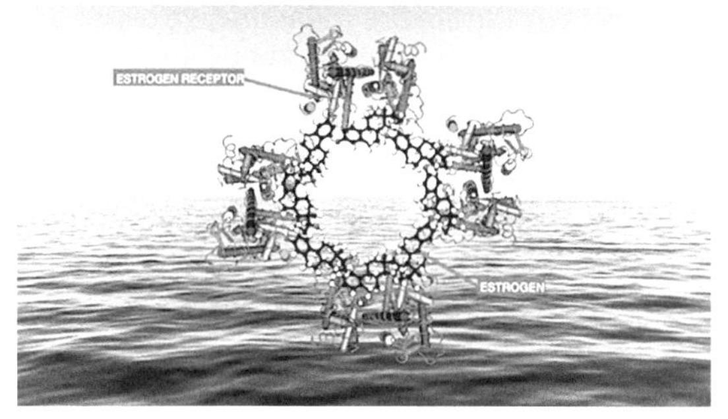

Figure 5. Digital illustration of estrogen receptor interactions under the molecular semiosphere. Image from "We're All Living in the Estroworld," a presentation by Mary Maggic, image courtesy the artist.

person has a unique combination of nose receptors that varies with their genetic makeup and lived experience. Like our bodies that constantly glitch under the molecular semiosphere, our olfactory senses and their neurological associations change with varied frequency. As we all perceive urinary hormones differently, so too do we differ in the way that we perceive and interpret the world. This short yet revealing smell exercise proves in many ways how we are all in a continuous negotiation between differing worlds.

EXTRACTIONS AND AMATEURISMS

Piles of papers lie scattered across the table as we awake from a hot afternoon nap, ready to tackle another dense reading of scientific papers on hormone extraction. Over and over again, the papers kept mentioning the use of C18 Cartridges, small pinky-finger-sized plastic tubes with a magical filter inside designed to trap endocrine-disrupting compounds. Available online only with industrial and academic licenses, the C18s are inaccessible to the average citizen or for any DIY purpose. We knew we wanted to substitute the contents of that magical filter for something cheaper. We looked again at the scattered papers with blocked exhales of frustration, our brains numb from dissecting scientific jargon. I started to roll loose tobacco between the thin paper in my fingertips. Holding one of those small cigarette filters between my thumb and index finger, my mind began to consider possibilities.

The "Urine-Hormone-Extraction-Action" protocol was first conceived in 2016 among friends and collaborators in the Hackteria community, a global and decentralized network for open-source biological art.

Description Fig. 5. A digital rendering of the molecular structure of an estrogen receptor is overlaid onto an image of a calm ocean. A label that reads "ESTROGEN" points to the black inner ring of the receptor that resembles the pattern of honeycomb, and another label that reads "ESTROGEN RECEPTOR" points to the outer tubular coils that line the inner ring.

The project began in June of that year during the collaborative residency Interactivos: Possible Worlds[6] at Medialab Prado in Madrid, where Canadian artist and professor Byron Rich, Gynepunk[7] practitioners Gaia Leandra and Paula Pin, researchers Carlos Gomez and Amanda Padilla, and I joined forces for the project *Open Source Estrogen*. Drawing upon working knowledge of the YES-HER Yeast Biosensors for detection, we knew we wanted to expand the scientific repertoire of *Estrofem! Lab* to include extraction from water-based sources under the premise that water is the universal carrier of industrial molecules.

The "Urine-Hormone-Extraction-Action" is based on column chromatograpy, a separation and selective method for chemical compounds. Like the C18 Cartridges, column chromatography can trap environmental pollutants using a long, expensive glass column packed with chemical substrates that attract the molecules of interest. Using the polar and nonpolar properties of hormones, we can isolate these molecules from our own urine. Hormones are part of a class of steroidal molecules characterized by a six-ring carbon structure. This structure gives hormonal molecules a nonpolar or hydrophobic property that allows them to diffuse across lipid-based cell membranes. That's why specific hormone therapies, such as the testosterone patch, are delivered through the surface of the skin. At the same time, hormonal molecules contain side chains that make them polar or hydrophilic, allowing these molecules to be carried by water. As I held the cigarette filters between my fingers, I suddenly thought to test the chemical properties of the filters. Adding a drop of acetone (the type of alcohol commonly found in nail polish remover) to the filters, they immediately liquified, proving that they contained nonpolar properties. Combined with silica gel, the substance commonly found in "DO NOT EAT" packets known to absorb moisture, we had the polar and nonpolar components for attracting hormonal molecules through the column chromatography method.

Using cigarette filters as the nonpolar substrate and silica gel as the polar substrate for the glass column, we felt we had successfully created a DIY version of the C18 Cartridges. As a substitute for the expensive laboratory glassware, we resorted to using recycled glass bottles and modifying them using a glass bottle cutter to etch a line along the circular edge. This bottle is then placed in water baths alternating between boiling water and ice-cold water, a process that shocks the glass to separate cleanly at the etched line. Now the column and its substrates are complete. Like a simple kitchen recipe, only four basic pouring steps are required to perform this protocol (figure 6): first, conditioning the column with methanol and water, then loading the urine sample, and then eluting with methanol. Elution refers to the process of drawing the hormonal molecules off the column's substrate using methanol as the solvent. Once the hormones havedissolved in the methanol, the final step is to evaporate the volatile alcohol, leaving behind the brown sticky substance at the bottom of those blue-cap test tubes.

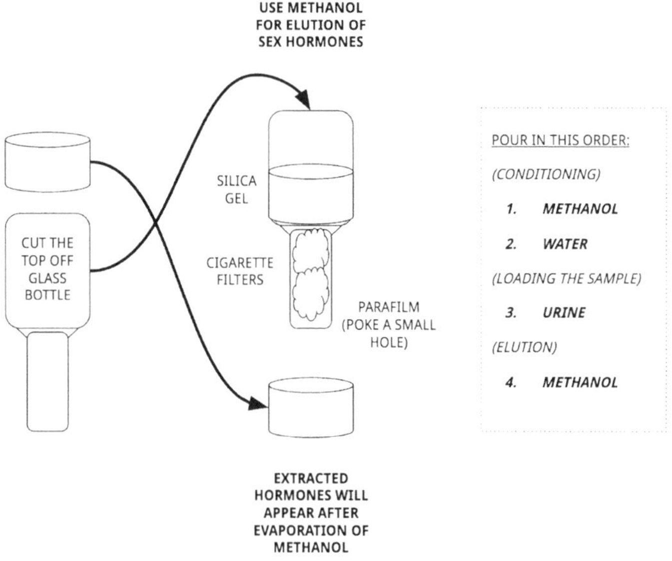

Figure 6. Diagram illustrating the protocol of "Urine-Hormone-Extraction-Action." Image courtesy of the artist.

Between the cigarette filters, crushed glass of wine and beer bottles, contaminated water samples, and spillage of sulfuric acid, our unruly knowledge production superseded the reading of dense scientific literature and the making of sterile laboratory conditions. We hacked in the spirit of public amateurism,[8] the subversive process of learning, doing, and failing in a noninstitutional setting. And while we hacked at the material, unboxing its molecular invisibility, we also hacked at its symbolic representations, unboxing its molecular meaning. Therefore, the practice of hacking produces knowledge on an existential level, inevitably leading to some form of world-making. This opens up ways of relating to the world that go beyond desires of purity and "save the earth" slogans. Despite our oceans of toxicities, we never stop "worlding" with molecules and engaging in a process of co-creation. It is only a matter of becoming aware of this invisible co-creative process and how this might change the way we perceive what is toxic or what is alien. With the

Description Figure 6. A diagram displays the tools and method of "Urine-Hormone-Extraction-Action." A glass bottle with the top cut off is used to extract the hormones after the evaporation of methanol.

“Urine-Hormone-Extraction-Action” protocol, I knew there was more to uncover beyond invisible molecules.

WORLDING WITH THE MOLECULAR

It’s hard to tell what we’re looking at. There is a disordered assortment of upturned folding chairs and table legs stacked on top of each other and fastened together precariously with cable ties and packaging tape. Oxygen masks connected to blue-cap test tubes are scattered across this strange scenography. Every object seems to lean on each other in a delicate balance. Upon closer examination, there are upside-down glass bottles connected to the chair legs with metal, three-finger clamps. The bottles, with their necks facing downward, appear to have shiny jewels on top of a layer of white cotton, as if to act as some kind of filtration device. With empty and half-filled plastic cups littering the floor, it looks like a ritual has already finished, leaving behind empty spaces that bodies used to inhabit.

In July of 2016 in Amsterdam, in a small corner of the Waag Society’s wetlab, artist Špela Petrič and I explored the urinary hormone extraction protocol for our then-collaboration with the laboratory theater collective, Aliens in Green (AiG).[9] Špela had been designing “milking” apparatuses for sucking urine through C18 Cartridges connected to large syringes with a constant tugging motion. Like a plastic chandelier, this array of large syringes hung over a medical IV stand became one of the main scientific props for the touring AiG participatory performance, *Xenopolitics #1: Petro-bodies and Geopolitics of Hormones*. Designed for twenty-five participants and spanning over six to eight hours, this workshop performance began by “abducting” the participants to trigger what we called “a crisis of the body.” We would then use this crisis, or corporeal vulnerability, as the starting point for creating new worldly constructions.

But why subject the participants, now called “abductees,” to a state of vulnerability? This crisis represents the panic and fear we commonly associate with becoming alien or becoming queer, trans, altered, orunsettled. Think about the word *disrupt* in the class of molecules called “endocrine disrupting compounds.” Think about the need to remove waste from a polluted land, only to relocate the pollution to a more marginalized land. Or the prophylactic need for cleanliness and sterility, when contamination is how we’ve adapted and survived throughout planetary history. Or how we label things as “toxic” is really the same as how we label anything that would classify as “the Other.” However, if we think through our vast entanglements under the molecular semiosphere, there are no such categories. *We are already alien.*

So how do we address these desires for purity and find commonalities with "the alien"? In these highly orchestrated workshop performances with AiG, abductees would chop up various foods of contaminated origins, grate-up plastic consumer products, liquify cosmetics and detergents, and role-play as different political and philosophical ideologists (figure 7). These exercises produce what AiG calls "cultivating an art of combinations," or an art of symbiosis that "recomposes the commons in an odd world."[10] Working with AiG was the moment I began to see the potential of biohacking and collective world-making and the possibility of neutralizing a deeply ingrained fear conditioned in us from birth. More importantly, I learned that only from this point of emancipatory neutrality, where the old world has been interrogated, deconstructed, and re-appropriated, can new imaginations emerge most freely. At this point, we can begin to ask ourselves, *do we want to be more alien than we already are?*

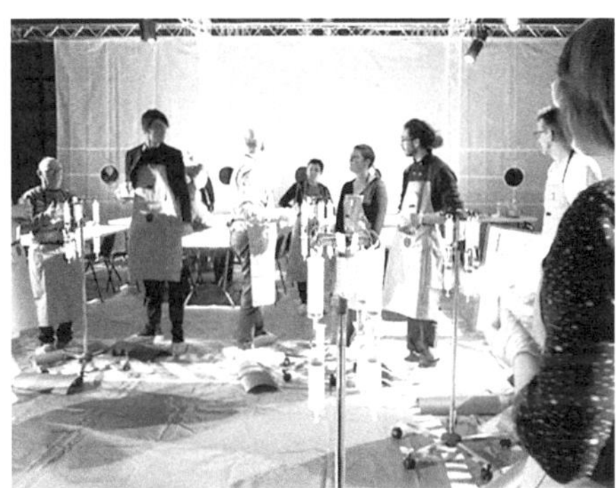

Figure 7. From the Aliens in Green workshop-performance Xenopolitics, a performative workshop on endocrine disruptors, presented at the 2019 PACT Zollverein Festival in Essen, Germany. Image courtesy of Aliens in Green.

In October 2021, the Institute of Anxiety in Prague hosted a two-day workshop event with urine hormone extraction followed by a hormone gastronomy dinner cooked together with all the participants. Paradoxically, I got hit with a panic attack on the day of the workshop that led to a significant breakthrough. Grasping for clarity, I found pieces of printed paper taped to a wall, possibly left over from a past visiting artist. The text read various theories on new materialisms, with paraphrased quotes from Karen Barad, Serpil Oppermann, and Jane Bennett that read, "For us to understand matter and embodiment, we need to see it as active, dynamic, and stemming from a primacy of relations," and,

Description Figure 7. A photograph of the workshop-performance Xenopolitics that is taking place against a backdrop of large white curtains. There are nine participants who seem to be listening to the instructor (the fourth from the left) and all are wearing bright green aprons and latex gloves. In front of them are poles that hold hanging syringes.

"Performativity is the dynamic core of mattering." Suddenly everything made sense. Breaking from the original workshop plan, I proceeded to grab chairs and table legs, assembling them into a random sculpture in the center of the room. I told participants that this represented the old world, and that today we would destroy this old world and build from its ruins. After the rushed and violent destruction, I then asked participants to assemble the new world in complete silence, allowing negotiations between each other to happen only somatically. Using silence to break the anthropocentrism of speech, we allowed the agency of materials, including the urinary molecules trapped inside the glass columns, to speak for themselves (figure 8).

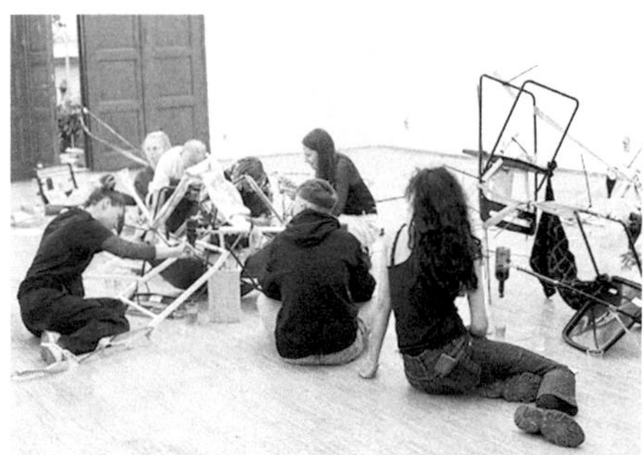

Figure 8. Open Source Estrogen & Estrofem! Lab. Two-day workshop presented at the Institute of Anxiety in Prague, Czech Republic, 2021. Photo by Karolína Matušková.

This workshop breakthrough helped me formulate and reflect on these questions, going beyond the didacticism of scientific protocols and the representations of structures and ideologies. Hacking molecules, hacking with participants, and hacking with collectives have shown me how much our world is itself a laboratory, experimenting with itself over and over again. And this experimenting is only possible because matter is agential, vibrant, co-generative, and disobedient. Whatever we find in landfills, ocean islands of garbage, abandoned sites of nuclear leakage, the bellies of whales, or black-market plastic trades has probably flowed through our own bodies at some point in our lifetimes. We glitch in every moment of the encounter. Every moment of the cell receptor binding to its molecule. There is no hard separation, clear boundary, or final destination in the form of an apocalypse, and perhaps we should all stop hoping for one. There are only relations—entanglements that transform us every day.

Description Figure 8. A photograph of the Open Source Estrogen & Estrofem! Lab where seven participants are sitting on the floor of a near-empty room and constructing complex structures from foldable metal chairs, wooden planks, and various other materials.

1 "Home," Odin, accessed July 24, 2024, https://www.the-odin.com/

2 Charles A. Miller et al., "Single Plasmids Expressing Human Steroid Hormone Receptors and a Reporter Gene for Use in Yeast Signaling Assays," *Plasmid* 63, no. 2 (March 2010): 73, https://www.ncbi.nlm.nih.gov/pmc/articles/PMC2819589/.

3 Jennifer E. Fox et al., "Detecting Ligands and Dissecting Nuclear Receptor-Signaling Pathways Using Recombinant Strains of the Yeast Saccharomyces Cerevisiae," *Nature Protocols* 3 (March 20, 2008): 637-45, https://www.nature.com/articles/nprot.2008.33.

4 Hui Wen Ng et al., "Versatility or Promiscuity: The Estrogen Receptors, Control of Ligand Selectivity and an Update on Subtype Selective Ligands," *International Journal of Environmental Research and Public Health* 11, no. 9 (Aug. 26, 2014): 8709-42, https://www.ncbi.nlm.nih.gov/pmc/articles/PMC4198987/.

5 Joseph W. Thornton, "Evolution of Vertebrate Steroid Receptors from an Ancestral Estrogen Receptor by Ligand Exploitation and Serial Genome Expansions," *Proceedings of the National Academy of Sciences* 98, no. 10 (May 1, 2001): 5671-76, https://doi.org/10.1073/pnas.091553298.

6 "'Interactivos?'16: Possible Worlds. Creative and Collaborative Uses of Digital. Collaborators Call," Metadero Medialab, accessed July 24, 2024, https://www.medialab-matadero.es/en/news/interactivos16-possible-worlds-creative-and-collaborative-uses-digital-collaborators-call-1.

7 The Gynepunk Lab consists of a "riot of bodies" researching the violent and patriarchal history of gynecology and various DIY protocols for gynecological health. "Gynepunk," Tumblr, accessed July 24, 2024, https://gynepunk.tumblr.com/.

8 Beatriz Da Costa, "Reaching the Limit: When Art Becomes Science," in *Tactical Biopolitics: Art, Activism, and Technoscience*, ed. Beatriz da Costa and Kavita Philip (Cambridge, MA: MIT Press, 2008), 365-82, http://doi.org/10.7551/mitpress/9780262042499.003.0021.

9 Aliens in Green (AiG, founded 2016) is a tactical theater group fighting the alien agents of xeno-anthrocentric power, using media communication, open science philosophy, and speculative fiction for critical interventions in public space.

AiG is a fluid formation of Ewen Chardronnet, Bureau d'Etudes (L. Bonaccini and X. Fourt), Mary Maggic, Julien Maudet, Špela Petrič, and other aliens.AiG is a fluid formation of Ewen Chardronnet, Bureau d'Etudes (L. Bonaccini and X. Fourt), Mary Maggic, Julien Maudet, Špela Petrič, and other aliens.

10 Aliens in Green, "Becoming Non-Alien," in *Synthetic Becoming* (Berlin: K. Verlag, 2022).

MEANS WITHOUT ENDS: LEARNING HOW TO LIVE OTHERWISE THROUGH ACCESS-CENTERED PRACTICE[1]

Taraneh Fazeli and Cannach MacBride

A note to readers who like to use text-to-speech software. Downloadable digital copies of this book in both PDF and ePub formats are available on Amherst College Press's website. The ePub has the greatest text-to-speech reader functionality so we recommend using that format.

Please read this essay's introduction carefully, it is not for everyone.

We, Taraneh Fazeli and Cannach MacBride, are friends and collaborators. I, Cannach, am a white Scottish queer trans artist and editor with chronic illnesses living in Rotterdam; I, Taraneh, am a queer chronically ill Iranian American curator living in Waawiiyaatanong/Detroit and Lenapehoking/New York. We are co-editing a field guide of accessibility practices for art and culture that emerges from the lessons and networks cultivated in *Sick Time, Sleepy Time, Crip Time: Against Capitalism's Temporal Bullying*, the peripatetic group exhibition that Taraneh curated from 2016 to 2020.[2] The book addresses issues that occur when ableist, modern-colonial cultural institutions attempt to "include" disabled, negatively racialized, and Indigenous bodyminds without addressing their own structures, and explores practices less reliant on institutions that are already in use to create accessible worlds.[3]

We begin by honoring the compassionate militancy and wisdom of disabled ancestors who came before us (and may not have assumed the identity but nonetheless lived disability experiences), our elders and peers in disability arts and organizing communities, and those yet to come.[4] There are disabled people in the future.[5]

Without the perseverance of all disabled and debilitated people alongside efforts to untangle disability's relations to necropolitics, none of these routes we investigate here to being the fullest versions of ourselves alongside others would be possible. As we write, the settler-colonial Israeli state escalates its long-term targeted debilitation of Palestinians, this time in response to Hamas's violence on October 7, 2023, with a disproportionately violent campaign supported by US military aid.[6] The death numbers tick rapidly further and further up. The number of the dead and accusations of genocide reverberate, rallying demands for a ceasefire. Those disabled or debilitated go uncounted by geopolitical powers. Those who are sick and die because they can't get medicines go uncounted. Those who can't move to safety when mobility devices won't work in a war zone go uncounted. We sit with both what disability frameworks and associated disability pride offer politically and their inadequacies.[7]

Our requirement of you is not contingent on you holding a disabled identity, being a part of disability communities, or experiencing "disability" described otherwise. We ask that, in entering this essay, you do not merely distill the offerings emerging from it for your needs and desires.[8] We ask you to commit to valuing the lives of the disabled people who created the resources shared here, and the people disabled and debilitated by state and corporate violence everywhere, by collectively resisting ableism in your actions.[9] In doing so, you'll uphold the values and lineages this text is shaped by. We follow abolitionist lawyer and organizer Talila A. Lewis's definition, "Ableism is a system of assigning value to people's bodies and minds based on societally constructed ide- as of normalcy, productivity, desirability, intelligence,

1 This title comes from artists Park McArthur and Constantina Zavitsanos: "We, very unreasonably, will be held. We are one another's means without ends." McArthur and Zavitsanos, 2016, "The Guild of the Brave Poor Things." In Reina Gossett, Eric A. Stanley, and Johanna Burton, eds.,*Trap Door: Trans Cultural Production and the Politics of Visibility* (Cambridge, MA: MIT Press, 2017), 238.

2 "Crip" is a reclaiming of the derogatory label cripple first popularized by disability activists. Our book expands on materials introduced in this essay.

3 "Bodymind" is a term often used in disability studies and disability communities to refuse the Cartesian mind body split that still pervades so much of Western culture. It was first elaborated on by disability studies scholar Margaret Price in *Mad at School* (Ann Arbor: University of Michigan Press, 2011).

4 From you, artists Frida Kahlo and Jim Flanagan, to you, art and organizing collectives Gran Fury and Sins Invalid, to you, writers Aurora Levins Morales and Naomi Ortiz, to you, justice warriors Audre Lorde and Harriet Tubman, to you, activists prostrate on steps in the 504 sit-ins and Black Panthers feeding them, to you, anti-austerity activists like Disabled People Against the Cuts and Dawn Foster, to you, all the activists chained to fences in front of incinerators, we strive to inhabit the creativity and community you cultivated in the face of so much violence when building on your practices. There are way more of you than we can name, but we honor the impact and power of the vast web.

5 Attempts to erase disabled people from the future are numerous. Leah Lakshmi Piepzna-Samarasinha, a powerful disability justice organizer and poet named their book *The Future Is Disabled* (Vancouver: Arsenal Pulp Press, 2022) in homage to disabled activist and writer Alice Wong's "crip oracle work." In linking futurity and disability positively, we intentionally align with others who have similarly faced eradication. We mirror the phrasing of artist Alisha Wormsley's project *There Are Black People in the Future* (2012-).

6 Current US government aid to Israel can be found here: "U.S. Foreign Assistance by Country (Israel)," US Department of State, accessed October 4, 2024, https://www.foreignassistance.gov/cd/israel/. Details of the most recent United States to Israel military aid package at time of writing can be found here: "US House Passes $14.5bn Military Aid Package for Israel," Al Jazeera, accessed October 4, 2024, https://www.aljazeera.com/news/2023/11/3/us-house-passes-14-5bn-military-aid-package-for-israel.

7 The US disability rights movement advocates for disabled people's unalienable citizenship rights, but not everyone living in the US has access to citizenship, the state enforces strict control over its borders and harms citizens of other nations through military operations, military aid, conditional international aid, debt, and carbon emissions. In *The Right to Maim: Debility, Capacity, Disability*, Jasbir K. Puar articulates that expanded care for disabled rights-bearing subjects under liberalism exists alongside the relentless pursuit of profit in racialized capitalism that creates debility for the slow depletion of marginalized populations not afforded these same rights. (Durham, NC: Duke University Press, 2017).

8 Too often we witness knowledge rooted in specific communities and needs grifted carelessly. In the early days of the COVID-19 pandemic, access practices that had previously been deemed "impossible" suddenly, temporarily proliferated because of the fears and needs of wealthier able-bodied people in certain regions of the world.

9 We haven't always resisted ableism or known how to best enable access. We've learned through struggles and joys in the specific disability, diasporic, and/or queer communities we are a part of. We are indebted to many

excellence, and fitness. These constructed ideas are deeply rooted in eugenics, anti-Blackness, misogyny, colonialism, imperialism, and capitalism .... You do not have to be disabled to experience ableism."[10]

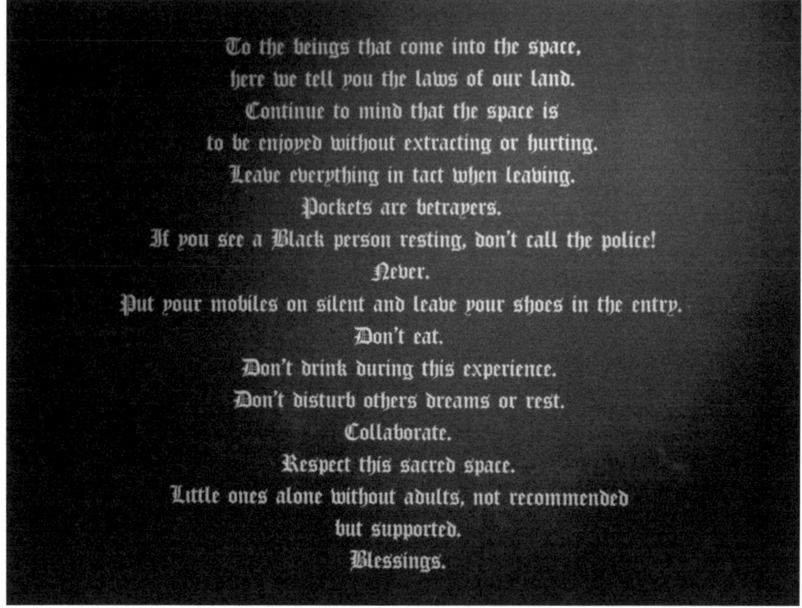

Figure 1. Navild Acosta and Fannie Sosa, *Black Power Naps*, 2017 (detail). Photo by Clare Gatto. Courtesy the artists.

Strategic boundary setting within situations of relatively open access (as we attempt here) is one means of affirming existences devalued through ableism by shifting the presumed center of a situation as well as whose access is prioritized. Navild Acosta and Fannie Sosa's *Black Power Naps* is an artwork that works in the material of policy to do this (Figure 1). The artists created this series of glittering Afrofuturist immersive napping environments and performances for Black people to germinate idleness, rest, and dream together alongside Brown, Indigenous, migrant, queer, and trans people. By offering spaces of reprieve from ongoing histories of strategic disruption of Black people's

Description Figure 1. Printed on a black gallery wall in light green gothic type is a center-justified block of text that begins: "To the beings that come into the space, here we tell you the laws of our land. Continue to mind that the space is to be enjoyed without extracting or hurting. Leave everything in tact when leaving. Pockets are betrayers. If you see a Black person resting, don't call the police. Never ...."

10 Available at "Working Definition of Ableism," Talila A. Lewis (blog), January 1, 2022, https://www.talilalewis. com/blog/working-definition-of-ableism-january-2022-update.

restorative sleep patterns to better subjugate and extract labor from them, they resist ableism as defined by Lewis.

Within the gallery, audiences are welcomed by a set of "rules" hanging atop an ancestral altar. Employing a form of policy drag, their détournement playfully embodies policy's language of command to mandate an ethic of relations while also using poetics to fundamentally question the way policy operates. Beyond the explicit conditions listed, for those in the know, aesthetic and tonal cues strategically deploy humor and queer Black aesthetics to center Black visitors without explicitly saying so. Visitors holding other identities that public spaces and institutions are not usually structured around may feel affinity with this recentering and therefore also feel invited in. Yet, for visitors who are used to their needs being addressed as a presumed default may perceive these cues, experience the heightened awareness that this space is not for them, and for them, and they may shift their behaviors accordingly.[11] The artists' approach centers access for some over others to provide better safety and care than is possible under "universal" access (which performs as an openness to everyone but often does not deliver). This form of reparative practice emerges from separatism.[12]

If you seek knowledge without responsibility, please skip past the section that follows.

11 For example, when Taraneh visited the installation at Performance Space New York, a small group of youth of color played on the beds while one middle-aged white woman stood to the installation's side, quietly spoke to a docent, and otherwise respectfully bore witness.

12 *Black Power Naps* was shown in *Sick Time, Sleepy Time, Crip Time* in 2019. The project's inclusion extended the frame of disability to better account for racialized forms of physical debilitation. Taraneh's intended curatorial approach (halted by COVID-19 closures) was to take the proposition that exists within the space of the artwork and extend it to its social and physical placement. After situating a version of *Black Power Naps* within the exhibition at Red Bull Arts Detroit's main galleries (purportedly open to all in the gentrifying Eastern Market area), the plan was to seat some exhibition programs within another installation in an existing space already tailored around people it was created for (a Black community organization outside the more-structurally resourced city center). Queer and disability studies scholar Amalle Dublon's thinking on partiality—organizing with those you are partial to for reasons that may include or exceed identity—helps us understand how strategically setting the frame of a social space supports the affective potential of what happens within, and how strategies of visibility and opacity function in relation to power. See Amalle Dublon, *Partial Figures: Sound in Queer and Feminist Thought* (PhD dissertation, Duke University, 2017).

We link art's recent heightened interest in protocols to the field's attention to the distribution of power in many forms of interaction. This "protological turn," occurring alongside a reckoning with the fundamental inequity of arts systems, often examines and reworks accepted ways of doing things to enable change toward social good.

In the background of these developments is the emergence of policy as a primary form of governance, the cultural seepage of computational logics into many fields, and wider awareness of infection control protocols prompted by COVID-19.[13] In each, in different ways, protocols systematize interaction to (re)produce behavior and action within controllable parameters that uphold established power dynamics and their values.[14] Whereas policies state an intention to make something happen, protocols are the sets of decision-making rules and instructions—the procedures and role allocations—for making the policy happen through action.

In our field guide, we share a range of resources to help users cultivate access practices—scores, guides, agreements, contract riders, value statements, poems, maps, exercises, reflections on efficacy, and more. From considering the differences in intention and operation across these forms, we now understand a "practice" as a set of considerations for doing something *and* the actions of doing it. Practices are remade iteratively through time by those doing them in response to context; they involve tacit knowledge, are learned through experience, and are rarely transmitted solely through written or oral language—expectations around them are shared implicitly or explicitly. Practices can involve, and sometimes may even depend on protocols, but always exceed what protocols can encompass.[15] In art, where artists make and remake their processes continually, the term practice has come to hold the integrated totality of an artist's work (and sometimes life); the multiplicity of everyday actions and interactions—creative, relational, organizational—that constitute it; and the ongoing craft of each type of action.

In the rest of this essay, we consider how protocols and practices function within artworks and interactions in the arts to analyze two models of accessibility.

Preparation for gathering: three invitations from public arts organizations[16]

Dear …

An invite is emailed by a curatorial assistant on behalf of the curator. Many others with email addresses from the same museum are cc'ed. They may or may not be introduced by name and position. The names mentioned all sound femme and Anglo.

13 This reading of policy as governance comes from our experiences as patients and care workers and from cultural theorists and Black studies scholars Stefano Harney and Fred Moten's *The Undercommons: Fugitive Planning and Black Study* (Wivenhoe: Minor Compositions, 2013). Policy can be situated in the ever-expanding dispersal of power extending from post-Fordist models, where all human activity is a potential site of extraction and every individual can be a deputy of power. Inherently resistive to policy and refusing its terms, Harney and Moten's "planning" maintains the essentials of a life lived between whole humans. Planning's ungovernable realm of social life occurs in the undercommons. Not merely a site of oppositional critique or antagonistic rebellion, the undercommons refuses calls of order that hierarchize some forms of being together as knowledge and others as not.

14 It is beyond the scope of this text to address the parallel and interweaving history and present of Indigenous protocols for gathering and being. These honor Indigenous sovereignties and center radically different onto-epistemological relations than are permissible under settler-colonial governance structures, which the access models of this essay and even access-centered spaces that try to build otherwise all fall under.

15 Norms around the use of different protocols, practices, and tools in art are continually shifting and depend on context. For example, community agreements are becoming a common addition to more-standard liability releases for events. This shift's roots and effects reflect evolving conceptions of community versus audience, with whom responsibility resides, and what one is accountable to across all stages of creating an artwork, exhibition, or event.

16 Art museums (and, by extension, art non-profit galleries) have long been lauded as unique sites of democratic public space in which the public is invoked, comprehended, and realized. For numerous reasons tied to what type of subject, citizen, or body this space imagines and creates, representation and access have long been contested: the museum purports to be open to everyone, but it never really is.

They float collaborating with you on an event at the museum in three weeks' time, which might turn into a group exhibition later. Your creative work syncs with their upcoming programming theme, which is an effort to make the museum more inclusive to all! They ask to meet online to discuss.

You have never met them before other than, possibly, briefly at their public events. Until the uprisings for Black liberation precipitated by George Floyd's murder in 2020, over 75% of art shown there was by white cis men.

They apologize for the short notice and offer you a couple of meeting times this week, all in the mornings.

You do not usually meet in the mornings due to the timing of your dialysis schedule.

Since it is the only option offered, you feel forced to agree and plan to stay off camera to maintain your privacy. You want to ask for more information about the possible fee, timeline, access, and what the event is, but it feels hard to respond to this vague email.

So you reply "yes" to meet, and they send an invite with a link to meet for forty-five minutes.

You get a message an hour before the meeting: they must cancel. They suggest meeting again next week, which is only one and a half weeks before the event.

They don't tell you that they are postponing because of multiple organizational and personal crises that the chronically overstretched and under-supported staff are unable to manage.[17]

You wonder if the nebulous opportunity is worth the clear tax it will take on your health.

Hello …

An invite is emailed by an assistant curator.

Many others with email addresses from the same non-profit gallery are cc'ed. They are introduced by full name and position at the onset and are all signatories.

They invite you to collaborate on planning an event for the thirtieth anniversary of the Americans with Disabilities Act in two months. They share that they have reached out to a local disability non-profit to explore if they want to partner. They have invited some artists already who they name; they'd like you to moderate a panel and brainstorm the remaining panelists.

They name a decent fee.

They say there will be access accommodations for the event but do not detail what these are beyond "American Sign Language (ASL) and captioning." Their website invites access requests, stipulating they be made well in advance of events.

17 The artistic director canceled for an emergency board meeting after a donor pulled out. Their workload is that of two positions, so they lack time to empower the staff. The curatorial assistant, despite their mother being evicted, took initiative to pitch this program. Their approach clashed with the director's thematic direction and the curator, who often advocates for the assistant, has a young child and limited capacity.

You have met the white cis woman who is the Community Engagement Director before and heard them ask thoughtful questions at events, indicating they listen deeply. To your knowledge, no one on the team is disabled like you.

They ask if you'd like to meet online to discuss and, if so, to suggest times and share your access needs for the meeting.

You reply, and a meeting link is sent with a brief agenda.

When you arrive at the meeting, everyone introduces themselves with their names, pronouns, the precolonial name of the land they are on, and their position within the organization.

You suggest an access check-in; they follow. They only detail being tired and possibly going off camera.

Hi ;)

An email, containing a voice memo and its transcription, arrives from a curator at a small community arts organization.

They open by saying they hope it was OK to reach out, asking if this method works and the timing is right. They say that oral communication is often preferred in their culture, but they understand that's not the same for everyone. You immediately feel like you can both have what you need.

You have met. They are not disabled like you, but they are also_____ (insert another shared identity or experience). Their internet presence shows you that they are experienced with working across difference in considerate, non-tokenizing, practical ways.

They invite you to collaborate on developing a program next fall. They have been building relationships with communities with disability experience (even if not named as such) through cross-disability, unhoused veteran, and environmental justice organizations for the past two years. They've offered them space to host meetings and events while quietly channeling money into some of those organizations' cultural programs. For programs, they request scent-free attendance, provide ASL and Arabic interpretation, travel funds, stim and prayer spaces, Halal and gluten-free food options, and sometimes CART[18] or childcare. You've noticed they offer these in a straightforward, non-performative manner.

They describe the multiyear program grant and their organization's overall funding structure. They offer to discuss the drawbacks of their funding sources, and have refused some partnerships despite potential retaliatory censorship around boycotts. In sharing plans to maintain ethical collaboration with the partners longer term, you understand how they approach their commitments to specific communities across differences and the land they work with and on through the lens of their family's displacement as settler-refugees.

They reflect on your past work in relation to what they are proposing in a way that demonstrates deep understanding.

18 CART is an acronym for Communication Access Realtime Translation, which is used to refer to live captioning of speech to text by captionists.

This all suggests that their accessibility practices—for you, themselves, and others—are embedded within and inseparable from the creative project they propose and their wider activities.

You reply with enthusiasm but explain that due to an upcoming surgery you can't meet for some time. You ask if they might be able to send some voice memos since you use a text to speech reader already; they ask what messaging platform is preferred.

POLICY AND DISABILITY

One common disability model used in policy is the social model. Emerging in the mid-twentieth century, it locates disablement within societal structures rather than disabled people's bodies.[19] Systemic barriers, derogatory attitudes, and social exclusion prevent disabled people from living their fullest lives, in part by impacting access to work, housing, education, transportation, and the public realm. This model values disabled bodyminds while upholding an individual's agency in choosing treatments, medical or otherwise. However, its systems orientation has difficulty addressing how symptoms of some chronic conditions, like pain, impact quality of life in ways that cannot be entirely resolved by social change.

With the social model's depathologization of the individual came the rise of disability pride. Adopting strategies from the civil rights movement, the disability rights movement mounted pressure to change political, economic, and social systems by seeking legislative change to obtain rights and institutional resources for access provisions.[20] Although the movement involved BIPOC people, like second wave feminism, it focused on disability as a single-issue identity and resisted addressing race.[21] Protests, including the 504 Sit-ins and Capitol Crawl, helped bring the Americans with Disabilities Act (ADA) into law in 1990.[22] To protect the rights of disabled people, the ADA prohibits discrimination and requires "reasonable accommodations" be provided in arenas like transportation, employment, telecommunications, and public services.[23] While its impact has been notable in removing some stigma and barriers, its protections can be hard to enforce without legal support or biomedical proof of disability.

POLICY AND ACCESS: REASONABLE ACCOMMODATIONS

"Access" has been used to characterize the relationship between disabled bodyminds and their environments since the mid-to-late twentieth century.[24] Accommodations-based access broadly follows the social model and is based on the idea that physical and social barriers to disability

19 The social model of disability is one of the more established contemporary modern models for constructing, regulating, and supporting disability in the US settler-colonial state. Other more recent disability models—including neoliberal universal design, services, rights, consumer, money, political-relational, cultural, radical—stem from extensions to the social model or critiques of its limits. Although new models often develop in critical response to existing ones, they do not entirely supersede each other and layer in complex ways. The social model itself can be understood as a critical response to the medical model of disability. In the medical model, human ability is understood as a spectrum with disability on the inferior end, which "impairments" should be cured or managed, as in the racist ableist pseudoscience of eugenics. This paternalistic model emerged in the nineteenth century when the scientific and technological developments of the Industrial Revolution brought a cultural shift in some contexts towards secular concepts of normalcy and abnormalcy, impacting perceptions of disability. The medical and social models of disability are rooted in modernity's ideas of individuality, autonomy, and bodily integrity (for some). These models were developed in transnational exchange between Western liberal humanist participatory democracies rooted in colonial structures and have circulated through globalization and neoimperialism, but do not necessarily fit the contexts they are transmitted to and remixed within.

Prior to this, disability was often understood through moral models that perceived disabled embodiments as shameful indicators of divine stigma or retribution for wrongdoing These may have grown from spiritual/inspirational models that also understood disability as an act of a divine being, taking disability as positive (indicating being blessed with special powers) and/or negative (indicating evil possession). Unlike moral models, these spiritual models do not necessarily attribute morality to the person experiencing disability. Spiritual models exist in many cultures and societies globally and often interact with kinship structures and their associated care practices differently than in places where the Western social and medical models of disability dominate. In these cases, whether care is violent or lacking or supportive is similarly shaped by one's status in embedded social relations determined by factors like race, class, caste, and ethnicity models. However, in societies that rely heavily on kinship structures, spiritual models can be more defined by culturally specific hierarchies dependent on collectivist orientation, gender, age, familial status, religious or spiritual roles and beliefs, trade, and more.

20 The main organizing frameworks for resisting ableism do not neatly graft onto disability models. For example, those invested in contemporary justice frameworks with abolitionist principles still rely on access accommodations that were won through disability rights activism and benefits from the service model.

21 Originating with war veterans pressuring the government for rehabilitation support in the first half of the twentieth century, the disability rights movement took hold in the 1960s and 1970s. The disability rights movement is both indebted to concurrent Black civil rights movements and has perpetrated anti-Blackness.

22 In 1990, after months of inaction by Congress on the proposition to make the ADA law, over 1,000 people marched on the US Capitol to protest the efforts within the government to stall this legislation. When they arrived, to make the violence of inaccessibility in public space evident, around sixty protestors got out of their wheelchairs or put down other mobility aids, many crawling up the Capitol steps. Several months later the ADA was passed. Predating the ADA, in the 504 Sit-in of 1977, protesters in San Francisco occupied a government building for twenty-six days to push for civil rights legislation Section 504 that would protect disabled people.

23 The ADA's attempts at inclusion for disabled people in key arenas of public life emerge out of the continued violent impacts of institutions, operative via the institutionalization of disabled people and the production of disability and debility by institutions. Institutionalization during the nineteenth century was often justified by the perceived social and economic good of turning disabled people into productive workers, "correcting" their prior grouping with criminals and the poor. The result was exclusion from society through custodial warehousing in institutions, many of which were sites of abuse. The paternalistic assumption was that disabled people needed protection, management, and segregation.
This was magnified when eugenics classified disabled populations as a social danger, resulting in moves towards sterilization and permanent incarceration (with overcrowding and abuse common). From the mid-twentieth century, disabled people, their families, and sometimes healthcare workers mobilized to demand

inclusion can be overcome via (ADA-mandated) accommodations—often retrofit adjustments, adaptations, or supplements—provided by public and private institutions and employers.[25] These include adaptations to the built environment such as elevators, curb cuts, and wayfinding; human access such as interpreters and access support workers; and assistive technologies like hearing loop systems. The ADA addresses physical disabilities more adequately than chronic illnesses, mental health disabilities, or neurodiversity.[26]

Access as accommodation positions access as inclusion within capitalist systems of labor, education, or consumerism.[27] Access is either granted via standardized accommodations to an abstracted universal disabled subject, or via personalized accommodations to individuals with access needs that exceed a rarely defined norm, who must often supply evidence of need.[28] Access as accommodation has, in application, often become technocratic, which both obfuscates and emphasizes embedded power relations.[29] Responsibility for providing access lies with institutional bodies or individuals employed within them, and is often only provided if disabled people advocate for themselves, often with legal support.[30]

This access cannot witness or heal the harm and violence that disabled people have experienced historically through forms of segregation, and still experience. Access as accommodation cannot truly value disability culture, joy, and knowledge of ways to live otherwise, as it is fundamentally a project of normalization that neutralizes the political world-building potential of access as it is and has been practiced between humans unmediated by vast organizational bodies. The ableist world is just fine as it is and surely everybody wants in, right?

DEBILITY AND DISINVESTMENT

Encompassing a wide array of embodiments and experiences, disability is a fluid category that can be situational, happen to any person, and fluctuate in and out over the course of a life. Debility is similar in these regards, but the two frameworks differ. Within disability studies, debility has been offered as a supplement to disability, which is rooted in the Western model of autonomous, bounded selves. Access to welfare, services, and accommodations still relies on being legally categorized as disabled (enough), regardless of how one experiences one's disability.[31] Debility, understood as a depletion of capacity in a person, operates on a continuum and usually does not integrate well with legal disability thresholds and their associated rights.[32]

In *The Right to Maim*, gender and ethnic studies scholar Jasbir K. Puar similarly uses debility to think beyond an able-bodied/disabled binary, but also engages debility as a continuum to think beyond necropolitics' life/death binary.[33] Mobilizing the concept to examine deinstitutionalization. Despite the progress of the independent living movement, many disabled people still live in institutions. Licia Carlson, "Institutions," in *Keywords for Disability Studies* (New York: New York University Press, 2015), 109-12.

24 Bess Williamson, "Access," in *Keywords for Disability Studies* (New York: New York University Press, 2015), 14.

25 The meaning of "accommodation" in disability rights coheres to the ADA mandate that there be "reasonable accommodations" in specific environments to make them accessible to disabled people and that failure to do so is a form of discrimination. Rights to accommodations for disability access have been supported by the US courts in a way that positions accommodation as an anti-discrimination measure. Accommodation in this sense is still viewed as positive by many within disability discourse. However, accommodation had a prior meaning within rights discourses around race following the abolition of slavery. The idea of racial accommodation—wherein Black people accommodated racist white society and the state—was associated with reformist and gradualist approaches like those of educator, writer, and orator Booker T. Washington who suggested that compromise would lead to gradual improvements to Black lives. This was substantially critiqued by other Black intellectuals and activists of the time like W. E. B. Du Bois. Elizabeth F. Emens, "Accommodation," in *Keywords for Disability Studies* (New York: New York University Press, 2015), 18-21.

26 These vital interventions in existing systems are the result of hard-won struggles by disabled people against endemic ableism, but even this legal minimum is precarious: although provision of accommodations is legally mandated with a threat of punishment for non-compliance, this law is often not enforced, and neither government nor businesses allocate adequate funding to meet the law fully.

27 Disability activist and writer Marta Russell's work offers an in-depth analysis of access, disability, and the limits of disability rights frameworks through a materialist Marxian reading. A good introduction is Marta Russell and Keith Rosenthal, *Capitalism and Disability: Selected Writings by Marta Russell* (Chicago: Haymarket Books, 2019).

28 The need to request accommodations in advance or provide evidence of need varies according to context and legal obligations. For example, educational institutions are legally mandated to provide "reasonable accommodations" on an ongoing basis for their disabled students when a student can provide medical diagnostic evidence. In a museum, access accommodations are not mandated for guests by law (beyond the accessible toilets and ramps that a new public building must have under the ADA) but may be offered to guests who request it without proof of need if the museum prioritizes this possibility in budget, staffing, policy, etc. Employees who need access accommodations to do their job may well need to evidence their disability to receive them.

29 Policy, amalgamated with protocols, guidelines, and procedures, aims to limit the variability of actions and therefore resulting outcomes by minimizing opportunities for autonomous thought and action outside what is scripted. An effect of this is that policy often ends up determining what is possible and is performed unthinkingly without care or responsiveness, whether it achieves what it was originally intended to or not.

30 Often access is imagined and granted by able-bodied or system-enabled people who do not experience the same kind of inaccessibility they are charged with remedying. While being disabled does not inherently bestow knowledge of how to support access needs outside one's own or mean participation in cross-disability communities, it does often bring awareness of what it means to need access support, navigate systems to get it, and experience access that feels good, adequate, and bad. Many people who are systemically enabled to exercise power have circumscribed technocratic roles and are not necessarily enabled to meet their needs or exercise their rights.

31 Rachel Adams, Benjamin Reiss, and David Serlin, "Disability," in *Keywords for Disability Studies* (New York: New York University Press, 2015), 9-14.

32 Debility does not necessarily end in disability.

33 Jasbir K. Puar, *The Right to Maim: Debility, Capacity, Disability*. (Durham, NC: Duke University Press, 2017). Whereas biopolitics examines how control of life through statistical management enables socio-political powers, necropolitics, a concept developed by Achille Mbembe, highlights how biopolitical frameworks fail to address state-sponsored death, with race a main determinant of who lives and who dies, (*Necropolitics*, Durham, NC: Duke University Press, 2019).

how it is intentionally produced globally, Puar focuses on debility's production in entire populations across the Global South and negatively racialized populations in the Global North who are excluded from accessing the benefits of disability rights and pride.[34] She writes compellingly on how Palestinian people are purposefully disabled and debilitated by the Israeli state, but only deaths are counted.[35] Debility, disability, and death are not only produced directly through militarized state violence but also through organized abandonment. This intentional disinvestment by the corporate-state matrix from certain communities and infrastructures is furthered by policy. Organized abandonment's deliberate depletion of infrastructure creates new

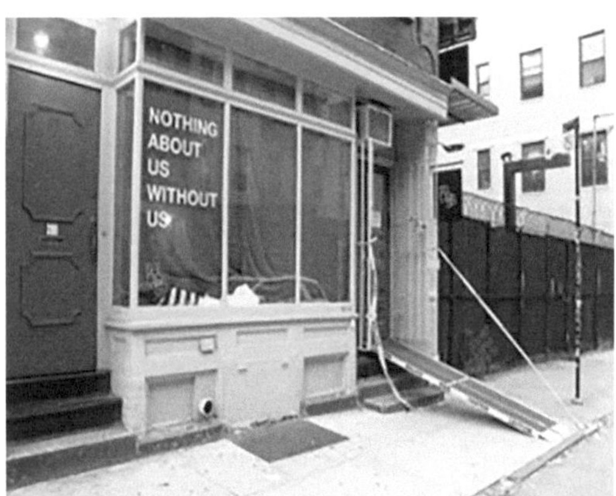

Figure 2. Outdoor view of Recess during the Canaries 2016 session *Refuge in the Means*, while *Slumber Party*, an event by Park McArthur and Constantina Zavitsanos, takes place inside.

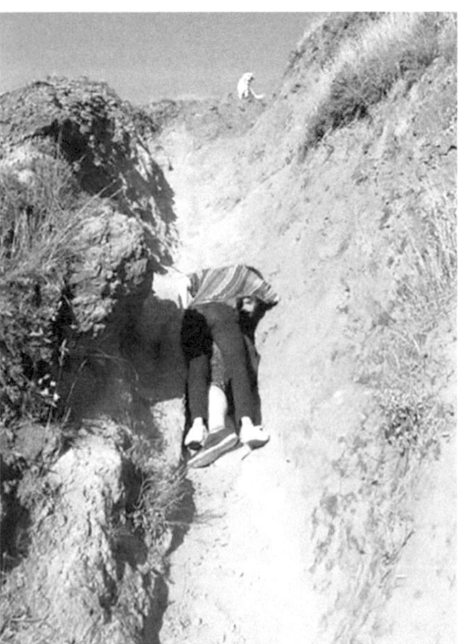

Figure 3. Amalle Dublon and Constantina Zavitsanos, *We already have the night*, 2014. Digital photo, dimensions variable. Courtesy of the artists.

34 While *Right to Maim* importantly challenges the epistemic whiteness of disability studies, there is an embedded tension in naming the production of certain types of disability as violent when one valuable contribution of disability studies has been to challenge the notion that disability is inherently undesirable. Puar often cites disability studies scholar Helen Meekosha's writing on how the dominance of scholarship from the Global North within disability studies has resulted in marginalization of experiences from the Global South; agendas of disability pride in the North stand in stark contrast to the need to prevent mass impairment caused by colonialism, war, industrial injuries, and pollution in the Global South. Helen Meekosha, "Decolonising Disability: Thinking and Acting Globally," *Disability & Society* 26, no.6 (October 2011), 667-82.

35 This reveals both the limits of necropolitical frameworks that emphasize death as the primary marker of violence and the limits of biopolitical frameworks' strategic use of measuring.

Description Figure 2 (top). View onto an urban storefront and adjoining sidewalk. A portable ramp leads from the street into the front door. It is covered with yellow caution tape. White vinyl text placed on the left window spells out the rallying cry for the right to self-representation emerging from disability rights, "Nothing About Us Without Us." The windows are occluded with magenta bed sheets, creating a space behind protected from gazing eyes and the need to represent outwards. These simple means of using bed sheets as curtains alongside the disability rights slogan hold the representational strategies of visibility and opacity in tension.

Description Figure 3 (bottom). Photograph with a view onto a chimney-shaped dry sandy path. The steepness makes it seem nearly unsurmountable. A little white dog peers down expectantly from the top of the trail silhouetted by a big blue sky. Two people wearing blue jeans are wedged in the middle of the path. One lies on top of another, their limbs are intertwined and it's hard to tease apart where one becomes another. They seem to be holding each other in place; it is unclear whether they are struggling or resting, or both.

opportunities for extraction and carceral control while attempting to crush resistive people power.[36] In such contexts of extreme inequity, greater accessibility for some can be used to mask dispossession and displacement for others.[37] For example, following organized abandonment, property developers sometimes access-wash gentrification by touting statement buildings utilizing universal design as inclusive.

DISABILITY JUSTICE AND ACCESS-CENTERED PRACTICE

Access needs—and people's options to access resources from institutions or make choices about engaging with them—follow spectra of oppression beyond disability.[38] Those most subject to the sharp end of this—disabled, poor, migrant, immigrant, trans, Indigenous, Black, and other negatively racialized people—know too well the necessity of interdependency to survive and find ways to live otherwise in spite of constraint.

The intersectional disability justice movement, with origins in San Francisco Bay Area organizing broadly and the collective Sins Invalid specifically, takes up the limits of disability rights.[39] This framework addresses the intersection of oppressions according to identities and experiences of race, ethnicity, gender, class, sexuality, citizenship, housing status, and more.[40] It is led by those most impacted (disabled LGBTQIA+ and BIPOC people), centers non-hypothetical bodyminds, focuses on immediate access formations and relationship building, and seeks to dismantle institutions while investing in community-focused solutions. In doing so, it recognizes the limits of how, in current systems, becoming an abstracted rights holder is the primary way to gain life-giving resources, yet does not address the ongoing exclusion of many from the position of rights holder within settler colonial states, or the fundamental ableism at the core of racial capitalism.

Access-centered practice is a term we and others working from disability justice principles use to describe intersectional, sometimes abolitionist, approaches and methods of access that address the co-constitution of ableism, racism, and settler-colonialism.[41] Within disability culture and communities, while there's still a reliance on accommodations and services, access encompasses a broader range of approaches, like creating disability access without the need for diagnosis and disclosure. It can also mean expanding access to better address intersectional disability experiences rooted in multiple communities and cultures, as well as access needs beyond disability, without trusting institutions or the carceral state to uphold access.[42] Knowledge of how to do this usually comes from affected communities or smaller organizations connected to them. Access extends beyond any one event, location, individual, or group into durable, flexible, pluralistic cultures. In practical

36 Ruth Wilson Gilmore, *Abolition Geography: Essays Toward Liberation* (New York: Verso, 2022).

37 Stacey Milbern, "Notes on 'Access Washing,'" Disability Justice Network of Ontario website, February 20, 2019, https://www.djno.ca/post/notes-on-access-washing.

38 Currently, rights and resources for some depend on policy's organization of debility, extraction, and abandonment for others. The need to sometimes prioritize certain forms of access over others relates to austerity's uneven impacts. Although many people have never been supported well or at all by state services and institutions, neoliberal austerity's privatization, deregulation, and withdrawal of the state from social provisions means that public institutions offer even less care and access. Prior to austerity, disabled people's needs had already long since been described as "too much" and the idea of what is "enough" weaponized against us. We refuse the foundational parameters of this thinking. Energetic imaginaries of other possible worlds live in community spaces. But even in the abolitionist futures that many imagine and build, where resources can be distributed more evenly and time is not based on maximizing production for the benefit of an elite few, access conflicts will still occur. In present conditions, one often has to make choices about what forms of access can be present with the resources available (time, money, knowledge, space). Disabled people already know so much about improvising in the face of difficult choices rooted in insufficient resources to meet needs. On the smaller scale where much access-centered practice currently happens, we encourage readers to make clear and brave imperfect choices that you are able to hold yourselves accountable to regarding who and what is centered with what you have.

39 Sins Invalid began in 2006 and is a "disability justice performance project that centers people of color, queers, nonbinary and trans people with disabilities." Their organizing, political education, and cultural work often creates liberated spaces to celebrate intersectional crip sexuality, beauty, and desire. Their "Ten Principles of Disability Justice" was foundational to disability justice (https://www.sinsinvalid.org/blog/10-principles-of-disability-justice). Initiatives like Krip Hop Nation, which was started in 2007 by Sins Invalid co-founder Leroy Moore, address what disability justice means specifically in relation to the conditions of Blackness.

40 Disability justice conceives of ableism as inseparable from racism, transmisogyny, sexism, imperialism, heteropatriarchy, classism, colonization, and police violence. It overlaps with anti-ableist forms of healing justice, which embrace non-Western traditional medicines in response to trauma produced by colonialism, racial capitalism, militarism, and imperialism. It also substantially overlaps with AIDS activism and reproductive, health, and environmental justice.

41 The earliest published use of the term "access-centered" we have found is rhetoric and composition scholar Tara K. Wood's "Access-Centered Pedagogy" (*Disability and College Compositions: Investigating Access, Identity, and Rhetorics of Ableism* [PhD dissertation, University of Oklahoma, 2014]), which proposes building cultures of access into ableist learning environments without relying on a "reasonable accommodations" framework. A disabled healing practitioner based in the Bay Area called Springlove has used the term online since circa 2015 (https://accesscenteredmovement.com/). Abolitionist disability justice organizer Dustin Gibson uses the term "access-centered cultures" (https://www.peopleshub.org/trainings-and-offerings/building-a-disability-politic-access-centered-cultures). (https://www.peopleshub.org/trainings-and-offerings/building-a-disability-politic-access-centered-cultures).

42 In the compliance model, the state "gives" access but only to those able to "receive" from the state. This doubly devalues life. For those who are at risk from the state, receiving access requires closer proximity to the institutions set up to harm you. For example, Black disabled people in crisis are disproportionately killed by police when simply needing healthcare. The compliance model cannot account for or value the different experiences of the "same" condition as lived in different bodies.

terms, this might look like committing to provide specific types of access consistently without the need for individual requests; being prepared to negotiate access conflicts; clearly explaining choices around which forms of access are provided; sharing knowledge to collectivize access; and learning through practice, including mistakes. Access-centered practices include protocols because certain needs are best met with consistent solutions (like ASL interpretation), but access overall can't be reduced to protocols.[43] When access practices are responsive to the nuance and mutability of needs, responsibility for access becomes collectivized into culture rather than held by experts or individuals with static roles in policy, protocol, and procedure.

Access-centered practice exceeds existing models of civic participation in dominant systems; it unfolds best within a party, a study group, a community meeting, a land defense process, a care collective, a memorial, a refusal, or an embrace.[44] Access-centered practice creates more self-determined alternatives to oppressive systems under, around, and in spite of them.

WHAT WE NEED AND WANT

Artists Park McArthur and Constantina Zavitsanos's *Score for Lift and Transfer* models the improvisational choreography and interdependence required to enact care that is intimate and, by exceeding the framing of care as event, labor, or exchange, ruptures capitalist value (see also figures 2 and 3).

McArthur describes this as "access shared by disabled people, constitutive of what we need and want, rather than mediated by an image of access that provides none," which we understand as access-centered practice.[45]

> "Ready?"
> "Ready."
> Work to deliver your bodies safely from platform to platform, surface to surface.
> Hold yourself; stand.
> Stand and hold yourself while holding someone else.
> Learn how the you of your body and me of mine work our mutual instability together. Learn how the instability of holding while moving is a moment.
> Learn that to move is to hold a we.[46]

Here the distinct "I"s become an inseparable "we"; dependencies are written in such a way that each line holds an action either person can experience; the way a reader chooses to inhabit the action facilitates

43 For example, when providing sign language interpretation there are timelines, steps, and technological integrations that don't vary widely. It is always advisable to work with interpreters who share a cultural and/or racial identity with the artists and/or audience, provide scripts or written materials for the interpreters to prepare with in advance, ask participants to speak at a slower speeds and pause the event if they forget, reserve seating in clear sight lines of interpreters, ask people to introduce themselves by name every time they speak, and so on. Policy and protocol on ASL provision needs to be combined with relationship building with D/deaf and hard of hearing communities, considering those who don't speak English or ASL, and support for the production of non-audist artworks. Beyond this is the intersection with other access needs and the opportunity to situate expansive access within the art itself.

44 In this we follow Harney and Moten's formulation of planning where "the plan is to invent the means in a common experiment launched from any kitchen, any back porch, any basement .... This ongoing experiment with the informal, carried out by and on the means of social reproduction ... is not an activity ... but the ceaseless experiment with the futurial presence of the forms of life that make such activities possible." (Harney and Moten, 2013), 74-75.

45 McArthur, in conversation with Amalle Dublon and Zavitsanos, "Dependency and Improvisation," *Art Papers* (Winter 2018/2019), https://www.artpapers.org/dependency-and-improvisation/.

46 This score has been excerpted for length. *Score for Lift and Transfer* is one of several choreographic scores published in an essay by McArthur and Zavitsanos that explores care, intimacy, labor, value, and dependency through their experiences together in McArthur's care collective. The essay examines how the possibility of harm or violence is present in any act of intimate care; other scores with more asymmetrical vulnerability between roles address fear, anxiety, desire, and expectation. McArthur and Zavitsanos, "Other Forms of Conviviality: The Best and Least of Which Is Our Daily Care and the Host of Which Is Our Collaborative Work," *Women & Performance: A Journal of Feminist Theory* 23, no. 1 (2013), 126-32.

noticing the roles one tends towards. The score plays with expectations around caregiving and receiving, remixing the unidirectional protocol of a typical lift and transfer into a multidirectional practice where agency and vulnerability are entangled.[47]

Embedded in McArthur and Zavitsanos's score is knowledge that the intimacy of moving with another bodymind is always weighted with the potential for connection *and* violence. This manifests across all scales of relation—interpersonal, institutional, and infrastructural. Dependency and interdependency are where we materially and affectively meet: our needs are what connect us to one another, they bring us into the vulnerabilities of both love and harm.

The expression of access in McArthur and Zavitsanos's scores (and Dublon and Zavitsanos's image) is co-created by interdependent humans seemingly unmediated in the moment by others; in witnessing, the audience is brought to *feel* something of the affective quality of that intimacy. These artworks hold the persistence and necessary creativity of access-centered life, embodying how disability justice organizer Mia Mingus's concept of access intimacy comes out of (conscious or unconscious) praxis. Mingus emphasizes the possibility for access intimacy to occur instantaneously between people without shared experience or political identity. This intimacy need not be communicated linguistically, offering an intuitive, non-identity based, affective lens onto modes of relation beyond policy.[48] Access intimacy centers the affective aspects of access essential to access-centered practice.

The moments and spaces where access-centered practice occurs are often provisional or messy. They unfold in artworks, needle exchanges, and spontaneous support groups; around hospital beds and in messaging threads; in spreadsheets, adjunct classrooms, public toilets, squatted community centers, and bedrooms. There is loitering, loving, fighting, kinship, gossiping, hanging out, grieving, pleasure, willful resistance, dreaming. Within, we learn each other's protocols (How do I inject you? When do you have to go to hospital despite the risks associated with being undocumented?). We cultivate practices of care that exceed what protocols encompass (What types of touch does my body welcome? Do you enjoy metaphors when I describe images to you? Who has space to host others?). Amongst, we fuck with policy—negotiate, circumvent, and refuse it. Work it, flip it, and reverse it.

Beyond policy or protocol, in the full aliveness of access-centered practice, we, as disability justice organizer Dustin Gibson says, build our political muscles.[49] We do so by embodying abolitionist futures everywhere, especially in fleeting moments and fragile spaces cultivated amidst state-sanctioned violence and institutions; we learn to work through conflict through repair, and show up and show love.[50] In cultivating access-centered cultures wherever we are, we work together to refuse ableist systems.[51]

47 In health and social care settings, a lift and transfer is a formalized procedure that is a part of care protocols. It dictates how one or several people can support a person who needs assistance to move, often from a chair to a bed, or a bed to a chair, or a chair to a shower chair. When taught as a care procedure, the focus is usually on the best biodynamics for the safety of all involved. However, the set of actions is typically written unidirectionally, addressing the person lifting rather than both parties. It assumes a certain capacity of both parties, circumscribing distinct roles and limiting their agency to step outside of them. Notably, the embrace required to lift and transfer a person is not so far from the type of embrace that happens in a hug. This highlights both the vulnerability of the (sometimes forced) intimacy of physical care and the strangeness of teaching a procedure to move a person understood as an abstract body rather than a specific person with distinct traits and preferences.

48 Disability justice and transformative justice organizer Mia Mingus defines access intimacy as “that elusive, hard to describe feeling when someone else ‘gets’ your access needs. The kind of eerie comfort that your disabled self feels with someone on a purely access level.” It can occur when not everything is accessible, you do not need a political understanding of disability to experience it, and the term is meant to describe all forms of access, not just those in relation to disability. “Access Intimacy, Interdependence and Disability Justice.” *Leaving Evidence* (blog), April 12, 2017, https://leavingevidence.wordpress.com/2017/04/12/access-intimacy-interdependence-and-disability-justice/.

49 The muscle building metaphor comes courtesy of Dustin Gibson who uses it when speaking about the way the disability justice framework supports us to build the muscle and skill to be able to deal with access conflicts when they arise as we develop practices rooted in self-determination through shared struggle rather than being granted things from the state. Access-centered practices therefore function as a form of abolitionist practice, where alternate forms of relation are learned and built in the present, thereby bringing abolitionist futures into being. Dustin Gibson, “Disability Justice and Intersectionality,” *What’s up WID*, World Institute on Disability podcast hosted by Ashley Inkumsah, October 8, 2021, https://wid.org/whats-up-wid-disability-justice-intersectionality/.

50 Affective access intimacy has political potential: although shared politics are not necessary to create it, the experience of it can build capacity for love and liberation within the liberatory praxis of disability justice. Mia Mingus, "'Disability Justice' Is Simply Another Term for Love," Leaving Evidence (blog), November 3, 2016, https://leavingevidence.wordpress.com/2018/11/03/disability-justice-is-simply-another-term-for-love/.

51 In the forthcoming *Sick Time, Sleepy Time, Crip Time* field guide, we more fully address lines of inquiry begun in this essay such as: “universal” access and public space, access-centered practice’s relationship to furthering systems change (including abolition), how values relate (or not) to practices and protocols, accountability, the benefits and pitfalls of disclosure, art’s role in interrogating the distribution of power in forms of interaction, and the politics behind representational strategies linked to disability, including separatism, partiality, visibility, and opacity. This analysis will sit alongside “tools” that help identify and adapt existing care and access structures, offering a variety of different practices not included here. Many tools begin with the needs of specific groups, like access riders made to support disabled artists or decolonial riders that support Indigenous artists. However, since ableism and colonialism harm everyone (although differently) these tools’ impacts are of benefit to all. Through analyzing specific tools and practices and how they relate to each other, we examine the ethics of sharing tools outside their original community of use.

II.
PROTOC
TRANSM

COLS OF
MISSION

This section addresses external protocols, i.e., the methods by which protocols are transmitted as a form of communication. It considers the technological, infrastructural, and environmental mechanisms and processes by which protocols are conveyed or articulated, with contributors considering ways of altering how we perceive the language of protocols in order to rethink how we relate to protocols within our built and natural environments through technology, sound, and time itself.

ON THE WEB: A PROTOCOL FOR CARE

Salome Asega

I was born the same year the World Wide Web as we know it was invented by Sir Tim Berners-Lee. Four years later, on April 30, 1993, CERN (the European Organization for Nuclear Research) put the web into the public domain, forever changing how we relate to each other. The internet has revolutionized how we communicate, access information, and conduct business. It has become an essential part of our lives, with billions of people using it daily. However, despite its tremendous benefits and social impact, the internet and the protocols that guide it are still a mystery to most.

One year in middle school, I spent the summer in Addis Ababa, Ethiopia, where my uncle Wondwossen had my brother and me take computers apart and put them back together again. We acted as his assistants while he was completing his computer science degree. I will never forget neatly placing components in orderly lines across my grandma's living room carpet while the smell of fresh rue, coffee, and incense filled the house. That summer was world opening for many reasons—I met many relatives for the first time, I traded my *NSYNC CD for my uncle's Tracy Chapman cassette tape, and it was the first summer I wasn't glued to AOL Instant Messenger because I only had access to the internet when we'd visit internet cafes. At eleven years old, I remember it taking a few weeks for me to wrap my head around the idea that having access to a computer and the internet are not one and the same.

The internet's physical infrastructure is completely invisibilized, and our metaphors for the internet don't accurately reflect its material architecture. The "cloud" has us look up when in fact, the internet is a complex, global network of interconnected fiber-optic cables, routers, switches, and other networking hardware that trail the ocean floor and emerge onto land.

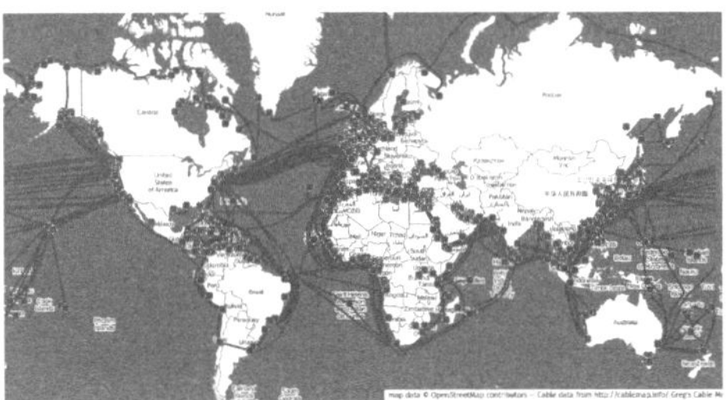

Figure 1. World map of submarine communication cables. Cable data by Greg Mahlknecht as of July 21, 2015. World map by Openstreetmap contributors. Courtesy Wikipedia Commons.

Artists have visualized and made this clear to me. Evan Roth and Trevor Paglen each came out with projects between 2015 and 2016 that

Description Figure 1. A world map is drawn in grey and the water is a darker shade of grey. Small red dots appear across the map in coastal areas and red lines connect them to each other, representing submarine communication cables.

documented the submarine network of cables that form the internet. Evan Roth's video and photo series *Internet Landscapes* captures contextual portraits of the exact intersection where the cables emerge from the ocean and meet the land, using infrared footage as a reference to the infrared laser light that is transmitted through fiber-optic cables.[1] Trevor Paglen's diptych series *Landing Sites* includes photographs of the NSA-tapped sites where multiple undersea cables come onshore and collages featuring documents from computer intelligence consultant and whistleblower Edward Snowden's archive and other sources generate a nonlinear historical snapshot of the internet's materiality. At once, Paglen makes the architecture visible and its tainted use by the state.[2]

One of the most striking features when studying landing sites or looking at the fiber-optic world map is the density of cables running through the so-called Global North compared to the scarcity in the Global South, despite the population and resource distribution of these regions. Educator and technologist Nabil Hassein makes this extremely clear using the following example: "So what this means in practice is that, let's say you're in Brazil and you want to send a message to your buddy in Nigeria, it's very likely that this message is actually going to … travel north to North America before going across to Europe and then down before it can travel to its actual destination in Africa."[3] The infrastructure and its limitations have predetermined the communication trajectory and centered the West as a hub through which all information moves, making the internet's architecture political.

In *Control and Freedom* new media theorist Wendy Hui Kyong Chun questions how the internet became accepted as a medium of freedom when it in fact thrives on control. For tech-savvy users, "at its birth, the Internet gave individuals great freedom of speech and privacy. This was because it was hard, under its original design, for behavior on the Net to be monitored or controlled."[4] The internet was publicly owned and controlled by governments and had a small audience as only government agencies or universities were allowed to go online. By the mid-nineties, the internet became privatized by way of commercial internet service providers (ISPs) like CompuServe and AOL, which increased access to the Web for a new audience and a growing global audience, which came with a tradeoff. Chun points to writer and computer programmer Alex Galloway's assessment of a new internet architecture, "In order for protocol to enable radically distributed communications between autonomous entities, it must employ a strategy of universalization, and of homogeneity. It must be anti-diversity. It must promote standardization in order to enable openness … computer protocols do not tolerate deviations—if not followed exactly, compatibility problems will (and often do) occur."[5] In other words, as access to the internet widens, control tightens.

Infrastructure and protocols are closely related concepts in the context of computer networks and communication systems. The choice of infrastructure has a direct impact on the protocols that are used to facilitate communication. For example, the type of network hardware used, such as routers or switches, affects the protocols used for routing and switching data. Similarly, the choice of software components, such as operating systems or applications, can affect the protocols used for data transfer and communication.

Protocols guide our everyday life in various ways, both online and offline. In general, protocols provide a set of rules or guidelines that help to ensure that distinct systems or individuals can work together safely, effectively, and hopefully with care. And by following protocols, we can avoid misunderstandings, conflicts, harm, or other issues that might otherwise arise. Internet protocols specifically are a set of rules that govern the communication between devices on the internet. They provide a standardized way in which data is transmitted and received. The purpose of internet protocols is to ensure that data is transmitted efficiently, accurately, and securely. However, these protocols are designed primarily for efficiency and speed, rather than for the safety and well-being of the users.

From the 1990s into the early 2000s, Web1, the first generation of the World Wide Web, was largely static, with read-only content that did not allow for user interaction beyond basic clicking and linking. The dominant protocol during the early days of the web was the **Hypertext Transfer Protocol** (HTTP), which allowed for the transfer of hypertext documents, such as web pages, between web servers and web browsers. Other widely used protocols started during this period include **File Transfer Protocol** (FTP) and **Simple Mail Transfer Protocol** (SMTP). Used for transferring files between devices on the internet, FTP allows users to upload and download files from remote servers. SMTP is used for sending email messages between devices on the internet. However, these protocols were relatively simple and lacked many of the advanced features that are now commonplace on the internet.

From the mid-2000s into the 2010s, the rise of social media and other interactive web applications during the Web2 era was accompanied by developing new protocols and standards to support these applications. One of the most important of these was the **Asynchronous JavaScript and XML** (AJAX) protocol, which allowed for real-time updates and interactive features on web pages. Some ever-present examples of AJAX in use include features like autocomplete on search engines or having the ability to upvote or like posts. Other protocols, like **JavaScript Object Notation** (JSON) and **Representational State Transfer** (REST), became widely used for data exchange and temporary storage between different web applications and services. Security protocols also became more critical as online commerce and other sensitive transactions became more common. Protocols using encryption, such as **Secure Sockets**

Layer and Transport Layer Security (SSL/TLS), protect data for secure communication over the internet.

The evolution of the internet from Web1 to Web2 has involved significant changes in the protocols used to facilitate communication and data exchange between devices. While the protocols used in the earlier generations of the internet are still in use today, newer protocols have been developed to meet the changing needs and demands of users.

Web2 gave rise to new internet companies like Meta and X (formerly Twitter) that serve as centralized platforms for easily sharing user-generated content but at the cost of packaging and selling mass amounts of users' data and activity. As awareness of how these platforms operate increases, internet users, programmers, cryptocurrency enthusiasts, and venture capital firms are all prompting the internet to undergo a paradigm shift that pledges to be people-centered, decentralized, secure, and more immersive. This next generation of the internet, Web3, goes by many names and definitions—an embodied internet, the convergence of physical and digital worlds, the Semantic Web or Spatial Web, and the metaverse, just to name a few. Some of the key internet protocols being developed for Web3 rely on blockchain technology and peer-to-peer networking protocols, which enable decentralized data storage, authentication, and communication. One example is Ethereum, an open-source blockchain protocol with **smart contract** capabilities, which are software programs that automatically self-execute when predetermined terms and conditions are met by all parties who set the contract. Another protocol, **self-sovereign identity** (SSI), is redefining data ownership by eliminating the need to store personal data on a central database. The data is instead stored on a blockchain like Ethereum and SSI references the data when needed for verification. While the promises are great and the opportunities even greater, the overemphasis on technical protocols makes the overall premise feel like a marketing tactic by those who have waged big bets. Web3's development is outpacing most people's understanding of it, so adoption feels reliant on an overly idealistic mission: "To free humanity not only from Big Tech domination but also from exploitative capitalism itself—and to do it purely through code."[6]

In his essay "Racial Justice in the Distributed Web," Taeyoon Choi writes, "The internet as we know [it] today ha[s] been developed by white male engineers working in academia and military-industrial complexes. It's not surprising the protocols and networks, as well as [their] epistemologies and [effects], are contained in their imaginations. To be more accurate, the internet has not been developed solely by the white male engineers, but the narratives of its development have been dominated by the triumphs of white male engineers."[7] As we move into this next chapter of the internet, there are many actors, big and small, carving out their space in Web3, and some already have robust infrastructure to push forward in their singular vision for the internet's future. At the helm of Meta, Mark Zuckerberg is unyielding in his quest to realize the metaverse and has put all his chips into Web3, despite the company losing more than $20 billion on the venture since 2021.[8] The promise for shared and distributed power is already fleeting.

In describing this Web3 moment, which feels newly thrust upon many of us, technology writer Gilad Edelman points to Gavin Wood, an English computer scientist who helped program the decentralized blockchain Ethereum and coined the term Web3 in 2014, the year Ethereum launched. "In [Wood's] view, Web 2.0's fatal flaw was trust. Everyone had to trust the biggest platforms not to abuse their power as they grew. Few seemed to notice that Google's famous early motto, 'Don't be evil,' implied that being evil was an option. To Wood, Web3 is about building systems that don't rely on trusting people, corporations, or governments to make moral choices, but that instead render evil choices impossible."[9]

The need for care-based internet protocols becomes more apparent as the internet continues to evolve and become an increasingly integrated part of our daily lives. By care-based internet protocols, I mean a set of rules and guidelines that prioritize the well-being of users, their privacy, and their security over other considerations such as convenience or profit. These protocols move us away from technical jargon and encourage access through consentful participation.[10] They question what is lost when English is the foundation of most programming languages and what is owed to people whose labor and land are mined in the name of technological progress. They also challenge power's ability to turn the internet on and off like a spout. They operationalize trust and are sustained by our interdependence. I'm moved by Spideralex and Mayeli Sanchez Martinez's reminder "La expresión 'Eres tan segura como la persona menos segura de tu red' permite resaltar en estos casos la importancia de la adopción de prácticas de seguridad colectivas" ("The expression 'You are as safe as the person most at risk in your network' is a 'traditional' principle for establishing collective security protocols and practices"[11]). We can't rely on any one individual or entity in the network to hold this work alone. Care work requires all of us tending to each other.

When I think back to my preteen summer in Addis Ababa, I'm reminded of a shared but unspoken agreement with my uncle to remain encouraged despite the complexity of the task. Care-based internet protocols don't exist as a formal standard, but considering most of the protocols shared above emerged just in my lifetime, the potential for evolving and new guidelines is not impossible. The task now is larger than deconstructing and reassembling a desktop computer. I'm talkin' bout a revolution.

1 Carey Dunne, "A Pioneering Net Artist Mourns the Unfulfilled Promise of the Internet," Hyperallergic, March 24, 2016, https://hyperallergic.com/283973/a-pioneering-net-artist-mourns-the-unfulfilled-promise-of-the-internet/.

2 Trevor Paglen, "NSA-Tapped Fiber Optic Cable Landing Site," *DIS Magazine*, February 2015, http://dismagazine.com/dystopia/73110/trevor-paglen-nsa-tapped-fiber-optic-cable-landing-site-%E2%80%A8mastic-beach-new-york-united-states/.

3 Nabil Hassein, "Computing, Climate Change, and All Our Relationships," Deconstruct Conference, April 23-24, 2018, https://www.deconstructconf.com/2018/nabil-hassein-computing-climate-change-and-all-our-relationships.

4 Wendy Hui Kyong Chun, *Control and Freedom: Power and Paranoia in the Age of Fiber Optics*, (Cambridge, MA: MIT Press, 2006), 69.

5 Ibid, 70.

6 Gilad Edelman, "Paradise at the Crypto Arcade: Inside the Web3 Revolution," Wired, May 18, 2022, https://www.wired.com/story/web3-paradise-crypto-arcade/.

7 Taeyoon Choi, "Racial Justice in the Distributed Web," Distributed Web of Care, January 11, 2019, https://distributedweb.care/posts/racial-justice/.

8 Sam Reynolds, "Meta Remains Committed to the Metaverse Despite $13.7B Loss in 2022, Mark Zuckerberg Says," CoinDesk, July 27, 2023, https://www.coindesk.com/markets/2023/07/27/meta-remains-committed-to-the-metaverse-mark-zuckerberg-says/.

9 Edelman, "Paradise at the Crypto Arcade."

10 "Consentful Tech Curriculum," Consentful Tech Project, March 28, 2022, https://www.consentfultech.io/.

11 Alexandra Hache and Mayeli Sanchez, "Women's Bodies on Digital Battlefields: Information Exchange and Networks of Support and Solidarity of pro-Choice Activists in Latin America," Tactical Technology Collective and Accion Directa Autogestiva, 2017, https://donestech.net/files/womensbodies_0.pdf.

LINES OF CONTROL: NAVIGATING TANGLED TIMELINES AND COLONIAL CARTOGRAPHIES[1]

Rasheedah Phillips

Humans have gazed up at the skies throughout the ages, using a myriad of devices to trace the patterns of the stars, the sun's rising and setting, and the cycling of seasons in order to measure the passage of time. As societies grew, traveled, and traded with each other, mathematicians began to unravel the complexities of time measurement, devising intricate calculations and equations that were scrawled on scrolls and manuscripts and eventually used to craft clocks.

The rapid expansion of commerce and travel, the growth of global capitalism, and the maintenance of global colonization by European nations over their colonized territories increasingly required clock and calendar time standardization. Eventually, power brokers negotiated and adopted a universal standard of time across industries, forcing nations and cultures to submit to a single global standard. Today, a system of twenty-four time zones is used to not only synchronize activities across and between continents, but also to control the activities and daily lives of billions of people across the globe.

In the mid-1800s, the idea that the world would be divided into time zones was first introduced. When delegates from twenty-five countries gathered in Washington, DC, for the International Meridian Conference (IMC) in 1884, they determined that the Greenwich meridian in southeast London would be the world's prime meridian—or the 0° longitude line of geographical reference—making it the standard reference point from which all of the world's twenty-four time zones were created.

The IMC is a critical point on the Western timeline for understanding the backward and forward-reaching impacts of time standardization and its resulting temporal oppression—the collapsing of natural time into capitalist time in ways that fundamentally shift humans' experience of, and relationship to, time itself. The IMC's decision had reality-altering political, legal, and social implications and consequences: Britain was chosen as the epicenter for a global timekeeping system, representing a reaffirmation of Western-centric power dynamics, and with it, a new way of perceiving and interacting with time.

MEASURING (OR LONGITUDES, OR COUNTING)

Before the international time zones and a single prime meridian to rule the globe could be established, cracking the mystery of accurate longitude measurement was a necessary first step in man's conquering of space-time. The development of advanced timekeeping technologies, including the chronometer, was pivotal in the expansion of European empires during the nineteenth century. These technologies enabled European explorers and traders to navigate the world's oceans more accurately, which facilitated the colonization and exploitation of distant (to Europeans) lands.

Clocks, time, maps, and global imperialism are intimately bound. As historian Giordano Nanni notes, “the science of horology was instrumental in the exploration and charting of the oceans and in the ‘discovery’ of the so-called New World.” The colonization of the Australian and African continents was enabled by the search for the invention of a device that could accurately measure longitude, making the clock as essential to colonization as the ship.[2]

For centuries, sailors struggled to determine their longitude when navigating the seas. Latitude, or a ship’s position north or south of the equator, could be determined relatively easily by observing the angle of the sun or the North Star. However, determining longitude, or a ship’s position east or west of a reference point, was much more difficult. Not having an accurate longitude measure significantly reduced navigational precision at sea, thereby increasing the risks associated with unknown coastlines, hazardous reefs, and other navigational hazards.

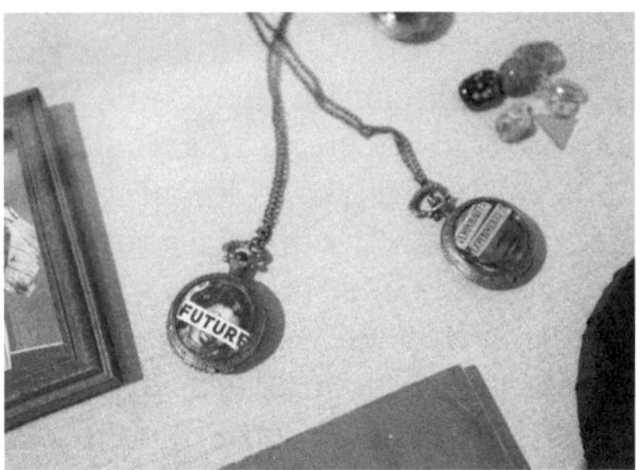

Figure 1. Rasheedah Phillips, Black Quantum Futurism: Time Zone Protocols. Installation view with detail of Dismantling the Master’s Clocks series. Sheila C. Johnson Design Center, New York, April 4-18, 2022. Presented by the Vera List Center for Art and Politics. Photo by Da Ping Luo, courtesy the Vera List Center.

Sailors often used a combination of hourglasses to measure time and a rope with knots to measure distance, but these methods often led to inaccuracies and land masses showing up in unexpected places.[2] Before the seventeenth century, clocks were large and expensive, and they were typically owned and operated by wealthy individuals or institutions such as governments or religious organizations. It was not until after Dutch scientist Christiaan Huygens invented the pendulum clock in 1656 that clocks became more accurate and affordable, making them more widely available to the general public. These early devices, however, were still not fit for sea travel and rough ocean waves. Sailors often had to rely on estimates or unreliable devices that were frequently inaccurate or

Description Figure 1. Two small, bronze, ornate pocket watches sit side by side on a beige linen background. The clock on the left has the word "future" typed in black sans serif capitalized letters overlaying a black-and-white image of a smiling woman's face. The clock on the right has the words "temporarlity experiments" typed in black serif captialized font over a yellowed photograph of a stoic subject.

deteriorated and rusted on the rough journeys. Ships were often unable to return to their home ports after long voyages.

Over nearly two centuries, rivaling imperial nations offered large financial rewards and prestige to whomever could develop a practical and reliable method for measuring longitude, including Spain in 1567 and 1598, and the Dutch Republic in 1600. Galileo Galilei even worked on the problem without much success, while Isaac Newton said no clockwork could succeed in finding longitude. The longitude problem became a popular obsession for people across nations ranging from renowned scientists to inventors to those considered scammers and madmen, breeding its own slang term, the "longitude lunatics."

Later in the 1600s, France and Britain tried to find another solution to the longitude problem by building observatories to assist sailors and navigators in making accurate astronomical maps and charts. France was first up with the establishment of the Paris Observatory in 1667, and then a few years later, in 1675, came the Greenwich Observatory in London—both observatories eventually came to play an important role in the Age of Exploration that brought the conquest, colonization, and exploitation of nations across the world.[4] The Greenwich Observatory's main instrument was the quadrant, a large measuring device used to determine the positions of celestial objects, providing the foundation for accurate navigational charts and significantly improving the safety and efficiency of long-distance voyages.

However, the problem still had not been fully solved by the erection of expensive observatories and technologically advanced instruments. In 1707, for instance, four warships in an English fleet were wrecked due to bad weather and miscalculations of its longitude, with an estimated loss of fourteen hundred to two thousand sailors. Large financial rewards and prestige were offered by rivaling imperial nations for whomever could develop a practical and reliable method for measuring longitude. The Longitude Prize was one such competition for a sum of £20,000 from the British Parliament in 1714 (worth about US $5 million today) for anyone who could determine longitude to within one-half of a degree of accuracy, or a margin of error of no more than three seconds every twenty-four hours.[4] British clockmaker John Harrison threw his hat into the ring. Harrison had spent many years studying the problem of longitude and concluded that an accurate timepiece was the key to solving it. In 1730, he built his first marine chronometer, which he called H1. H1 was a large, heavy instrument that used a balance wheel and spring to regulate its timekeeping. Although it was accurate, it was too bulky and impractical for use on ships.

Over the next few decades, Harrison continued refining his design, building smaller and more accurate sea clocks, watches, marine timekeepers, and chronometers. His H4 marine chronometer, which he completed in 1759, was a breakthrough in accuracy and reliability. It was small enough to be carried on a ship, was less subject to deterioration, and was highly accurate, matching the land-based clocks within a few seconds per day.

The chronometer had a quick and profound impact on navigation. With an accurate chronometer, sailors could determine their longitude by comparing the time on the ship's chronometer with the time at a known reference point, such as the Royal Observatory in Greenwich, London. With this tool, ships could more accurately plot their course and avoid getting lost, which allowed for longer and more extensive sea voyages. This, in turn, enabled exploration, colonization, and trade with other continents.

A replica of Harrison's H4 chronometer, the K1, would eventually be used to help complete Captain James Cook's second and third voyages to Sydney Cove, Australia. After Cook's voyage, the British government commissioned further expeditions to explore and chart the coast of Australia, with the aim of claiming the land for the British Empire. In 1788, the First Fleet arrived in Botany Bay, New South Wales, establishing the first British colony on Australian soil. This marked the beginning of European settlement in Australia, eventually leading to the displacement and dispossession of Indigenous Australians. Cook's voyages to Australia also had wider geopolitical implications, giving Britain a significant new territory to claim and exploit and helping to cement its position as a major global power.

Chronometers were a crucial technological development that also aided the exploration, exploitation, and mapping of Africa by imperial interests. Chronometers enabled explorers and cartographers to create more accurate maps of all continents. David Livingstone, a Scottish explorer considered to be one of the first medical missionaries to travel extensively throughout Africa in the mid-nineteenth century, used a chronometer to accurately determine his longitude, and his surveys and maps of the continent helped fill in gaps in the existing knowledge of Africa. The British Empire also commissioned Henry Morton Stanley to lead a number of expeditions to explore the interior of Africa and map its resources.

In a clockwork, Newtonian universe where God is the ultimate clockmaker, setting the zero point for the world's time was the earthly counterpart and institutionalization of a God-like infinite power over time and space. On the surface, the creation of time zones was an attempt to create a unified system of time measurement that would simplify communication, transportation, and trade among nations. However, it was also an exercise in power. International time zones emerged as part of a larger imperial project and a reflection of the prevailing power structures of the era. It also functioned as an assertion of the West's dominance over other regions, and the enforcement of its own standards and values around the world.

From October 1 to 22, 1884, forty-one all-male delegates from twenty-five countries in diplomatic relationships with the United States convened in Washington, DC, by an act of US Congress "to fix on and recommend for universal adoption a common prime meridian, to be used in the reckoning of longitude and in the regulation of time throughout the world."[6] The purpose of the conference was to determine a single prime meridian or a reference line from which longitude could be calculated, for the entire world. It would eventually be used as the basis for standard time zones for the coordination of global transportation and communication.

At one point, there were at least twenty prime meridians in the world. At the time of the International Meridian Conference, many different prime meridians were still in use, including the meridian that runs through the Royal Observatory in Greenwich and the meridian through the Paris Observatory in France. The US utilized two at the time—one in DC for astronomical observations known as the American Meridian, and the Royal Observatory in Greenwich for geography and navigation. The IMC was meant to be a formality where diplomats from the world's most powerful nations would come together to confirm what had already been decided at two previous conferences (the Geographical Congress at Venice in 1881 and a meeting of the Geodetic Association in Rome in 1883) on the matter of the universal meridian: that the world's prime meridian would lie at the Royal Observatory in Greenwich.

The IMC resulted in seven resolutions laid out in the Final Act of its Protocol Proceedings, which included a recommendation for the official adoption of the Royal Observatory as the prime meridian and a recommendation to rearrange the astronomical and nautical days to begin at mean midnight. The conference established the Greenwich meridian as the global standard of time. This meant that all time zones would be based on the Greenwich meridian, allowing people to calculate time differences between locations easily. The conference also established the twenty-four-hour clock, which is still widely used today. The International Meridian Conference eventually accepted the Greenwich meridian and a universal day of twenty-four hours beginning at Greenwich midnight. However, the conference specified that the universal day "shall not interfere with the use of local or standard time where desirable."

The IMC was ill-planned and politically fraught among the various nations represented. During the IMC and after, some nations argued that they should not have to adapt to Greenwich Mean Time. Nations like France and Brazil abstained from the final vote to fix the meridian in Greenwich, while San Domingo (now the Dominican Republic) voted against. France wanted a neutral meridian that did not pass across any continent (a resolution that was supported by Brazil and San Domingo), while "delegates at the meridian conference had no authority to commit their nations to any resolutions." Some countries chose to ignore the conference's declarations, instead choosing to adopt a time zone based on their own observatories and the time of their capital cities. These countries often referred to this as "local mean time" to differentiate it from Greenwich Mean Time.

Although the resolutions were not immediately adopted or acted on by the representative countries given that the delegates had no authority, some countries began setting their times in accordance with Greenwich Mean Time about a decade after the IMC. By 1929, most major countries in the world had accepted the time zones. Despite the world's slow adoption, the establishment of the Greenwich meridian as the world's prime meridian in 1884 had significant consequences for the rest of the world, effectively placing Britain at the center of a global timekeeping system, perpetuating the idea of British superiority and reinforcing the notion that British customs and laws should be adopted by other countries. All other longitudes were measured relative to the prime meridian, and countries around the world had to adjust their standard time zones to align with the new reference line. This process led to the adoption of standard time zones around the world, which are still in use today, where "the worldwide system that was established in the years following the International Meridian Conference has proved to be enduring, despite radical changes in the worlds of politics and commerce."[7]

The IMC established the Greenwich meridian as the universal barometer of time and, in tandem with its spatial counterpart, the Berlin Conference, prodded the standardization of timekeeping to foster a global system of space-time to encourage capitalism, white supremacy, and its stranglehold over the world. Consequently, the uniformity of time zones blazed a trail for telecommunications networks and industrial capitalism in the late nineteenth and early twentieth centuries, which unsurprisingly facilitated the economic and political conditions that maintained and grew colonialism and imperialism internationally.

The agreements made at the Prime Meridian Conference have had immense implications that extend far beyond navigation: they effectively created a new form of colonial power structure over time. Establishing a single, global temporal reference point essentially flattened all other forms of timekeeping—communal, personal, spiritual—into that which serves a state and global functions. This temporal colonialism has ushered in the current era of globalization, where different cultures are increasingly interconnected under one universal concept of time.

This temporal imperialism continues to produce its own set of unique challenges. Traditional forms of timekeeping have been left behind in favor of an overly convenient universal system that does not account for regional or cultural particularities; this homogenization has caused many communities to lose an important element of their cultural identity.

The timeline from the so-called ending of chattel slavery to the present reflects a society designed to systematically leave Black diasporic people and families locked out of the future. Western capitalist and colonialist timelines exploit, injure, and reduce the lifespans of Black people, denying us an opportunity to thrive in a future of our own making. Every second feels as if it has been designed to leave us behind, as if every hour has been set against us, as if every year is a dare for us to continue to exist. Black people recognize this timeline as a weapon used to restrict and control our lives.

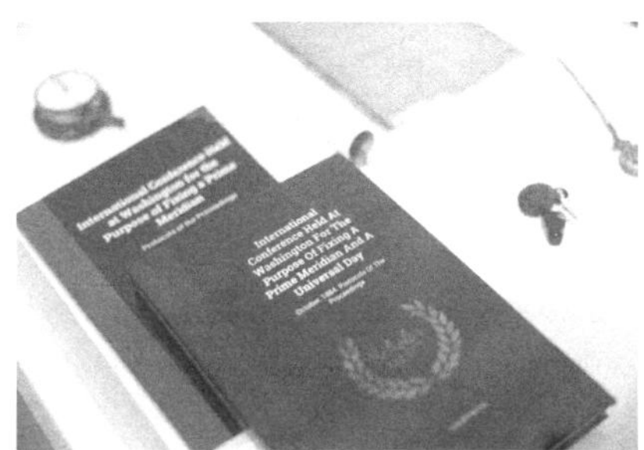

Figure 2. Rasheedah Phillips, *Black Quantum Futurism: Time Zone Protocols*. Installation view. Sheila C. Johnson Design Center, New York, April 4-18, 2022. Presented by the Vera List Center for Art and Politics. Photo by Da Ping Luo, courtesy the Vera List Center.

TIME ZONE PROTOCOLS

Redesigning the collective timeline cannot be accomplished by a single, solitary voice or action, nor by a small group of individuals. It requires shared responsibility and agreement from multiple communities and their branching timelines. It calls for the collaboration of multiple forces from different times, spaces, and narratives. Our position in time influences our connection to the past and future. Communal time is formed from a diverse range of times and narratives. Time Zone Protocols is a long-term and ongoing project to rewrite the protocols of time, realigning and restitching the fabric of our temporal-spatial consciousness. It unmaps the global imperialist colonization of time, ushering in a new era with a Black futurist lens and Colored People's Time as an ontology. In 2022, during the COVID-19 pandemic, the Vera List Center for Art and Politics presented the *Time Zone Protocols* exhibition and conference that I had curated as part of my Vera List Center Fellowship.[8] For the three-day hybrid online and in-person event called the *Prime Meridian Unconference*, I brought together Black artists, architects, musicians, and scholars of physics, geography, technology, and African American studies to explore how space-time can be reimagined using unique Black social, cultural, and geographical frameworks. Discussions were held,

Description Figure 2. Two copies of the "Protocols of the Proceedings" from the International Meridian Conference, October 1884.

workshops were facilitated, panels were convened, performances were staged, and plenary sessions conducted.[9] From their various disciplinary backgrounds, the participants considered new ways of understanding our relationship to space-time, utilizing unique Black social, geographical, and cultural frameworks that sought to unmap Black temporalities from the Greenwich Mean Timeline, and shifted the standards and protocols of time that leave Black people locked out of the past and future and stuck in a narrow temporal present, enabling us to reimagine our relationship with space-time. During the *Unconference*, we collectively developed protocols, resolutions, temporal tools, alternative time zones, and new markers of time that were compiled and shared for people to utilize in their communities with a commitment to working toward creating liberated futures, new space-times, and environments where these shared principles can be utilized and honored.

Leading up to the TZP exhibition and *Prime Meridian Unconference*, I convened the Time Zone Protocols Surveyors Discussion Group—a gathering of twenty-one individuals to analyze and debate TZP research materials, including an archive of readings, images, sounds, and videos on time zones, time, temporality, prime meridian, temporal oppression as experienced by Black communities, and social, political, and cultural concepts of time and temporality. The discussion over several meetings centered on new ways of understanding our relationships to space-time, utilizing specific social, geographical, and cultural frameworks that depart from colonial linearity and shift the standards and protocols of time. Our collective sharing produced a set of alternative principles, protocols, and/or values that reshape, remap, transcend, deconstruct, or dismantle and create new and equitable time zones or protocols of time based on Black communal tools, temporal technologies, ancestral techniques, and philosophies. Several of them informed the Unconference.

One of the workshops featured at the Unconference was "The Black Fugitive Infrastructures and Cross-time Space Routines," developed and presented by Celeste Winston. This workshop offered an exploration of fugitive infrastructure as a cornerstone of Black freedom struggles throughout history. Infrastructures, typically understood as material systems that organize and sustain everyday life, took on a new dimension within the context of "fugitive infrastructures." This concept encompasses the material arrangements created by ordinary individuals, pooling their efforts to sustain life when survival seems impossible.

The workshop provided a protocol for locating and identifying sites and possibilities of fugitive infrastructure across time. It encouraged participants to engage with a series of prompts, including identifying present-day anti-Black or violent systems, understanding their historical connections to slavery, colonialism, or imperialism, and critically examining popular solutions for reforming or abolishing these systems and who they originate from. Participants were also encouraged to envision space routines that demonstrate longstanding infrastructure that refuses and pushes back against oppressive systems.

Another workshop featured at the *Prime Meridian Unconference* was Danielle M. Purifoy's session titled *Dead Line? On Slowing Down in Black "Space-time."* This workshop took participants on a transformative journey through four poignant scenes set in the US South and Midwest during the 1990s–2010s. By exploring these scenes, the session illuminated the concept of Black "space-time" as both a rupture from the lineage of plantation time and a dedicated practice of nurturing relationships with people, land, and livable futures.

One key aspect of the workshop was the exploration of the term *deadline* within both a historical and metaphorical context. Purifoy delved into the working definition of the deadline as the latest time by which something should or can be completed, highlighting its connection to the legacy of plantation time. Additionally, the historical definition of a deadline as a boundary drawn around a prison, beyond which prisoners were at risk of being shot, provided a stark reminder of the literal implications of such boundaries on Black lives.

Within this framework, participants were invited to create their own representations of space-time disentangled from racial capitalist patriarchy. They were encouraged to imagine and visualize a space-time that transcends oppressive systems and structures through a series of reflective questions exploring the aesthetics and sensory experiences of their alternative space-time, such as: What does it look, sound, smell, and taste like? Who is present within this space-time? How do individuals choose to act or refrain from certain actions? And most importantly, how do they feel within this space-time free from the constraints of racial capitalist patriarchy?

The digital space www.TimeZoneProtocols.space continues and documents the *Time Zone Protocols* research and exhibition, the *Prime Meridian Unconference* presentations and protocols, and ongoing iterations of the project. It harbors a substantial collection of protocols to be expanded on, adapted, and implemented. *Protocols*, as I use the term, means a draft set of agreements, approaches, strategies, tactics, lenses, experiments, rituals, and/or tools, in accordance with its etymological origins as a first draft (or first glue) and not in its more modern sense as "proper conduct." These protocols are merely a starting point and roadmap for a collective journey and not the final destination. Protocols, resolutions, and practices are meant to be replicable and will be revisited at some collectively agreed-upon time and space.

1 An expanded version of this essay appears in Rasheedah Phillips's *Dismantling the Master's Clock: On Race, Space, and Time* (Chico, CA: AK Press, 2025).

1 Giordano Nanni, *The Colonisation of Time: Ritual, Routine and Resistance in the British Empire* (Manchester: Manchester University Press, 2012), 1.

2 Robert Gardner, *Experimenting with Time* (London: Franklin Watts, 1995), 117-19.

3 David Rooney, *About Time: A History of Civilization in Twelve Clocks* (New York: W. W. Norton, 2021); Joseph Mazur, *The Clock Mirage* (New Haven, CT: Yale University Press: 2020).

4 Dava Sobel and William J. Andrewes, *The Illustrated Longitude: The True Story of the Lone Genius Who Solved the Greatest Scientific Problem of His Time* (New York: Walker, 1998), 72.

5 *International Conference Held at Washing for the Purpose of Fixing a Prime Meridian and a Universal Day* (Washington, DC: Gibson Bros., 1884), https://www.gutenberg.org/files/17759/17759-h/17759-h.htm#Page_1.

6 Karl Benediktsson and Stanley D. Brunn, "Time Zone Politics and Challenges of Globalisation," *Tijdschrift Voor Economische en Sociale Geografie* 106 (2015): 276-90, https://doi.org/10.1111/tesg.12114.

7 *Black Quantum Futurism: Time Zone Protocols and the Unconference*, Sheila C. Johnson Design Center, New York, April 4-18, 2022, and presented by the Vera List Center for Art and Politics at The New School, https://www.veralistcenter.org/exhibitions/black-quantum-futurism-time-zone-protocols.

8 See the related contributions by Asia Dorsey (p. 94) and V. Mitch McEwen with Nadir Jeevanjee (p. 168).

ON CLOUD TIME AND PROTOCOLS

V. Mitch McEwen in Dialogue with Nadir Jeevanjee

As climate becomes human[2]—affected by the complete human sphere of politics, urban and regional planning, logistics, economy, and revolt—it seems important to discuss climate as something other than a problem. We can be subsumed in the totality of this problem if we lack a space to think or feel outside of it. The matter of thinking "outside of climate" might be articulated through the concept of time—not only "past time" or "out of time" but another time.

The speculations presented here follow Black Quantum Futurism's prompt to consider and resist Greenwich Mean Time as an instrument of colonialism and globalization. The ubiquity of Greenwich Mean Time plays that colonial trick of naturalizing itself so completely that any alternatives quickly demand a remaking of the world.[3] At my convening with climate scientist Nadir Jeevanjee at the Vera List Center for Art and Politics, we invited alternative time protocols toward superseding or evading the colonial temporal order. We ventured into the question of cloud temporality: How do clouds matter in something other than the matter of solid substance, certainty, and earthiness, where "earthiness" can mean something different from soil, rock, land, and extracted minerals? How do clouds constitute another earthiness, another real, which might invite cloudy ways of conceiving space-time?

Temperature defines the strata of space within clouds. This is the first significant way of knowing clouds that I learned from Jeevanjee.

The quantification of clouds in physics is based on dynamic moving aspects of air and water—pressure, temperature, and evaporation.[4] Defining clouds by their distance above us allows cloud movement and temperatures to be calculated in relation to strata of air pressure. But the cloudiness of clouds—their fuzzy edges, their drifting—makes these calculations infinite. Until Jeevanjee's work, most cloud scientists described clouds through their linear distance from the water—water being both a flatter surface than land and directly related to how clouds emerge. Within a distance-centered framework, clouds are generally grouped by height, and their temperature explains their air pressure and evaporation rates. Jeevanjee's research flipped that paradigm. By replacing one category of markers with another, he completely changed the protocols of cloud descriptions. His research took the idea of temperature dynamics and advanced the concept of "temperature coordinates," in which the location of clouds can be described via temperature. Not a cloud one mile above us, but a cloud in a drifting clump of forty degrees. When was the cloud? Where was the cloud? How warm was the cloud? These become deeply interrelated questions and shift the protocols for cloud science.

Jeevanjee made pages of formulas to answer these quetions, which become measurable through considering temperature as a space-time of cloud formation. Most of the Earth is composed of tropical oceans, he points out. This planetary space of tropical oceans is called the troposphere. Our limited understanding of clouds, oceans, and the troposphere as earthy entities may be due to the difficulty to lay claim on them—to define them in terms of property, extraction, or another form of colonial expressions. But what does "earthy" mean? Why does it mean soil and not clouds?

As an architect, I am not often called on to consider cloud-time and what it might mean for human collective time or space-time. And yet it is extremely relevant to political empowerment: the relationships between poetry and revolution, between music and social movements are precisely "cloudy," in this way of cloud time. In a coherent movement or a critical mass, one recognizes the exchange of feelings and energy as both a tempo and an emotional state. This poethic[5] temperature (let's call it that) makes clusters of experience legible to a collective in motion. Usually, you have to be there—at the protest, the sit-in, the riot, the hours-long activist meeting—in order to be there. But sometimes, you can be almost-there, in the wake of it. There is something of a temperature-based constitution of the where and when of social political movements. This may be cloud-time.

Nadir Jeevanjee: I'm at the Geophysical Fluid Dynamics Laboratory, a national climate modeling center associated with Princeton University. Before I was a scientist, I was a drummer and kept time. Then as a physicist, thinking about time, and space, and relativity, it is space-time that I hear cropping up a lot.

When talking about the concept of how to coordinatize space-time, the key question is how to assign numbers to where and when things happen. There are deep connections to Einstein's physics of relativity, essentially pointing out that the way we assign the coordinates is arbitrary.

V. Mitch McEwen: We're going to get into cloud-time! But first, I think one of the most important things is that the planet is mostly ocean, mostly water. When talking about climate, we're talking about atmosphere, we're talking about anything planetary, we're really talking about water. What you talk about is a troposphere, the lowest region of the atmosphere extending from the Earth's surface.

One of the things that is really important in terms of this geography of time is that when you're thinking of the planet as a troposphere, as this most "earthy" space, if I understand it correctly in, it is actually a tropical space. It's a tropical ocean space. And the temporality of clouds invites us to "feel" time and to do that in a way that makes temperature and embodiment a part of how time becomes instantaneous and accessible to multiple entities. That there are multiple temporalities in the ocean. There's deep space in the ocean where things change at different rates.

Nadir Jeevanjee: When I transitioned from music to physics, and then finally to earth science, it was illuminating to think about the center of the Earth as a tropical ocean. If we had to boil the Earth down to one geographical space, from a climate point of view, it would be a tropical ocean. Why is that? I'm a native Californian living on the East Coast; I have always lived in the middle latitudes that many of us are familiar with. The tropics work fundamentally differently. The tropics is where most of the sunlight comes in. It's where most of the rain falls.

The places we live in here in the middle latitudes stay warm because of the tropics, where the sun evaporates water from the ocean and then that water gets transported to the middle latitudes. That water, as it rises, cools, and condenses, makes raindrops. Those raindrops are actually concentrated sunshine. They release heat energy when they condense, and the heat they release is the same heat that went into evaporating those water molecules off the ocean surface.

You get that heat back when you make the raindrop. That raindrop heats the air that then gets sent our way up here in the middle latitude. The tropics is really the furnace for the whole planet. That's where all the heat is generated.

In this process, the sunlight comes in and then, as you say, creates two layers of the ocean through the process of evaporation. First, we have this shallow ocean box and then this deep ocean box. The first one is maybe a few hundred feet down. The second one goes down thousands and thousands of feet. The bottom of the ocean is ten thousand feet down or more. The sunshine comes in, and then where the clouds come into it is where you get this evaporation off the surface as little water molecules.

I'll draw them as little H2O molecules, little Mickey Mouses, and then they rise and make clouds (figure 1). When they do that, when they condense to make raindrops, there's heat that gets released, the same heat that came from the sun to evaporate them in the first place.

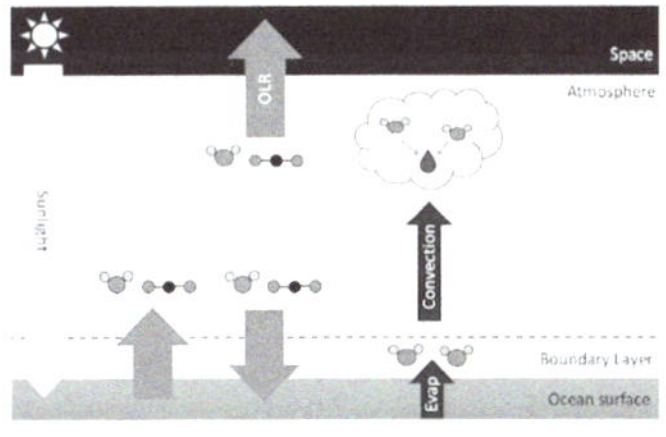

Figure 1. Schematic of energy flows through the climate system. Sunlight heats up the surface (yellow arrow), but this energy cannot be radiated away because it is blocked by greenhouse gas molecules (red arrows at bottom). So, the surface cools off by evaporation, and these evaporated water molecules eventually condense higher up to make clouds, giving off a heat of condensation in the process. Schematic courtesy of Nadir Jeevanjee.

V. Mitch McEwen: When I think about the sky in a pictorial sense, I think about a horizon line over land, where clouds blend into the land. In a way, one could imagine the ownership of the land extruding up into the sk. And that the terms of landed property could be extrapolated to the sky in a sense that ties into the history of landscape painting and Manifest Destiny. For me, part of what is so significant about this is that the physics you are diagramming is all related to the ocean. This is all still the troposphere, this whole dynamic of what makes the atmosphere.

Nadir Jeevanjee: Definitely, and in most places, the land gets its water from the ocean. My motivation for studying climate science is, of course, climate change. What you see here in this diagram is the shallow ocean, the deep ocean, and then this arrow represents the heat that we're trapping from carbon dioxide.

This diagram is describing that you've got a shallow and a deep ocean, which means that there's a shallow and a deep time of climate change. Because, as we all already know, if you've got a small pot of water, you can heat that quickly. If you've got a big pot, it takes longer.

We've got this heat that's being trapped in this shallow layer, which warms up pretty fast, on a time scale of maybe three to five years, but this deep ocean, four thousand meters/twelve thousand feet down, this takes hundreds to thousands of years, although even minuscule change may have enormous impact since the temperatures down there are normally so stable. There is definitely a deep time of climate change that we often don't think of. This deep time shows that while the temperature changes may be minimal, we'll have an impact thousands of years into the future, even if our civilization and humanity are gone (figure 2).

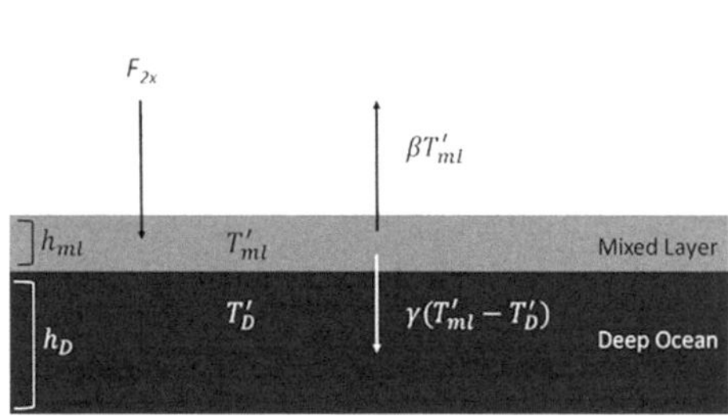

Figure 2. Schematic of the shallow ocean ("mixed layer") and deep ocean. The "F2x" arrow indicates the trapped heat from CO2. The downwards white arrow represents the slow transfer of this heat to the deep ocean. Schematic courtesy of Nadir Jeevanjee.

There's also a deep time of the CO2 that we put in the atmosphere. We dug it up from underground, and it took tens of millions of years to sequester it down there, and in a matter of decades, we suck it up, and we blow it into the atmosphere. That means there's a deep time to the changes that are coming. There are some that we feel soon, but then there are others that will take centuries or millennia to fully realize, which we, as humans, may no longer experience. That's where the time and the physical space meld together.

V. Mitch McEwen: We can already recognize that whole systems are failing—or that they produce failure by design, that they produce disruption by design. Now I want to take a moment to highlight where I think we can make connections to the troposphere and clouds that we can bring into human practices and consciousness. One is this presumed space that we were talking about in this diagram and how it disrupts something like a horizon line and the significance of land because disrupting land also disrupts colonial land and its terms.

Thinking about the idea of surface temperature, you talk about boundary layers, these slow timescales. What is the potential of a coordinate space that is no longer spatial but actually based on temperature? In other words, if we switch some of the protocols of cloud data capturing in theoretical physics, can we better understand climate change? Can we shift from a coordinate space to a coordinate temperature?

I'm going to pass it back to you, but first, let me unpack this a bit. It relates to the flux divergence that you talk about. There's a way that in order to measure clouds, we need to measure our own experiences, our own feelings. I don't know about you, but sometimes I feel cloudy to myself, right?

Part of what is at stake with clouds is what I would call individuation. I know you use your own language around things like bulk plumes, fluxes, and flux divergence, but really, the science of clouds is a science of flows. I'm thinking of individuation in the way that poet Fred Moten talks about it in terms of Blackness as a universal machine.

That part of the thinking of Blackness in terms of Black studies is something other than the individual biography, individual greatness, or the individual artist being an individual genius. I think we're all invited into something other than individuation in this symposium with the mode of artistic practices. Part of what I hear from Nadir's cloud science is also a science of collectivity. That collectivity is a protocol for conducting science.

There's a way in which the science of flows and collectivity is already temporal and part of the science that you're doing on clouds. I think you're doing science around these systems that are changing drastically because it allows you to also map these broken systems. The Greenwich Meridian Time, for instance, is a broken system because of white supremacy, which is also a broken system because of colonization. I want to shift from this map of the troposphere to discuss this GIF.

Nadir Jeevanjee: This is a simulation using computer models that we develop of this tropic's only picture of the world (figure 3). The surface is there in blue, those colors that you see are the amount of rainfall hitting any point of the surface at any time, and then that moisture gets transported up by the clouds. You've got this whole population of individuals, but they are all part of the same cycle of energy and water.

That is the climate, that is how the energy flows from the sun through us. We take our portion of it and then the rest flows out to space in the form of infrared energy. These clouds are key. Each individual cloud is a key component of this process, but it turns out that in science, and perhaps more broadly, it makes sense to describe these collectively. Each individual cloud, as you can see, it's kind of chaotic. They all have their small differences, but it turns out that they actually have a lot in common. The best way to describe it is by thinking of them as one collective entity and describing their behavior collectively.

You can actually take this, which is simulated on a supercomputer. It's complicated, and you can boil it down with pencil and paper, where at each sort of level in the atmosphere, whenever there's a cloud, it turns out that the amount of moisture it has, its temperature, is pretty similar at a given height, no matter which cloud or when the cloud is. It could be a cloud here at this point in space and time or one later, but if you look at it at the same height, it's got the same properties.

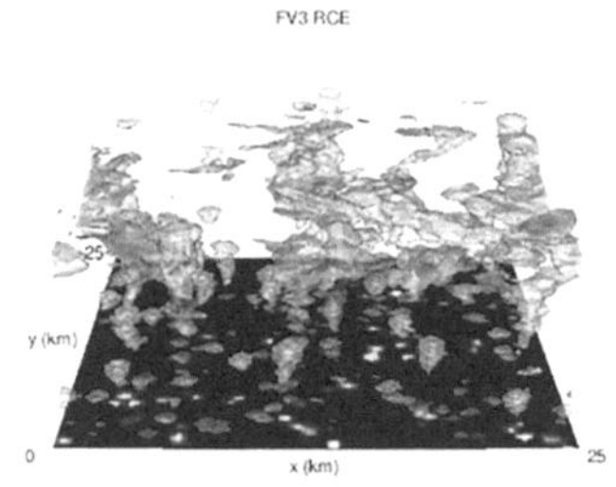

Figure 3. Snapshot of simulation of a "tropics-only" world with widespread clouds and convection. The ocean surface is blue, with other colors representing intensity of rainfall at the surface. The clouds flow individually but act collectively, and share many characteristics (humidity, density of cloud drops) especially when viewed in "temperature space" rather than in height or pressure space. Simulation still courtesy of Nadir Jeevanjee.

Now we can go back and touch on coordinates and temperature. The way that people usually coordinatize this and in ways, and remember time is a coordinate, we have our space coordinates and that's just a theme of this conference is what do these coordinates mean. They have an intrinsic meaning. Are they arbitrary? What are other coordinates that we could use?

V. Mitch McEwen: We're going to make a radical—it's just a little bit of a rupture, but I want to shift from cloud time in the pure theoretical physics to cloud time as something that maybe is already practiced in a Black reality. The way Rasheedah Phillips talks about that, we as Black people have needed to navigate Greenwich Mean Time, similarly to how our ancestors navigated through the stars in terms of locating fugitive potentials. Protocols navigate metrics. We have mostly been talking about metric systems, which arrange protocols but cannot be reduced to them.

From there, I want to ask you about the instantaneous because this is something that you work on. You have taught me about the distinction between steady-state and equilibrium. Within this temperature temporality, there is a temporality of what is instantaneous that actually takes time.

Nadir Jeevanjee: It relates to that shallow, deep ocean thing that we were talking about before in that the climate is the whole system and the pieces are coupled, but they're coupled on different timescales. The surface ocean and atmosphere appear to communicate quickly, but then in the deep ocean, it takes hundreds of years to know and truly feel the changes that are happening up here and come into a steady state with them, where the energy they're receiving is the same as the energy they're putting out. In that way, what we consider instantaneous depends on a reference frame.

The three to five years that it takes the surface ocean to adjust to what's happening in the atmosphere is instantaneous from the point of view of the deep ocean; three to five years is nothing. When we're thinking in terms of this deep climate time or this deep time, again, relative to a concrete change that's happening here, the adjustment time here is invisible. It's instant. Obviously, from the point of view of the ocean, that takes three to five years to change. There are atmospheric changes that happen on the time scale of weeks, and those are instant.

V. Mitch McEwen: We might consider the way that we learn from and feel each other's knowledge also in cloud-time. The way that a conversation can happen over the course of an hour, be transcribed over the course of weeks, edited over the course of months, and read by a reader outside of this room, in a manner of minutes—that also traverses time. There is energy dissipated and condensed at various moments of that process.

1 This text is an edited and condensed excerpt of McEwen and Jeevanjee's exchange on clouds, offered at Black Quantum Futurism's Prime Meridian Conference and presented by the Vera List Center for Art and Politics at The New School in 2022.

2 The term Anthropocene emerged from scientists at the opening of this century to demarcate significant human impact on Earth's geology. There are other terms and other ways of understanding this crisis, whether Plantationocene or simply Modernity, but they share an entanglement with questions of what it means to be human.

3 The premise of the Prime Meridian Unconference resonated with what philosopher Denise Ferreira da Silva calls Black Poethics, a consideration of aesthetic and ethical intentions. "What is the Black Poethic Intention? Is it an ethics, which, instead of the betterment of the World as we know it aims at its end?" Denise Ferreira da Silva, "Toward a Black Feminist Poethics: The Quest(ion) of Blackness Toward the End of the World," *The Black Scholar* 44, no. 2 (Summer 2014): 82.

4 See Nadir Jeevanjee and David M. Romps, "Mean Precipitation Change from a Deepening Troposphere," *Proceedings of the National Academy of Sciences* 115, no. 45 (November 6, 2018): https://orcid.org/0000-0002-6657-896X.

5 Ferreira da Silva, "Toward a Black Feminist Poethics."

SONIC PROTOCOLS

Shannon Mattern

I was jolted awake this morning by a rapid succession of discordant beeps. They started off strident and pugnacious, then tapered off in a hasty decrescendo—much like a rapidly accelerated radar ping. The pattern repeated until I hit the snooze button. Last night I had carelessly set my iPhone's alarm without changing its default sound, "Radar," regarded by some sleep researchers as one of the worst possible overtures to a new day.[1] According to Stuart McFarlane, who studies auditory perception and cognition, Radar's rhythm and metallic timbre resemble those used in emergency alarms.[2] Its heavy initial attack connotes and incites panic, prompting our reticular activating system—the neural network that regulates sleep and arousal—to stir us for battle, framing morning itself as an arena of circadian warfare. Had I chosen a more melodic iPhone alarm option, like "By the Seaside" or "Uplift"—or had I owned a Samsung, with its much more effervescent suite of options—I could instead be enticed and eased into wakeful activation.[3]

For eons, our "internal clocks" (and those of other fauna and flora) have responded to visual, thermal, and sonic cues in regulating our metabolic processes. Leatherback turtle embryos use chirps, grunts, and pulses to coordinate a time when they'll simultaneously emerge from their shells, allowing them to march en masse toward the ocean.[4] Humans, once settled in agricultural communities, counted on the rooster's crow to prepare them for the sun's impending rise. We've long deployed bells to carve sacred time from the profane, to call citizens to take caution or take up arms, and to create a sonic-temporal signature for the towns and villages in which they resound.[5] I recently moved to Center City, Philadelphia, where a large central clock chimes out the hours, synchronizing calendars and quickening footsteps within earshot. A few days after our arrival, I noted on Twitter that "I've never lived in a place where a big, central bell with a deep timbre and long decay marks the hours, bouncing off building facades and vibrating your guts. It's really nice" to experience synchrony as an embodied, environmental phenomenon.[6] Meanwhile, the whistle and alarm have, according to many theorists, marked the compartmentalization and commodification of time and emblematized the asymmetry between our circadian rhythms and capitalism's 24/7 churn of production and consumption.[7]

Today, our phones seem to be contrived for such circadian contradiction, to mediate between competing temporal logics and operational protocols. While their productivity apps compel us to optimize our waking hours and burn the midnight oil, and their tiny screens emit blue light that keeps us from dozing off, shortens our REM-stage sleep, and suppresses the secretion of melatonin, their *sounds* often promise a synesthetic corrective. We can download a flock of apps that play binaural beats or pink noise to "soothe the brain," or we can install tools that track our tossing and turning and surveil our snores, helping us monitor our sleep quality and gently waking us at the optimal time. The phone serves as a visual, haptic, and sonic interface between sleeping and waking, both as we get into bed and rise out of it. But it's also more than that: its material properties and symbolic content—especially its sonic qualities—have physiological and psychological effects that qualitatively and quantitatively alter the relationship between our horizontal and vertical hours.

The rooster's crow, the bell's chime, the whistle's screech, and the alarm's blare exemplify how we've created new sounds or manipulated existing ones that prompt us to execute various protocols governing our individual behavior and social interactions. To a sociologist, a protocol is an accepted or established code of behavior or etiquette within a given group or situation. To a technologist, a protocol is a set of rules governing data exchange. To a scientist, a protocol is a method for carrying out an experiment or procedure.[8] Sonic protocols are all three: they're social, technical, and methodological. Literary scholar Jennifer Lynn Stoever describes sonic protocols as "culturally specific and socially constructive conventions that shape how sound is indexed, valued, and interpreted in any given moment."[9] Those sonic conventions also intone how we index, value, interpret and execute myriad practices within our social and cultural worlds—from labor to leisure, war to worship. Let's listen to a few more such protocols.

Our objects and environments are often designed to offer sonic cues that regulate the way we interact with or function within them. A few years ago, I published an essay that explored "how we rely on our gadgets, from tea kettles to Twitter, to [sonically] signal their needs, to announce their approval, or displeasure with, our actions, and to confirm that we've pressed the right buttons, that we've gotten the job done."[10] Sound design thus constitutes a protocol for communication between us and the engineered world, and it signals to us how to function properly as the executor of particular operational protocols. Yet those sonic protocols aren't merely functional; they're also cultural and political. These resounding things, I wrote, "are designed to interpellate, placate, motivate, even manipulate use—and, increasingly, to record and process the sounds *we* make, too."

Tupperware containers, with their "burping" seal, were designed to assure the conscientious housewife that she was protecting the freshness and quality of her family's food and, at the same time, to appeal to her motherly instincts. Vacuum cleaners and espresso machines and combustion engine-powered cars likewise lend themselves to sonic diagnostics: an attuned ear can hear when they are or aren't operating properly. As we've swapped our mechanical tools for digital gadgets—many of which are tightly sealed typological novelties that veil their internal parts and operations—we're relying more and more on haptic and sonic cues to provide affirmative feedback. ID card or retina scanners at our building lobby turnstiles and UPC scanners at the store self-checkout beep to let us know that we've correctly validated our identities or registered our purchases. That beep reminds us that we, like our toilet paper and orange juice, can be reduced to a machine-readable essence. Our phones, the same gadgets that initiate a protocol for our passage into wakefulness, are bursting with pings and whooshes to confirm that we've sent that email, completed that transaction, snapped that pic, matched with a potential mate. The quality of those sounds—including the alarm that assaulted me this morning—cultivates particular affective relationships both with our gadgets *and* with the functions they facilitate. While it might have taken me ten torturous minutes to successfully enter that virtual meeting about budget cuts, now that I'm here, after passing through a hall of transcendent wooshes and encouraging dings, it sure does sound like a place of fellowship, play, and possibility!

In myriad professional environments, creating and listening to sound are integral components of method, of executing operational protocol, of exchanging information between various parties. I've written elsewhere about what engineers and maintenance workers learn by listening to dams and bridges and various other infrastructural installations; they rely on sound to confirm structural stability and functional integrity.[11] On the battlefield, soldiers have long listened for distant gunfire and approaching aircraft in order to adjust their strategy in response to enemy forces that cannot be seen.[12] Instrumental marches have regimented the troops' corporate movement. On the factory floor, managers have strategically deployed music to regulate the execution of labor.[13] In the courtroom and wedding chapel, speech acts—"I promise," "I do"—obligate participants to publicly affirm their intention to uphold the institutions' established protocols.[14] In border stations, immigration officers execute forensic listening protocols to determine the veracity of asylum claims, by ensuring that immigrants' vocabularies and accents match those indigenous to the geographic loci referenced in their testimony.[15] Philosopher of language Emily Apter notes that these immigration interpreters are often subcontractors performing their work from a distance, "without the supplementary information provided by facial and bodily cues or nuances of affect."[16] Their sonic protocols reduce the voice to a "smoothed out, partial object," an impoverished proxy for the life stories it ostensibly documents. In the counseling room, meanwhile, the psychotherapist practices a protocol of diagnostic listening that recognizes the corporeality of talk. And in the doctor's office, physicians have long performed auscultation, listening to sounds within the body, to diagnose ailments of the lungs, heart, and digestive system.[17]

The corporeality and spatiality of sound are particularly apparent in religious spaces. While church bells, the Islamic Adhan, and the Jewish Barechu summon believers to worship, sounds woven throughout religious service also cue attendees into liturgical protocols. Religious studies scholar Ashon Crawley has been studying the role of the Hammond B-3 organ in Black Pentecostal worship.[18] The instrument, used in storefront churches and megachurches from the United States to Africa, "has been taken up in Blackpentecostal spaces as the instrument, as the sound, of the movement."[19]

Crawley quotes musician and critic Salim Washington, who proposes that "music in the Holiness churches can be used simply as a transformation of the mood and/or mind-set of the participants, but in the case of the 'shout'"—wherein God inhabits the corporate body, melding sound and movement—"music is used as a technology, through which a direct cause and effect take place."[20] The Hammond organ is a technology that impels the execution of what Crawley calls a "choreosonic itinerary and *protocol*."[21] Its ubiquity throughout the worship service continually evokes the presence of ghostly forces and reinforces worshippers' faith in the unseen. The Hammond is a "tonewheel" organ composed of spinning, notched metal disks, which generate a sound more "alive and organic" than an electronic organ could produce. It also features drawbars that allow organists to control loudness, tone, and percussiveness; in moments of "intense emotionality," Crawley reports, musicians often "pull out all the stops" to create as much volume as possible.[22] Plus, the organ's "fast attack," or quick response to touch, makes it "perfect for the intense and quick 'movement of the Spirit' in Blackpentecostal spaces."[23]

The B-3 is the keynote, the root tone, in a whole protocological environment. Crawley writes:

> The sound of the B-3 participates in a relationship with the other sounds in the space, that the musician enacts—along with the architectonics, the noise and murmuring, the conversations and glossolalia, the foot stomps and vocable expirations—and this participation is the horizontal emergence for [a] mode of coming together in otherwise, uncapturable, anti-institutional configurations with each sounded out chord.[24]

The B-3 sounds out the overtones of protocol. Its warble and wail suggest that protocol is not simply about control and regimentation. Protocol can instead underscore a method of abandon; an etiquette of excess; a joyful, uncapturable exchange between bodies and spirits. It can make possible the creation of an "otherwise world of possibility."

If we can attune ourselves to the ubiquitous resounding of protocols in our daily lives, if we can discern the contexts of their composition and the various behaviors and interactions they're meant to underscore, perhaps we can also audiate their overtones and the "otherwise" worlds they might ring into existence.[25] Musicians like Oneohtrix Point Never and Matmos regularly extract protocological sounds from the realm of functionality and efficiency and mix them into *musique concrète* compositions that invite contemplation and curiosity. Matmos's "Ultimate

Care II" (2016) reveals the sonic protocols governing the operation of their Whirlpool washing machine: "Its rhythmic chugs, spin cycle drones, rinse cycle splashes, metallic clanks and electronic beeps are parsed into an eclectic syntax of diverse musical genres."[26] Oneohtrix Point Never, meanwhile, in "The Weather Channel" (2021), remixes familiar beeps and pings into an ethereal soundtrack that simply floats and swirls rather than moving toward any form of productive resolution. Creative technologist Brian Moore marshals those same sounds to simulate protocological excess: his Busy Simulator app layers notification sounds—email dings, text message pings, Discord blips, calendar chimes—to disrupt the sociotechnical protocols of teleconference calls.[27] All those phony sonic appeals make it impossible for your interlocuters to hear you, rending the meeting unproductive, and suggest that you're drowning in demands for your labor, which might elicit a temporary reprieve.

Or, what if rather than remixing and repurposing existing protocols, we orchestrated new ones—protocols that, instead of summoning us into productive labor, compliant tool use, or compulsive consumption, cultivate a soundtrack for camaraderie or care or caprice? Can we imagine an alarm clock whose aubade, or morning song, awakens us into an otherwise world of possibility?

1 James Picken, "Struggling to Wake Up? Try Changing Your Alarm Tune," *Startle*, November 16, 2022, https://www.startlemusic.com/blog/struggling-to-wake-up-change-alarm-tune; Mia Armstrong-López, "The Reason the Default iPhone Alarm Is So, So Terrible," *Slate*, October 15, 2022, https://slate.com/technology/2022/10/radar-iphone-alarm-apple.html. And speaking of suboptimal waking conditions, I must note that my own suboptimal *working* conditions while writing this piece required that I adapt my standard writing protocol. A new job, a hasty move, and a lack of available contractors to renovate our new home have impeded access to my books and research materials and a suitable workspace. Thus, this essay is the product of an improvisatory compositional protocol.

2 Quoted in Haley Henschel, "iPhone Alarm Sounds, Ranked," Mashable, April 17, 2022, https://mashable.com/article/best-and-worst-iphone-alarm-sounds-ranked.

3 Adam Entertainment, "Evolution of Samsung Galaxy Default Alarm," YouTube, January 16, 2022, https://www.youtube.com/watch?v=fVNYlbSLBys; Stuart J. McFarlane, Jair E. Garcia, Darrin S. Verhagen, and Adrian G. Dyer, "Alarm Tones, Music, and their Elements: Analysis of Reported Waking Sounds to Counteract Sleep Inertia," *PLOS One* (January 28, 2020), https://journals.plos.org/plosone/article?id=10.1371/journal.pone.0215788; Stuart J. McFarlane, Jair E. Garcia, Darrin S. Verhagen, and Adrian G. Dyer, "Auditory Countermeasures for Sleep Inertia: Exploring the Effects of Melody and Rhythm in an Ecological Context," *Clocks & Sleep* 2, no. 2 (2020), https://www.mdpi.com/2624-5175/2/2/17.

4 Camila R. Ferrara, Richard C. Vogt, Martha R. Harfush, Renata S. Sousa-Lima, Ernesto Albavera, and Alejandrao Tavera, "First Evidence of Leatherback Turtle (*Drermochalys coriacea*) Embryos and Hatchlings Emitting Sounds," *Chelonian Conservation and Biology* 13, no. 1 (2014): 110-14.

5 Alain Corbin, *Village Bells: Sound and Meaning in the 19th Century French Countryside* (New York: Columbia University Press, 1998). Portions of these few paragraphs are adapted from my "Time's Interfaces" presentation, which I shared at the DESIS Philosophy Talks @Studio Time at The New School on March 7, 2017. See "Time's Interfaces," Words in Space, accessed August 3, 2024, https://wordsinspace.net/2017/03/07/times-interfaces/#_edn3.

6 Shannon Mattern, X, November 3, 2022, https://twitter.com/shannonmattern/status/1588170934195830785.

7 Jonathan Crary, *24/7: Late Capitalism and the Ends of Sleep* (New York: Verso, 2013); E. P. Thompson, "Time, Work-Discipline, and Industrial Capitalism," *Past & Present* 38 (December 1967): 56-97.

8 "Protocol," n., Oxford English Dictionary, accessed August 5, 2024, https://www.oed.com/dictionary/protocol_n?tab=factsheet#27963133.

9 Jennifer Lynn Stoever, *The Sonic Color Line: Race and the Cultural Politics of Listening* (New York: New York University Press, 2016): 24. Richard Cullen Rath also refers to sonic protocols in *How Early America Sounded* (Ithaca, NY: Cornell University Press, 2003). He describes how encounters between First Nations people were prefaced and programmed through sonic protocols: war songs, yells, and other acoustic markers of aggression. See also Samantha Pinto, "'I Love to Love You Baby': Beyoncé, Disco, Aesthetics, and Black Feminist Politics," *Theory & Event* 23, no. 3 (July 2020): 512-34; and Sterre Gilsing, "The Power of Silence: Sonic Experiences of Police Operations and Occupations in Rio de Janeiro's Favelas," *Conflict and Society: Advances in Research* 6 (2020): 128-44.

10 Shannon Mattern, "Things that Beep: A Brief History of Product Sound Design," *Avant*, August 22, 2018, https://web.archive.org/web/20220520030808/https://avant.org/project/things-that-beep/. Portions of this paragraph and the next are adapted from the *Avant* essay.

11 Shannon Mattern, "Ear to the Wire: Listening to Historic Urban Infrastructures," *Amodern* 2 (October 2013), http://amodern.net/article/ear-to-the-wire/; "The Pulse of Global Passage: Listening to Logistics," in *Assembly Codes: The Logistics of Media*, ed. Matthew Hockenberry, Nicole Starosielski, and Susan Zieger (Durham, NC: Duke University Press, 2021): 75-90; "Sonic Archaeology," in *The Routledge Companion to Sound Studies*, ed. Michael Bull (New York: Routledge, November 2018): 222-30.

12 See, for instance, J. Martin Daughtry, *Listening to War: Sound, Music, Trauma, and Survival in Wartime Iraq* (Oxford: Oxford University Press, 2015); Steve Goodman, *Sonic Warfare: Sound, Affect, and the Ecology of Fear* (Cambridge, MA: MIT Press, 2010); Charles D. Ross, *Civil War Acoustic Shadows* (Shippensburg, PA: White Mane, 2001).

13 See, for instance, Nicola Dibben and Anneli B. Haake, "Music and the Construction of Space in Office-Based Work Settings" in *Music, Sound, and Space: Transformations of Public and Private Experience*, ed. Georgina Born (Cambridge: Cambridge University Press, 2013), 151-68; Keith Jones, "Music in Factories: A Twentieth-Century Technique for Control of the Productive Self," *Social & Cultural Geography* 6, no. 5 (2005): 723-44; and Marek Korczynski, "*Stayin' Alive* on the Factory Floor: An Ethnography of the Dialectics of Music Use in the Routinized Workplace," *Poetics* 39, no. 2 (2011): 87-106.

14 J. L. Austen, *How to Do Things with Words: The William James Lectures Delivered at Harvard University in 1955* (Oxford: Clarendon Press, 1962). Of the myriad applications of speech act theory, you might consider Susan E. Provenzano, "Can Speech Act Theory Save Notice Pleading?" *Indiana Law Journal* 96, no. 4 (2021), https://www.repository.law.indiana.edu/ilj/vol96/iss4/5/.

15 See Régine Debatty, "Shibboleth: The Geopolitics of Phonetics," We Make Money Not Art, February 15, 2022, https://we-make-money-not-art.com/shibboleth-the-geopolitics-of-phonetics/; Michael Erard, "Immigration by Shibboleth," Legal Affairs, November/December 2003, https://www.legalaffairs.org/issues/November-December-2003/story_erad_novdec03.msp; and the work of artist and VLC Fellow Lawrence Abu Hamdan. "Conflicted Phonemes, 2012," Lawrence Abu Hamdan, accessed August 5, 2024, http://lawrenceabuhamdan.com/conflicted-phonemes.

16 Emily Apter, "Shibboleth: Policing by Ear and Forensic Listening in Projects by Lawrence Abu Hamdan," *October* 156 (Spring 2016): 105.

17 See, for instance, Jonathan Sterne, "Mediate Auscultation, the Stethoscope, and the 'Autopsy of the Living': Medicine's Acoustic Culture," *Journal of Medical Humanities* 22 (2001): 115-36.

18 See also Ashon Crawley's Hammond Gospel Organ Oral History Project, "Hammond Organ Research," Ashon Crawley, https://ashoncrawley.com/hammond-organ-research-participate.

19 Ashon Crawley, *Black Pentecostal Breath: The Aesthetics of Possibility* (Durham, NC: Duke University Press, 2016), 253.

20 Salim Washington, "The Avenging Angel of Creation/Destruction: Black Music and the Afro-Technological in the Science Fiction of Henry Dumas and Samuel R. Delany," *Journal of the Society for American Music* 2, no. 2 (2008): 239.

21 Italics mine.

22 Crawley, *Black Pentecostal Breath*, 253.

23 Crawley, 254.

24 Crawley, 268-69. See also Maurice O. Wallace, *The King's Vibrato: Modernism, Blackness, and the Sonic Life of Martin Luther King, Jr.* (Durham, NC: Duke University Press, 2022).

25 "Audiation" is music theorist Edwin Gordon's term for hearing sounds that are not present or may never have been present. "Audiation," Gordon Institute for Music Learning, accessed August 5, 2024, https://giml.org/mlt/audiation/.

26 Matmos, "Ultimate Care II," bandcamp, accessed August 5, 2024, https://matmos.bandcamp.com/album/ultimate-care-ii.

27 "Busy Simulator," Busysimulator.com, accessed August 5, 2024, https://busysimulator.com/.

SOUND OF THE UNDERGROUND

Underground Resistance

The following playlist by Detroit-based techno collective Underground Resistance members Cornelius Harris and Nomadico (aka DJ Dex) unfolds as a new sonic protocol, one owed to the experimentation, riffing, and decentralized access to technology that manifested techno as a genre.

bitly

Words from Atlantis / Atlantis, Underground Resistance, 1:53
Free Your Mind and Your Ass Will Follow / Funkadelic, 10:07
City, Country, City / War, 13:24
Return Of The Dragons / Galaxy 2 Galaxy, 7:14
Computer Incantations for World Peace / Jean-Luc Ponty, 5:41
The Theory - Mind Mix / Galaxy 2 Galaxy, 2:29
Gamma Player - Blue Potential Version / Jeff Mills, 6:59
See This Way - Blue Potential Version / Jeff Mills, 6:02
Medieval Overture - Instrumental / Return To Forever, 5:13
Techno City '95 / Audiotech, 7:16
Kaotic Harmony / Derrick May, 6:35
Neptune / Model 500, 12:25
A Delicate Balance / The Infiltrator, Underground Resistance, 4:45
Controlled Substance / Perception, Underground Resistance, 1:15
The Fugitive from Tibet (Healing) / The Infiltrator, Underground Resistance, 2:24
Birdland / Weather Report, 5:56
Cosmic Raindance / Cybotron, 4:00
Frustration / Carl Craig, 6:58
Aqua Worm Hole / Drexciya, 5:29
Aquabahn / Drexciya, 2:08
Atomic Dog / George Clinton, 4:47
Hardcore Hip-Hop / Mantronix, 6:18
Song for the Hmong / Perception, 090, 3:55
Angkor Wat / DJ Dex, Underground Resistance, 4:23
Still Cruisin' / Nomadico, 5:04
Electric Night / Model 500, Mark Taylor, Juan Atkins, Mike Banks, DJ Skurge, 4:11
Don't Cry / J Dilla, 1:59
The Twister (Huh, What) / J Dilla, 1:16
Power to the People / Public Enemy, 3:50
Lethal Weapon / ICE-T, 4:33
Deep Space 9 / Galaxy 2 Galaxy, 5:43
Burning Spear / Mad Mike, Trinity, 4:27
I Wanna Be There - Edit / Model 500, 6:44
The Final Frontier - Nomadico Remix / Underground Resistance, Nomadico, 6:57
Backyard Trippin' / Nomadico, 5:07
Tazumal / Underground Resistance, 5:17
Baghdad Express / Underground Resistance, 5:22
Death of My Neighborhood / Underground Resistance, 3:13
Chaos & Order / Mad Mike, Atlantis, 5:45
Cargo Cult (Last Days) / Suburban Knight, Underground Resistance, 2:55
Fuji (The Peace Within) / The Deacon, Underground Resistance, 4:34
Starlight / Model 500, 6:26
Strings of Life / Derrick May, 6:02
Windchime / Galaxy 2 Galaxy, 6:09
Metamorphosis / Galaxy 2 Galaxy, 3:25
No UFO's (D-Mix) / Model 500, 8:17
Transition / Galaxy 2 Galaxy, Cornelius Harris, Christa Robinson, DJ Dex, 6:25
Thought 2 / Underground Resistance, 4:17

The Beginning / Derrick May, 5:28
Blakula / Innerzone Orchestra, 9:04
Frankenstein / The Edgar Winter Group, 4:44
Peaches En Regalia / Frank Zappa, 3:38
Motor City Madness - Underground Resistance Remix / Waajeed, Underground Resistance, 6:31
Snake Eyes / Waajeed, 5:32
Think Twice / Detroit Experiment, 6:18
Share My Life - Kenny Larkin Remix / Kevin Saunderson, paris grey, 5:49
King of Light / Mark Flash, 7:20
Blackwater - 128 full strings instrumental / Octave One, 8:31
Dem Young Sconies / Moodymann, 5:19
Manufactured Memories / Innerzone Orchestra, 4:50
Dance Sister Dance (Baila Mi Hermana) / Santana, 8:14
Knights of Jaguar / The Aztec Mystic, 6:38
Jingo - 12" Version / Candido, 9:53
Song 4 Sydney / Mr.De', 5:29
Zombie / Fela Kuti, Afrika 70, 12:25
Central Nervous System / Los Hermanos, 6:49
Resurrection / Los Hermanos, 5:00
In Deeper Presence / Los Hermanos, 4:35
Birth of 3000 / Los Hermanos, 5:12
Let's Start the Dance / Bohannon, 5:52
I Would Die 4 U / Prince, 2:58
Chase / Giorgio Moroder, 8:26
Hi NRG / Model 500, Mark Taylor, Juan Atkins, Mike Banks, DJ Skurge, 4:38
TECHNOPOLIS / YELLOW MAGIC ORCHESTRA, Norio Yoshizawa, 4:14
Get the Balance Right! - Combination Mix / Depeche Mode, Daniel Miller, 7:58
Frequency 7 - The Dance Version / Visage, 4:57
Europe Endless - 2009 Remaster / Kraftwerk, 9:41
Metropolis - 2009 Remaster / Kraftwerk, 6:01
Theme from the TV Series *Cosmos* (Heaven and Hell, 3rd Movement) / Vangelis, 4:04
The Gumbo Variations / Frank Zappa, 12:54
Journey of the Dragons / Galaxy 2 Galaxy, 6:44

NOTES ON METHOD: NARRATIVE AS CRITICISM

Emmanuel Iduma

When I began writing about art, I didn't give much thought to what I was getting into. My ambitions, during the years I studied law, mostly involved publishing fiction and poetry. Indeed, I completed a novel while I prepared for my bar exams. Yet, a few months before the novel was published, I participated in a project that changed the trajectory of my writing. I embarked on a road trip with a group of photographers—traveling from Lagos, Nigeria, to Addis Ababa, Ethiopia, under the auspices of the nonprofit organization Invisible Borders.[1] From then on, the concerns of my writing—its stakes and possibilities, predilections, idiosyncrasies, and protocols—were transformed.

I am considering these things in retrospect, of course, particularly from the vantage point of a decade and half of thinking of myself as a professional writer. I have time to think about the protocols I have worked with, through, and against—that is, the conventions of a career spent trafficking between critical and imaginative writing.

I didn't think, while in Addis Ababa in late 2011, that my writing could be described as "art criticism." I had been invited to participate in the trip on the basis of a short story and an essay—an essay written in response to a review of the five short stories shortlisted for that year's Caine Prize for African Writing. And so, in the strictest sense, the writing samples I submitted didn't qualify as examples of art criticism or art writing. Yet, invited to join the trip and required to write on a daily blog about the journey as it unfolded, I began to understand that my real task was to reconcile art with experience. The experience I had was traveling with photographers.

I participated in the trip three more times after 2011—from Lagos to Libreville, Gabon, in 2012, Lagos to Sarajevo, Bosnia, in 2014, and a trip within Nigeria in 2016. What made me return, despite the hecticness of the endeavor—the difficulties, for instance, of finding the solitude I required to write while traveling alongside nine or ten others—was the capaciousness I felt in relation to the forms of writing I could practice.

In an important sense, experience became my genre, one in which I could fit reflections on what it meant to watch photographers work, what it meant to reconcile their working methods with what and where they shot, and how it felt to be in the places where they worked. From this womb of method, place, and artwork, my criticism and essayism were born.

My years on the road were influenced by another experience: studying for an MFA degree in art criticism and writing at the School of Visual Arts (SVA) in New York City. I didn't know such a graduate program existed until the American photographer and organizer Eric Gottesman introduced me to David Levi Strauss, who had been his teacher at Bard College, and who now taught at SVA.

When I was accepted to SVA in 2012 but couldn't begin my studies that fall due to financial constraints, David Levi Strauss sent me a short essay he wrote at the prompting of Irving Sandler. "Dear Irving," the essay began, "If it's not good writing, it can't be good criticism." Thus began my apprenticeship, nearly a year before I eventually resumed my studies. That sentence—paraphrased from Walter Benjamin—became, and remains, a defining statement of my work. I needed a lodestar, and Strauss was it, together with the unforgettable and nonpareil constellation of writers and critics he assembled to teach seminar courses during my two years at SVA—Charles Stein, Claudia La Rocco, Dejan Lukic, Jennifer Krasinski, Lynne Tillman, Nancy Princenthal, Susan Bee, Susan Bell, and Thomas Beard. Together, they articulated for me that the practice of criticism was never far from the rigor of writing, draft after draft, and that a grasp of theory was never a shorthand for obfuscation in an essay.

And hence, once I became a student at SVA in 2013 and graduated in 2015, all the work I strove to accomplish while writing about the Invisible Borders road trips—whether for the blog or for publications or in curatorial statements—drew from the eclecticism of my graduate studies. I was like a dog sniffing a field.

The most consequential writer to me at the time was John Berger. He is perhaps the writer whose work I have read most. Berger had written the following of Joyce: "It was he who showed me, before I knew anything, that literature is inimical to all hierarchies and that to separate fact and imagination, event and feeling, protagonist and narrator, is to stay on dry land and never put to sea."[2] The statement was clarifying, to some degree. I had a sense of what it meant to resist hierarchies (one of my favorite statements at the time was made by Claudia La Rocco, attributed to Frank O'Hara, to the effect that a writer must be content to make distinctions, not hierarchies). But what would it mean not to separate fact from imagination, event and feeling, protagonist and narrator? What would it mean to produce writing categorizable both as narrative ("imagination," "feeling") and as criticism ("fact," "event")?

As I sought a response in the years immediately following my time at SVA, I made the mistake of considering the practice of "narrative as criticism" as a foray into an altogether different—and therefore unheralded—genre of art criticism. I was caught in a dense debris of hubris in my mid-to-late twenties. I wanted to hold up my writing as an example of something new—a genre within a genre. I was wary of editors or publications that worked with a "house style," who reached for a particular standardized voice, whether it was one close to academic writing, or one that required the fact-based rigors of journalism. And so, it began to increasingly seem that I had arrived at a neat demarcation between pieces of writing that hewed close to my literary sensibilities in poetry and fiction and those that paid attention to traditions of criticism and commentary both in the United States and Nigeria. I began to see that I favored the former; only sometimes did I take on more conventional commissions simply because I needed to pay the bills, producing texts that seemed like ballast on my journey to find my voice as a writer.

Yet, after years of producing texts for journals, monographs, and catalogues, I realized that I had not learned the lesson I advocated for: to make distinctions, not create hierarchies. I recognized that my enthusiasm could be as particular as it was general. I could reach for the best practices in both literary nonfiction and art criticism; I could let each project dictate its own methods.

Distinctions, not hierarchies: I am dealing with how I might define the scope of my writing. This requires, I believe, a worldview—to be a writer is a way for me to be in the world, to find an aesthetics that proceeds from an ethics, and to unite medium with message and meaning. This is the foundational basis on which every piece of my writing takes shape. I also proceed with the sense that to make a distinction between the forms of writing I work in, is also to seek overlaps between them.

Considering overlaps between art criticism and literary nonfiction requires, in the first place, articulating what good writing, regardless of genre, can aim for and achieve. And so, for example, I now believe that since my education and experience made it inevitable for me to write about art, it also became inevitable for me to use art—particularly photography—as an entry point into investigations outside the scope of art criticism. This transdisciplinary reach is what makes good writing.

In a sense, this realization was informed by a question I have struggled with for most of the pandemic: What is the value of art criticism? I thought then, and still think, that if I can answer it with some degree of honesty, I will illuminate my interest in forms of writing that put narrative techniques at the service of criticism and vice versa.

To be clear, I do not begrudge the field, and I am full of gratitude for all I have been given and how I have been recognized. Yet, around the time I began work on my most recent book[3]—a family memoir about the aftermath of the Nigerian Civil War, a book that has little to no analysis of, or response to, art in it—I realized that I was beginning to think of art writing as too narrow for my interest in narrative, by which I meant fiction, personal essays, and history. Too narrow? Does this refer to the modes of publication and distribution, to the journals and galleries that commission me? Is this in connection to the readers who are drawn to my work—that is, those who read the work I publish in limited-edition books, for instance, and how they engage with such "marginal" writing? I mean both of those things.

I have felt that my ongoing concerns—the themes I return to in my work, primarily the nature of the past and home—are occasionally too wide to fit within the scope of writing that responds to artists and their work. And, equally, by looking closely at artworks and the ideas surrounding them, I might find a font of specifics for those themes.

So, at this point in my writing practice, I am looking for opportunities that allow for equivocation in relation to both assertions. I can no longer sum up my identity as an "arts writer" or an "art critic." I want to claim a descriptor that is not genre specific: to say that I am simply a "writer." I intend no simplification. To consider the overlaps between art criticism and literary nonfiction is to note that those overlaps are defined by giving sense and scope to method, which happens for each piece of writing. Ultimately, to write under any genre is to define and delimit, to work with a set of formal constraints.

In February 2022, I launched *Tender Photo*, a newsletter on contemporary African photography, hosted on Substack. My immediate interest was to find a new frame for my writing, to practice an engaged criticism that makes me a kind of middleperson in the exchanges between a photograph and a photographer. Yet each edition of the newsletter, taken together, constitutes "notes on method," weekly protocols of attentive writing that might prepare me to work on a book-length essay on African photography. Is it still necessary to think about photography within a geographic framework? If so, will more complex, sub-disciplinary methodologies emerge to present photography produced on the continent?

To address these questions in an essay, I intend to stay with the geographic framework for two reasons, one aesthetic and the other political. My aesthetic reason has to do with the constraint of subject matter: I need to direct my impressions to photography produced within the region. My political reason, following from that, is informed by the scarcity of books on photography that use photographs taken on the continent—by photographers born or based there—as illustrative of what the medium is. I am not referring to scholarly studies on African photography, of which there are a good number of important books. I am thinking of books like Roland Barthes's *Camera Lucida* and Geoff Dyer's *The Ongoing Moment*, in which the authors are mindful of literary style in their analysis of photography.

Yet, this is an aside. What interests me most, at this stage of conceptualizing my book on photography and producing the *Tender Photo* newsletter, is that the photographs and photographers I choose to engage with matter for reasons besides a trend or an aspect of African photography. I do not expect anyone to read my monograph as a survey or tight selection of important photographs; my aim is to use the photographs as touchstones for my sensibilities. I know, in the first place, that I will select the photographs in response to a narrative. What this narrative is—whether it is based on a historical event or several remembered experiences—I do not yet know.

If I were to find a narrative structure, the next thing to deal with would be how to distribute the photographs within the text. How do I use the photographs as transition points in the narrative, both in the way I describe them and how I analyze them?

I am working with photographs, yes, but I am also working, primarily, with narrative. I want to tell a story that will elicit emotion from the reader, to point to the extraordinariness of lived, idiosyncratic life. And I find that lived life can be encountered in photographs: in the cool yet disturbed landscapes of Jo Ratcliffe; in Dawit L. Petros's images of men holding mirrors as they stand on sparse territory; in the photographs of women in Malick Sidibé's studio with their backs to the camera. And so forth. I want the reader to note that the experience I describe in the monograph is contiguous with the photographs.

Most of all, if art criticism aspires to the best of literary nonfiction—and if literary nonfiction aspires to the best of art criticism—then a writer who is also a critic should develop the sensitivity required to make literature matter. At the end of it all, the muscle I hope to develop in writing this monograph is a moral one. To point to the beauty of photography, its consolatory power, its sense of justice. It is the idea of at once trembling "with indignation every time an injustice is committed in the world," a quote attributed to Che Guevara in Chris Marker's 1983 film *Sans Soleil,* and finding the opportunity to transmute that into literature. And it is to respond to a question from an essay by Amitava Kumar: "What can you write that will make anyone reading you give a dying man a drink of water?"[4]

That this question is rhetorical assumes a protocol more personal than prescriptive, which means that I hope to respond to it in a way altogether different from the way another writer might. In other words, a moral muscle is not an ethical one. This view necessarily distinguishes between an external protocol—one defined by a universal ethos to engage with the world—and an internal or personal one. The latter reckons writ small with images or themes or people, finding the precise entry point that makes subtle distinctions between generally held views.

Consider this photograph of three open notebooks (figure 1): The focus is on the one in the foreground, and if I strain my eye, I can make out my scribbles on it. The farther I look, the more indistinct my letters are. Yet it is the farthest notebook that matters most to me: I have written in it every day for a month, preparing, as it were, for the memoir I am writing—outlining the plot, typifying the characters, copying out sentences from my research that might inform the historical background, writing test paragraphs. Each day, especially after I have taken photographs of the desk, I write in the notebook. How I have managed to do that all month takes me by surprise. I have never undertaken such an activity, habitually skirting through several notebooks as though incapable of regimen. I imagine this sudden focus has to do with five years of attempting to write a novel—novels, in fact, at one point, coming to forty thousand words—and failing to see the point, the throughline to connect story with imperative.

I am most attentive after I have taken photographs. In the moment between my glimpse and the records I make, I stretch the lining of the present, honoring what outlives a moment. Just as the soldier who, as Andrei Tarkovsky recounts in *Sculpting in Time* is walking around in circles.[5] He and others are lined up against a hospital wall, about to be shot for treason in front of the ranks. They have been ordered to take off their coats and boots. But the ground is full of puddles. The condemned man, wearing socks full of holes, spends a long time looking for a dry place to put down his coat and boots—coats and boots he will not need a few minutes later.

I take photographs of my notebook in the same month I write in the notebook, one regimen overlapping with the other. It is like a photographer I know, who has worked with the same medium format camera since the late '70s. His camera is not so much a device that takes pictures of what is visible, but one through which he learns what is peculiar about a place. Or perhaps it is that, by using a camera for that long, he understands his special relationship with the world, as if the rays of light cast on his eye refract in a unique manner. Think about this. It is like two people reading the same book, imbibing its ideas in the same sequence. Yet, do they raise their head in miscomprehension at the same sentence or nod at the acuity of the same phrase? After these monthlong exercises, it seems OK to take shelter in the process. OK, to make a pact with an elusive narrative, to keep track of its mutability. I want many more months like this, filled with arbitrary protocols. Not just so I can know for sure when I am ready to write the book without stopping, but simply for the pleasure, and indeed intensity, of a daily regimen. Like Robinson Crusoe, that famed voyager, making a table on his new island. An attempt to render the basic and necessary. In the notebook, I have made no rule except that I write today's date. And to pay heed to Anne Carson, in a note on her method: "Copy down whatever vibration you see while your attention is strong."[6]

You know, I keep these notes as a compromise in case I never get to the main thing. The main thing, what I pass on occasionally in vignettes, will soon be known to me. My notes are daily sweepings to clear the ground for a story on the horizon.

A version of this essay was delivered as a speech on May 2, 2022, during a virtual talk organized by AICA-USA, commemorating the Irving Sandler Award for New Voices in Art Criticism.

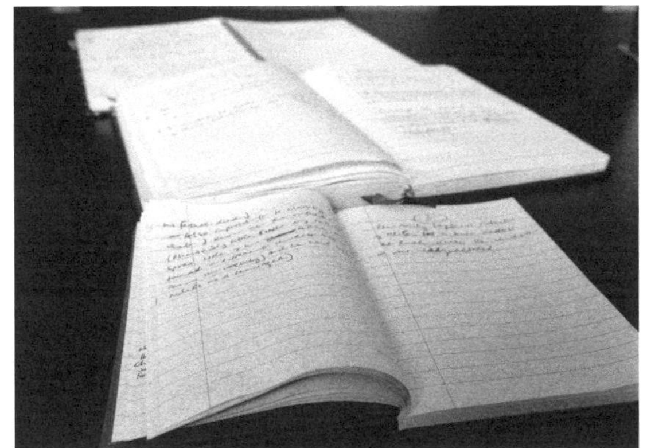

Figure 1. Emmanuel Iduma, *Untitled*, 2021.

Description Figure 1. Three open notebooks spread out vertically inline on a black surface. The writing inside, written in blue ink, is mostly illegible.

1 In 2020, Invisible Borders was appointed a Jane Lombard Fellow by the Vera List Center for Art and Politics.

2 John Berger, "Forthflowing on a Joycean Tide," in *Landscapes: John Berger on Art* (London: Verso, 2016), 85.

3 Emmanuel Iduma, *I Am Still with You* (New York: Algonquin, 2023).

4 Amitava Kumar, "I'm Writing a Novel, but There Is the News," *Brick*, September 10, 2019, https://brickmag.com/im-writing-a-novel/.

5 Andrei Tarkovsky, *Sculpting in Time: Reflections to the Cinema* (Austin: University of Texas Press, 1987, 2019), 26.

6 Anne Carson, "Note on Method," *in Economy of the Unlost (Reading Simonides of Keos with Paul Celan)* (Princeton, NJ: Princeton University Press, 2009), viii.

FRAGILE GLASS AT THE TEMPLE: ON ECONOMIC AND ACADEMIC VULNERABILITIES IN CONTEMPORARY ART MUSEUMS IN THE UNITED STATES

Pablo Helguera

The most important job interview of my museum career—for a leadership position at a major art museum—was my final meeting with its director. I had thought long and hard about the kinds of questions I would be asked regarding management philosophy, academic interests, or even fund-raising skills, and spent a good deal of time in advance of the interview rehearsing in my mind many of the responses I planned on providing. I entered the director's office, he greeted me, and we sat down. However, instead of initiating the interview in the usual format, he said nothing. He only made a gesture with his hand, indicating "Please go ahead and talk."

The gesture was completely unexpected and threw me off balance. I proceeded to speak about why I was interested in the position, but it was an exceedingly challenging task; it felt like the equivalent of walking through a pitch-black, darkened tunnel. I was not sure exactly what to talk about, nor for how long. The director sat stonefaced throughout my speech, showing no reaction whatsoever, which added to my uncertainty. I had no idea if what I was saying was at all of any interest to him or if I was bringing up any points that felt relevant; I did not know if my words would be viewed as a tired pitch or a series of platitudes. In retrospect, it was a brilliant interview strategy, as it forced me as the job applicant to make a choice as to which type of character I thought the director wanted me to perform. Clearly his assessment would be based not only on my understanding of the job but also on how I performed the role I thought he wanted me to perform.

As I look back, the experience made me reflect on the paramount importance of the cautiously mimetic behavior that dominates the art museum profession. To be clear, I am no novice in this art (and, just for context, I did get that job, although I believe my performance at that particular interview did not play much of a role in the end), but the process by which I and all of my colleagues have to navigate the art world was nothing anyone had formally taught us: this is on-the-job training that commences before one has a job or, at best, at the very junior level of the museum hierarchy.

In the art museum field, particularly at high-level institutions, a rigorous set of criteria goes into the hiring process. As in any other field, most involve the routine assessment of knowledge and work history of the applicant, but an almost equally important category, which is never explicitly mentioned in job applications, is the degree by which the applicant fits into "the culture" of the institution. This is an intentionally vague concept that is often invoked internally but in practice manifests the way in which the applicant will conform to the largely corporate dynamics of the institution. A very outspoken individual might be seen as "too disruptive" and not "a team player"; someone who appears to desire a high leadership position when applying for a mid-level job could be seen as problematic or "not a good fit." But mainly, the interview process explores the potential capacity of the applicant to adapt to the required interpersonal, social, class-based, value-driven, and professional protocols that rule a particular organization, explicitly or not. At the museums where I worked, for instance, discretion and restraint were seen as really valuable attributes; the ability to know not to speak out of turn was crucial. The quiet curatorial assistants who put their heads down to work would gradually be rewarded with more responsibilities, culminating in a promotion. The ability to be attentive and at ease among high-level donors was similarly valued, which is also why those who were hired generally came from high-income families.

To be clear, the type of performing speech I am referring to here is different from the public voice of the museum—that is, the interpretive narratives that are shared with visitors, and even the curatorial writing (whether in the form of exhibition essays or museum labels) that is put out there for public consumption. The same goes for marketing or PR language. What I'm referring to is a structure of internal deliberation that is, in fact, key for the day-to-day function of a museum and the many programmatic decisions that its leadership makes. The process requires adept learning and strategic employment of these protocols and language in order to advance the institution's ideas and policy. The job interview I partook in was, in fact, a screen test—the test being that I needed to ad-lib a character without a given script.

I admit, not without certain shame, that I was an active participant in the perpetuation of the protocols of that very culture, which I grew accustomed to over many years. These unspoken criteria applied not just to job interviews but to all kinds of curatorial closed-door meetings where we would discuss research, invite scholars to speak on certain topics, or discuss issues connected with exhibitions. Those gatherings would be conducted mostly in staid, sober, and gray corporate-style meeting rooms, which added to the sense that, as a university classmate in a dense semiotics class once remarked, "you need to rehearse in advance in your mind what you are going to say." Over the years, I adopted the common language shared among us and practiced it with the caution it required. Competition was always present through the introduction of terms, names of artists, and other references that served as proof of erudition, awareness of art projects and exhibitions, as well as the latest advances in related scholarship, but also through the way such knowledge was articulated.

While I suspect the dynamics I am describing are not exclusive to art museums, it does appear that the particular role of the art museum as a tastemaker, gatekeeper, and arbiter of high-end culture has created the demands of a particular economic and cultural model and its intrinsic protocols that, as I will try to argue, are highly fragile and, because of their fragility, highly conservative in their financial and intellectual ambitions. Such observations became particularly apparent during the COVID-19 pandemic. But in order to understand the delicate balance that museums have to enact, it is important to understand their institutional roots.

Going back to the nineteenth century, museums in the United States are built on a dual model of educational institutions and philanthropic initiatives. In a Brookings Institution book on philanthropic foundations, David C. Hammack and Helmut K. Anheier characterize the role and history of advocacy within foundations in the United States:

> As symbols and embodiments of private power, religious authority, modernism, and capitalism, America's philanthropic foundations have always attracted strong views .... America's foundations first appeared in the wake of the American Revolution and played important roles throughout the entire nineteenth century—including key roles in building the nation's "mainstream" Protestant denominations. Carnegie and Rockefeller did not invent the American foundation, though their funds did do remarkable things, especially in the first three decades of the twentieth century.[1]

This advocacy was not only for science or social causes but also for the arts as an avenue to knowledge and social betterment—in a country that was assumed to be "empty," a "new world." American art museums were largely privately funded institutions that collected and promoted different kinds of art for the benefit of the public's own social advancement and skill-building. Since their origins in the nineteenth century, American museums have thus prioritized their educational role while needing to be financially self-sustaining. As with anything in America, including nonprofits, there is always the ambition to grow and lead (or proselytize, as Hammack and Anheier argue), and as a result of that desire, the financial section of museums tends to resemble corporate structures and hierarchies (such as the top-down organization chart and departmental configuration of a company) while the programmatic sector (curatorial and education) tends to resemble academic structures and hierarchies (such as peer review processes and live presentation formats proper of academia). The separation between both areas is key to ensuring that the institution retains a degree of credibility; whenever it becomes clear that financial motivations drive the curatorial program, this spells reputational doom for any museum.

Working inside museums, I regularly observed the dynamic of one side aiming to safeguard the financial viability of the institution while the other ensured that it is a reputable "thought leader" in the field. (The term, which made its appearance in the business world in the 1990s and was later on mocked and satirized in the press, made its way to senior management meetings during my years in museums.) So, in a way, one can say that the museum, since its beginnings, is required to function similarly to both a business (i.e., generating revenue) and a university (i.e., generating knowledge) without properly being either of those things.

However, such aspirations of the museums, to be both financially sustainable and culturally relevant are enormous challenges to establishing themselves as credible organizations in the United States. When it comes to modern and contemporary art, legislators, speaking on behalf of "the American public," (a term more used in politics and not inside the culture world) have historically displayed indifference or lack of understanding about why the arts matter for society. While many agree that the arts offer value to society, they put the arts as among the least important activities in terms of their impact on American lives (as shown in a 2021 study[2] commissioned by the American Academy of Arts and Sciences). Several more polls emerged during the COVID-19 pandemic where the arts were listed as the least essential activities.[3]

For this reason, arts advocates try to find the most compelling arguments for the importance of the arts, most of which, inevitably, speak to their financial impact. The National Endowment for the Arts, for example, advocates for the arts in those terms, arguing that they bring more to the economy than agriculture or transportation.[4] The downside of this argument is that for a successful campaign, arts advocates must de-emphasize the confrontational and critical aspect of art making as expressions that can upset the status quo and propose new ways of thinking. Instead they have to emphasize the more traditional notion of art as a force of good that provides much needed enjoyment, beauty, and fun for the public. This essentially political strategy served Broadway theaters well during the COVID-19 pandemic. As Broadway and other performing arts organizations in America were positioned as not only good for tourism and jobs but also entertainment, they were able to receive funding through the US Senate's Save Our Stages Act,[5] one of the largest single-time infusions of federal funds into the arts in the United States.

This type of advocacy is not new. For many years, museums have faced the challenge of appealing to a wide nonart specialist public (usually tourists) who can see the museum as a source of enjoyment and, sometimes, a social activity. Programming often serves the purpose of attracting this public (such as through blockbuster exhibitions). This revenue-generating public, in turn, helps finance the more experimental or scholarly activities of the museum, which allows the institution to position itself in a leading intellectual capacity in the field. This approach evokes the phrase "robbing Peter to pay Paul." What is important to note is that there is a delicate balance between revenue-generating and experimental/scholarly programming.

On the academic front, precisely due to the widespread skepticism of the relevance of the arts beyond entertainment (especially in determining the value of contemporary art), the discourse around art practices is often highly esoteric. Academic jargon can often serve as a defense mechanism by indirectly emphasizing the complexity and, therefore value, of art for a nonspecialist public. The notion of the white cube, referring to the aspiration to create a neutral space separated from the "real world" where art takes place, serves as a territory reserved for a specialized type of conversation. Meanwhile, within the specialized professional realm of art—and this is something I observed directly for years—there is a quiet tension between museum curators and scholars, where curators yearn for the academic respect that some art historians attain with their writings. In contrast, art historians yearn for the public visibility that curators receive with their exhibitions. As the museum seeks to emulate the university environment, curators adopt behavior and language that reflects it.

On the financial front, museums often adopt corporate structures where most important decisions are made by the executive director and the finance office. While programming decisions regarding exhibition, acquisition, and education are usually part of a deliberative process among the curators and other senior museum leadership, it is understood that the budget sets the real limits of what is possible. In this sense, budget *is* policy.

I encountered this reality when I was ordered, as a senior program manager, to end all the part-time museum educator contracts, two weeks into the COVID-19 pandemic. These individuals, mostly women of color who received a modest hourly wage without health benefits, were let go during the worst health crisis of our generation and thrown into great uncertainty and a fearsome situation. Later that summer, after the murder of George Floyd, art institutions responded with a knee-jerk reaction in their programming, emphasizing the presentation of Black artists and turbo-charging their exhibition and hiring policies to support Black communities—actions that, while significant, can't mask inequities such as the firing of part-time educators or the long-standing realities of a white-majority board and leadership.

Both events, which took place during the watershed year of 2020, symbolize a cultural moment best illustrated by two interrelated concepts: "racial capitalism" (as coined by Cedric Robinson[6]) and "white fragility" (as articulated by Robin DiAngelo).[7] The hard-earned attainment of cultural and economic status by art museums in the United States has been accomplished by separating its programmatic voice (for example, presenting exhibitions of artists of color) from its governance practices (including Black voices in their boards and ensuring that its top leadership reflects the diversity of the city and the country). In fairness to museum leadership and following on the role that I found myself trying to play within that environment, those working within museums know very well this is a problem, but they do not see a clear path to properly address it. I do believe that museum directors, senior curators, and museum boards would be well served by reflecting on how racial capitalism and white fragility still determine the programmatic and financial structures of their museums, not unlike the white, heteronormative rules that continue to dominate the discourse within corporate culture and academia. To begin dismantling these rules, a first step, I am convinced, is to observe and critique the language and performative protocols that characterize these fragilities.

On one occasion during my museum career, I encountered an instance where transparency and the acknowledgment of not-knowing led to a rewriting of scripts. Connie Butler and Luis Pérez-Oramas, curators of MoMA's Lygia Clark retrospective (2014), approached us in the education department to help address the question of how to present Clark's therapeutic practice to the public—a practice of hers developed late in her career in which she used objects for therapeutic exercises that she had publicly declared to not be art anymore. In addition to not being an ostensibly exhibitable aspect of her work, Clark's therapies were private, not something that could be presented to large audiences. We traveled to Rio de Janeiro to meet with Lula Wanderley and Gina Ferreira, Clark's studio assistants and the only people she had approved to continue doing her therapies, to work with us and our educators to find a solution to present the spirit of Clark's work. In the end, we did so by inviting the public to experience her "relational objects" (objects that she created prior to her therapeutic work) and witness the therapies as one educator would perform them on another. While there's no way to know if Clark herself would have approved this approach, the final presentation was the result of a rigorous process of research and collaboration with the closest living specialists around this aspect of Clark's work, and we were certain that we arrived to the most accurate illustration of her process while acknowledging the impossibility of reproducing the original experience. None of this would have been possible if the entire team (curators, educators, and Clark's assistants) had not undertaken the task with humility, transparency, and the full willingness to accurately honor Clark's legacy.

I'm reminded of one of Miguel de Cervantes' most memorable *Novelas ejemplares* (*Exemplary Novels*), "El Licenciado Vidriera" ("The Lawyer of Glass"), the story of a man who, after drinking a love potion, develops the delusion that he is entirely made of glass and at risk of breaking into a thousand pieces. No one is allowed to get close to him, he believes he can only eat bland foods, and he sleeps inside a stable amid a mound of hay. His story is a parable of how our own delusions make us fragile and incapable of dealing with the real world.

As cultural workers, we are now in another crucial, collective job interview where, again, there are no guiding questions. It is up to us to construct the right protocols for confronting our weaknesses, to recognize the roles we play, and to allow for a new script to be written.

1 Helmut K. Anheier and David C. Hammock, *American Foundations: Roles and Contributions* (Washington, DC: Brookings Institution Press, 2010).

2 "What We Value: American Opinions about the Work of Artists," American Academy of Arts and Sciences News, October 19, 2021, https://www.amacad.org/news/american-opinions-about-artists.

3 José da Silva, "How Beret Dare They: Survey Says Artists Are the Most Non-Essential Workers," *Art Newspaper*, June 16, 2020, https://www.theartnewspaper.com/2020/06/16/how-beret-dare-they-survey-says-artists-are-the-most-non-essential-workers.

4 "The Arts Contribute More than $760 Billion to the U.S. Economy," National Endowment for the Arts, press release, March 6, 2018, https://www.arts.gov/news/press-releases/2018/arts-contribute-more-760-billion-us-economy.

5 "Save Our Stages: Cornyn-Klobuchar Bill Providing Relief for Independent Entertainment Venues Expected to Pass Today," United States Senator Amy Klobuchar, press release, December 21, 2020, https://www.klobuchar.senate.gov/public/index.cfm/2020/12/save-our-stages-cornyn-klobuchar-bill-providing-relief-for-independent-entertainment-venues-expected-to-pass-today#:~:text=In%20June%2C%20Cornyn%20and%20Klobuchar,affected%20by%20the%20coronavirus%20pandemic.

6 Cedric J. Robinson, *Cedric J. Robinson: On Racial Capitalism, Black Internationalism, and Cultures of Resistance*, ed. H. L. T. Quan (London: Pluto Press, 2019).

7 Robin DiAngelo, *White Fragility: Why It's So Hard for White People to Talk About Racism* (Boston: Beacon Press, 2018).

OF

THE

some notes:

. these are erasure poems made from redacting UNESCO's Intangible Heritage documents (ITH/12/7.COM/11 ADD.3; Convention for the Safeguarding of the Intangible Cultural Heritage / Intergovernmental Committee for the Safeguarding of the Intangible Cultural Heritage

. film stills from *O dust* (2022), which I filmed at the UNESCO headquarters in Paris, FR; in the Intangible Heritage archives, conference rooms, through the interpreters' booths and machines; in order to make another kind of speech—one that evades the bureaucratic narrative
one for my late grandmother
one that I utter to myself
one that remembers the forgotten, the inherited (lyrics)

the impermanent, and the untranslatable—
like the utterances, hums, 혼잣말, and murmurs carried across tongues, breaths, and time

INTAGIBLE

Jesse Chun

OF THE INTANGIBLE

movement of living
inherited repertoires thousands of tunes
a thousand place
hundred thousand thousands of tens of
thousands

strips of ribbon

raise altars along the route; steeped in

transmission of memory

Inscribe

mountain in their ancestors and pray for good weather,

beginning of

the key rite

bearers

chanting,

courage

there is no evidence of the free

bearers

in

chorus
collective fishing,
the sacred bond between

spirits
coming

coming

forth

the same

inappropriate vocabulary,

spirit of

proper place

the desired
place

the Body, the absence

even disappearance

to the tangible
'whose existence is
words

I   singing,

                                    voices
stand in a tight semicircle   singing

without the help of notation
and
    inherit

(-making) and
the unique
jargon

poetry

the island

, a
fire

Coming forth

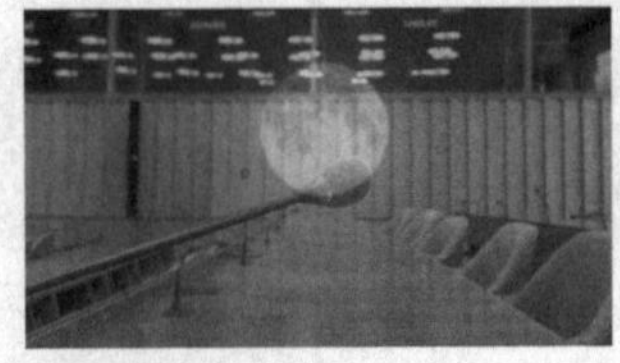

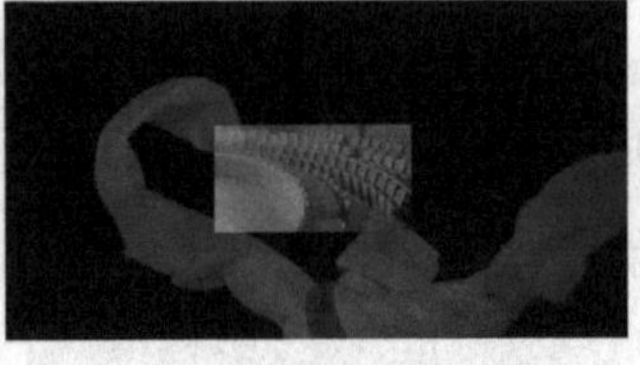

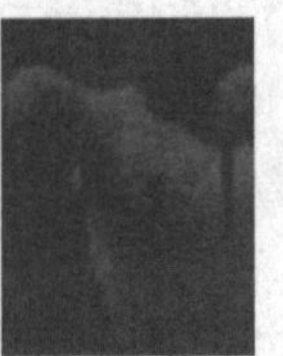

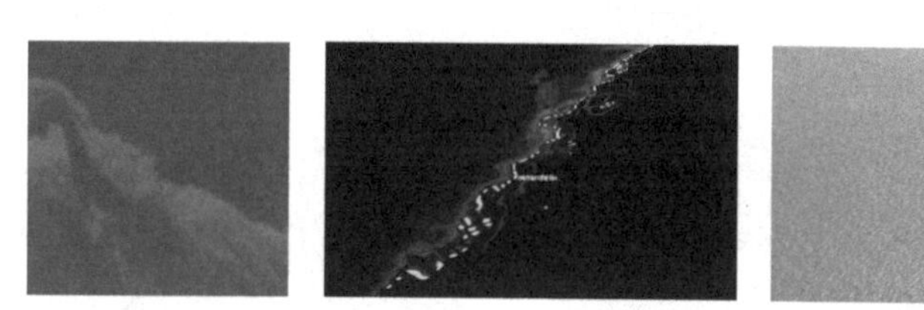

AS FOR PROTOCOLS: A CURRICULUM

Two years of programs, seminars, fellowship projects, publications, exhibitions, and prize initiative form the basis for this book. What follows is a noncomprehensive listing of the work presented by the Vera List Center for Art and Politics as part of the *As for Protocols* Focus Theme. We present it here not as an archive but as a constellation of interrelated ideas and exchanges between artists, writers, and peer organizations on the topic of protocols as practice. All of the public programs are recorded and available at veralistcenter.org.

2020-2022 VLC Fellows

Carolina Caycedo, Borderlands Fellow
Maria Hupfield, Borderlands Fellow
Etcétera, Boris Lurie Fellow
Adelita Husni Bey, VLC Fellow
Rasheedah Phillips, VLC Fellow

2020-2022 Jane Lombard Prize for Art and Social Justice

Avni Sethi, prize recipient

Jorge González, Jane Lombard Fellow
NayanTara Gurung Kakshapati, Jane Lombard Fellow
Emeka Okereke, Jane Lombard Fellow
Underground Resistance, Jane Lombard Fellow

Prelude, *Training for the Not-Yet: Protocols in the Making*, May 19, 2020, online.

With artist Jeanne van Heeswijk, musician Angel Bat Dawid, artist Adelita Husni Bey, designer Sandra Lange, and artist Joy Mariama Smith.

***Seminar 1: Protocols as Language and Communication*, September 14, 2020, online.**

With Shannon Mattern, Professor of Anthropology at The New School; artist, educator, and activist Taeyoon Choi; artist Jesse Chun; Meredith D. Clark, Assistant Professor of Media Studies at the University of Virginia; and blind tech educator and activist Chancey Fleet.

***Vera List Center Forum 2020: As for Protocols*, October 6-10, 2020, online.**

Performance, *The Berger Object: A Tribute to Maurice Berger, Part I*, October 6, 2020, online.

With Molly Rose Kaufman, co-director, University of Orange; public health practitioner and Ultra-red member Michael A. Roberson; and Robert Sember, Ultra-red member and VLC Fellow, 2009-2011.

Panel, *On Race, Representation, and White Lies: A Tribute to Maurice Berger, Part II*, October 6, 2020, online.

With Kinshasha Holman Conwill, Deputy Director, National Museum of African American History and Culture; Courtney R. Baker, Associate Professor, Department of English, University of California, Riverside; Lonnie G. Bunch III, Secretary of the Smithsonian Institution; Nona Faustine, photographer and visual artist; David Gonzalez, journalist and co-editor, the *New York Times Lens* blog; and Sarah Lewis, Associate Professor, Department of History of Art and Architecture, Department of African and African American Studies, Harvard University.

Performance, *Palais de Mari: A Tribute to Maurice Berger, Part III*, October 6, 2020, online.

With Sarah Rothenberg, pianist, artistic director of DACAMERA, and 1995 VLC Fellow.

Conversation, *Borderlands: VLC Fellow Carolina Caycedo in Conversation with Natalie Diaz*, October 7, 2020, online.

Artist Carolina Caycedo, 2020-2022 VLC Borderlands Fellow, and Akimel O'odham poet Natalie Diaz.

Screening and Dialogue, *Gathering: VLC Fellow Adelita Husni Bey in Dialogue with Robert Sember*, October 7, 2020, online.

Artist Adelita Husni Bey and Robert Sember, Ultra-red member and former VLC Fellow 2009-2011.

Conversation and Performance, *From Errorism to NEO-EXTRA-ACTIVISM: VLC Fellow Etcétera and Jennifer Ponce de León*, October 8, 2020, online.

Artist collective Etcétera and Jennifer Ponce de León, Associate Professor of English at the University of Pennsylvania.

Conversation, On *Protocol: VLC Fellow Maria Hupfield in Conversation with Leanne Betasamosake Simpson*, October 8, 2020, online.

Artist and Borderlands Fellow Maria Hupfield and scholar, writer, and musician Leanne Betasamosake Simpson.

Lecture, *Towards a Temporal Rezoning: Unmapping the Time Zones. A Talk by VLC Fellow Rasheedah Phillips*, October 8, 2020, online.

Artist and lawyer Rasheedah Phillips and Mia Charlene White, Assistant Professor of Environmental Studies in the Environmental Studies Program at The New School.

Keynote, *The Computable and the Uncomputable, October 9, 2020, online.*

Alexander Galloway, media theorist and Professor in the Department of Media, Culture, and Communication, New York University.

Convening, *What Protocols Are Needed Now? & Announcement of 2020-2022 Jane Lombard Prize for Art and Social Justice*, October 10, 2020, online.

With Ivet Ćurlin, curator, WHW; Natasha Ginwala, curator, Gropius Bau; Candice Hopkins, Director and Chief Curator, Forge Project; Carin Kuoni, VLC Senior Director/Chief Curator, Tamara Oyola-Santiago, public health educator and activist, Director of Wellness and Health Promotion at Student Health Services, The New School; and Shuddhabrata Sengupta, artist, Raqs Media Collective.

***Seminar 2: Protocols for Community and Equitable Networks* [*as Applied to Education*], October 19, 2020, online.**

With artist and former VLC Fellow Robert Sember and art critic Jennifer Kabat; artist Shani Peters of The Black School; Tsige Tafesse of the collective BUFU (By Us For Us); and artist Caitlin Cherry, founder and co-director of Dark Study.

Book Launch and Conversation, *The Idols of ISIS: From Assyria to the Internet*, November 1, 2020, online.

With artist Michael Rakowitz, writer Rijin Sahakian, writer and scholar Aaron Tugendhaft, and scholar Wendy M. K. Shaw.

***AICA-USA Distinguished Critic Lecture: Carolina A. Miranda: Going Local*, November 11, 2020, online.**

With Carolina Miranda, arts journalist and *Los Angeles Times* columnist.

Seminar 3: *Bring Forth the Body: Biopower, Protocol and Plagues*, November 16, 2020, online.

With Josh Scannell, Assistant Professor of Digital Media Theory, The New School; Anthony Ryan Hatch, sociologist and Associate Professor and Chair of the Science in Society Program at Wesleyan University; Ronak K. Kapadia, Associate Professor and the Director of Graduate Studies in Gender and Women's Studies, University of Illinois at Chicago; and Jasbir Puar, theorist and Professor and Graduate Director of Women's and Gender Studies, Rutgers University.

Book Launch, *Forces of Art: Perspectives from a Changing World*, November 26, 2020, online with the Prince Claus Fund, Hivos, and the European Cultural Foundation.

With journalist Aldith Hunkar; artist Heba Amin; artist Pierre-Christophe Gam; and writers and editorial team members Jordi Baltà Portolés, Nora N. Khan, Carin Kuoni, and Serubiri Moses.

***Seminar 4: Reimagining Protocols: Reclaiming, Challenging, and Queering Surveillance Protocol and Plagues*, February 8, 2021, online.**

With Fabiola Hanna, Assistant Professor of Emerging Media, The New School; artist and The New School faculty member American Artist; Shaka McGlotten, Purchase College Professor of Media Studies and Anthropology; Margaret Laurena Kemp, UC Davis Professor of Theatre and performer; and new media artist Abram Stern (aphid).

Panel, *Climate Relations: Indigeneity in Activism, Art, and Digital Media*, February 11, 2021, online.

With artist Maria Hupfield; curator and activist Regan De Loggans; Mikinaak Migwans, Assistant Professor of Indigenous Contemporary Art in Canada at University of Toronto; Anne Swartz, Savannah College of Art and Design; Connie Tell, independent curator, The Feminist Art Project; Jennifer Wemigwans, Assistant Professor in the Department of Leadership, Higher and Adult Education, Ontario Institute for Studies in Education.

Panel, *Communication After Refusal: The Turn to Love and Polyvocality*, February 22, 2021, online.

With artist Deanna Bowen; editor and producer Camille Crain Drummond; writer Anaïs Duplan; and artist Rasheedah Phillips.

***Seminar 5: Protocols of Revolutionary Feminisms to Re/make the World*, March 8, 2021, online.**

With Ujju Aggarwal, Assistant Professor of Anthropology and Experiential Learning, Schools of Public Engagement, The New School; Laura Y. Liu, Associate Professor of Global Studies and Geography, Eugene Lang College, The New School; Loira Limbal, film director and producer; Nadine Naber, Professor, Gender and Women's Studies and Global Asian Studies, University of Illinois at Chicago; Paula X. Rojas, midwife and community organizer;

and Robyn Spencer, historian, Associate Professor, History, CUNY, Lehman College.

Conversation and Reading, *Strategies for Survival: Black Feminist Manifestos*, March 13, 2021, online with Weeksville Heritage Center.

With readings by Cassandre Davilmar, Adina English, Danielle Moulton, Ebony Noelle Golden, Anika Paris, Nina Pluviose, Marguerite Thompson, Paige Wint and Olaronke Akinmowo, artist, scholar, cultural worker, founder of the Free Black Women's Library; a conversation with Aiesha Turman, founder of the The Black Girl Project, Gabriela López Dena, program curator, Zakiya Collier, Project Archivist, Weeksville Heritage Center; and workshop facilitation by Alyssa James, co-host, Zora's Daughters Podcast, Brendane Tynes, co-host, Zora's Daughters Podcast.

Screening, *Helene Kazan: Frames of Accountability*, March 15, 2021, online with UnionDocs.

With 2018-2020 VLC Fellow Helene Kazan and Soyoung Yoon, Assistant Professor and Program Director of Art History and Visual Studies at the Department of the Arts, Eugene Lang College of Liberal Arts, The New School.

Conversation, *Jorge González Brown Bag Lunch*, March 18, 2021, online.

With artist and Jane Lombard Fellow Jorge González.

***Seminar 6: Lab Work: Art of the Experiment*, April 5, 2021, online.**

With Jeannine Tang, Assistant Professor of Modern/Contemporary Art History and Visual Studies, The New School; artist fields harrington, artist Mary Maggic; artist Claire Pentecost; and Deboleena Roy, Dean of Faculty and Professor, Neuroscience and Behavioral Biology and Women's, Gender, and Sexuality Studies, Emory University.

Laboratory, *NO WORK, NO SHOP: Socio-Environmental Imagination and Pedagogies of Action*, April 22-23, 2021, online.

Keynote, *Extrativismos y Desarrollo | Alternativas y Desobediencia*, April 22, 2021, online, with Eduardo Gudynas, Director and Senior Research, the Latin American Center on Social Ecology.

Introduction by Mariana Amatullo, Vice Provost for Global Executive Education and Online Strategic Initiatives, The New School. Closing remarks by Leonardo E. Figueroa Helland, Chair, Environmental Policy and Sustainability Manage-

ment/Chair, Indigeneity, Decolonization and Just Sustainability Section, Tishman Environment and Design Center, The New School.

Conversation, with Boris Lurie Fellow and artist collective Etcétera (Loreto Garín Guzmán and Federico Zukerfeld); artists Eduardo Molinari and Azul Blaseotto; Steve Lyons, Director of Research, The Natural History Museum; philosopher Brian Holmes; and artist Claire Pentecost.

Symposium, *As for Protocols—To Hold Things Together,* May 20-21, 2021, online with BAK basis voor actuele kunst.

Panel, *Affective Protocols of Locality,* May 20, 2021.

With Mitchell Esajas, The Black Archives; Maria Hlavajova and Rachel Raekes, BAK basis voor actuele kunst; Elizabeth Povinelli, Karrabing Film Collective; and Norberto "Pee Wee" Roldan, Green Papaya Projects.

Discussion, *On Artistic Coalition and Institutional-Communal Nodality,* May 20, 2021.

With VLC Fellow Adelita Husni Bey; Carin Kuoni, VLC Senior Director/Chief Curator; artist and co-founder of Invisible Borders Emeka Okereke; Rolando Vazquez and Rosalba Icaza, Maria Lugones Decolonial Summer School; and Gudskul members Angga Wijaya, farid rakun, Gesyada Siregar.

Panel, *Hél čhaŋkú kiŋ ȟpáye (There lies the road). A Dialogue About Making Art in a Good Way,* May 20, 2021.

With Oglála Lakȟóta artist Suzanne Kite; Anishinaabe artist Scott Benesiinaabandan; Clementine Bourdeaux, Sičáŋ u Oglála Lakóta, Postdoctoral Fellow University of California, Riverside, UCLA; and Jason Edward Lewis, Hawaiian and Samoan digital media theorist, University Research Chair, Concordia University.

Seminar, *Spectral Labor and Unpayable Debt,* May 21, 2021.

Stefano Harney, author and researcher, Royal Holloway, University of London; Massimiliano Mollona, writer, filmmaker, and anthropologist, and Senior Lecturer, Goldsmiths College, University of London; and Denise Ferreira da Silva, Professor and Director of the Institute for Gender, Race, Sexuality and Social Justice at the University of British Columbia, Vancouver.

Ceremony, *LOS QUE MUEREN POR LA VIDA, NO PUEDEN LLAMARSE MUERTOS! (Those Who Die for Life, Cannot Be Called Dead!)*, September 18, 2021, El Museo del Barrio.

With VLC Fellow Carolina Caycedo; Tania Aparicio Morales, VLC Graduate Student Fellow, The New School; musicians Daphne Faulkner Valiente and Jessica Valiente; composer Rick Faulkner; Susanna Temkin, Curator, El Museo del Barrio; and artist Cecilia Vicuña.

***Seminar 7: Drones and the Bird's-Eye View*, September 20, 2021, online.**

With Melanie Kress, High Line Art Associate Curator; Heba Y. Amin, artist, Professor of Art, ABK - Stuttgart State Academy of Art and Design; Peter Asaro, Associate Professor, The New School; and Roger D. Connor, Curator, Smithsonian National Air and Space Museum.

Forum, *Vera List Center Forum 2021: As for Protocols*, October 12-16, 2021, online and at The Clemente Soto Vélez Cultural & Educational Center, The New School, UnionDocs, and Weeksville Heritage Center.

Exhibition, *Owed to a Certain Emptiness: Infra-structuring the Conflictorium*, October 9-24, 2021, Arnold and Sheila Aronson Galleries at Parsons School of Design, The New School.

Catalogue, *Vera List Center Forum 2021: As for Protocols*. Essays by Salome Asega, Adil Hossain, Michelle Marxuach, Naeem Mohaiemen, Eriola Pira, and Avni Sethi. 2021.

Conversations on Infrastructuring, October 9-24, 2021, Arnold and Sheila Aronson Galleries at Parsons School of Design, The New School.

With Avni Sethi and Manan Ahmed, historian and Associate Professor, Columbia University; Kemi Ilesanmi, former Executive Director, The Laundromat Project; Emily Johnson, dancer, writer, choreographer and activist; Carin Kuoni, VLC Senior Director/Chief Curator; Shaun Leonardo, artist and co-director of Recess; Shannon Mattern, former Professor of Anthropology, The New School for Social Research; Paloma McGregor, choreographer, artistic Director of Angela's Pulse; Tamara Oyola Santiago, public health educator and activist; VLC Curator Eriola Pira; Robert Sember, former VLC Fellow and member of sound-art collective Ultra-red; Radhika Subramaniam, Associate Professor, Visual Culture, Parsons School of Design; Jennifer Tipton, lighting designer; and Hrag Vartanian, Editor-in-Chief and co-founder of *Hyperallergic*.

***VLC Forum 2021 Day One: Invisible Borders Trans-African Photographers Organization*, October 12, 2021, online and at UnionDocs.**

Workshop, *Invisible Borders Trans-African Photographers Organization*, October 12, 2021, online, with artists and members and collaborators of Invisible Borders Trans-African Photographers Organization including: Reem Alfahad, Tope Adegoke, Uche James Iroha, Mathangi Krishnamurthy, Sadia Marium, Yemoh Odoi, Emeka Okereke, Zaynab Odunsi, Tom Saater, and Kay Ugwuede.

Screening and Conversation, *Coming Together,* October 12, 2021, UnionDocs, with artists and members of Invisible Borders Trans-African Photographers Organization James Uche Iroha, Emeka Okereke, and Kay Ugwuede.

***VLC Forum 2021 Day Two: Nepal Picture Library*, October 13, 2021, online.**

Screening, *Nepal Picture Library: A Presentation,* with photographer Nayantara Gurung Kakshapati.

Workshop, *Artist Books for Children* with the Center for Book Arts, with artist and educator María Verónica San Martín.

***VLC Forum 2021 Day Three: Underground Resistance*, October 14, 2021, Weeksville Heritage Center, Brooklyn.**

Conversation, *Underground Resistance and Friends:* A Conversation, with Underground Resistance members Cornelius Harris and Nomadico; educator Daniel Zarazua; and multidisciplinary artist Shyboi Yulan Grant).

Performance, *DJ set: UR presents Nomadico,* with Underground Resistance member Nomadico.

***VLC Forum 2021 Day Four: Conflictorium*, October 15, 2021, online.**

Conversation, Jane Lombard Prize recipient Avni Sethi and Amar Kanwar, artist and filmmaker.

***VLC Forum 2021 Day Five: Escuela de Oficios*, October 14, 2021, The Clemente Soto Vélez Cultural & Educational Center.**

With artist Jorge González and artists Monica Rodriguez (La Germinal) and Kultura Dyad.

Seminar 8: *Work in the Cultural Economy We Want: Cooperatives*, November 8, 2021, online.

Caroline Woolard, artist, Co-Founder, Project Development and Research Steward, Art.coop; Pia Mancini, co-founder and CEO, Open Collective;

Ramsey Nasser, computer scientist and game designer, co-founder of Emma Technology Cooperative; Daniel Park, US Federation of Worker Cooperatives.

Lecture and Performance, *RESPONSE ABILITY* A Manifesto on Ecocide*, November 19, 2021, online with ArtsLink Assembly 2021.

With Etcétera and Jay Bernstein, University Distinguished Professor of Philosophy at The New School, and performance artist L. M. Bogad.

Lecture, *AICA-USA Distinguished Critic Lecture: Legacy Russell*, November 29, 2021, online.

With curator and writer Legacy Russell.

Exhibition and Performance, *Hél čhaŋkú kiŋ ȟpáye (There lies the road)*, December 3-12, 2021, PS122 Gallery.

With Oglála Lakȟóta artist Suzanne Kite.

Catalogue, *Kite: Hél čhaŋkú kiŋ ȟpáye (There lies the road)*. Essay by Riel Bellow, accompanied by a digital project with sound contribution by Kite. Designed by Bobby Joe Smith III. 2021.

Seminar 9: *Bridge: Protocols of Jazz and Modernism*, December 6, 2021, online.

With curator Serubiri Moses; performance artist Raymond Pinto, Tendayi Sithole, Associate Professor, Department of Political Sciences, University of South Africa; and Yoko Suzuki, saxophonist and scholar.

Symposium, *Rethinking Residencies Symposium*, December 8-10. 2021, online in partnership with Abrons Arts Center, Eyebeam, Fire Island Artist Residency, Flux Factory, International Studio & Curatorial Program (ISCP), Lower Manhattan Cultural Council (LMCC), Queens Museum, Pioneer Works, Recess, Shandaken Projects, EFA Project Space's SHIFT Residency, Triangle, Wave Farm, Wave Hill and W.O.W. Project.

With Jamie Blosser, Executive Director, Santa Fe Art Institute; artist Eve Biddle; artist Tania Candiani; curator and writer Kari Conte; artist Lizania Cruz; arts administrator Christina Daniels; artist Robin Everett; curator Dylan Gauthier; Gabriel de Guzman, Director of Arts and Chief Curator, Wave Hill; Susan Hapgood, Executive Director, International Studio & Curatorial Program (ISCP); artist Laila Hida; artist Emily Jacir; interdisciplinary artist Jeff Kasper; cultural producer and educator Irmeli Kokko; artist and educator M. Carmen Lane; artist Catherine Lee; curator Eileen Jeng Lynch; curator Francesca Masoero; Sally Mizrachi, Executive Director and

General Coordinator, lugar a dudas; VLC Curator and Director of Programs Eriola Pira; Emily Pethick, Director, Rijksakademie van beeldende kunsten; artist Howardena Pindell; interdisciplinary art worker Sanna Ritvanen; artist Mierle Laderman Ukeles; arts worker Stephanye Watts; and Nick Weist, director of Shandanken Projects.

Symposium, *Remote Control: Surveying Drones and Culture Today*, February 9-11, 2022, online in partnership with High Line Arts.

With Spencer Ackerman, journalist and author; Saks Afridi and Ali Rez, artists and collaborators; Raven Chacon, artist, composer; Christoph Cox, philosopher, critic, and curator; Sam Durant, artist; activist Monther Etaky; Omer Fast, artist; Guillermo Galindo, composer and artist; Aziz Hazara, artist; activist Kathy Kelly; Sonia Kennebeck, filmmaker and journalist; Melanie Kress, High Line Art Associate Curator; Erik Lin-Greenberg, Assistant Professor, Political Science, Massachusetts Institute of Technology; Muheb Esmat, writer and curator; Arthur Holland Michel, writer and researcher; Chantal Meloni, International Crimes and Accountability, European Center for Constitutional and Human Rights (ECCHR); Hina Shamsi, Director, ACLU National Security Project; and filmmaker Alon Sicherman; Lucy Suchman, Professor Emerita, Anthropology of Science and Technology, Lancaster University, United Kingdom; Madiha Tahir, journalist and filmmaker; artist Sean Vegezzi; artist Hajra Waheed; activist and Women's Indigenous Media director Brooke Waukau; and researcher Taniel Yusef.

Exhibition and Programs, *Adelita Husni Bey: These Conditions*, February 8-April 10, 2022, Brooklyn Army Terminal.

Catalogue, *Adelita Husni Bey: These Conditions*. Libretto by artist. Designed by Other Means. 2022.

Study Group, *On Necessary Work: Robert Wallace*, February 17, 2022, online with the Department of Drawing and Printmaking, Victorian College of the Arts.

With Adelita Husni Bey and Rob Wallace, evolutionary epidemiologist with the Agroecology and Rural Economics Research Corps in St. Paul.

Workshop, *Family Prop-making Workshop with Adelita Husni Bey*, February 19, 2022, Brooklyn Army Terminal.

Poetry Reading, *A Reading in These Conditions*, February 24, 2022, Brooklyn Army Terminal.

With Adelita Husni Bey and poets Hannah Black, Benjamin Krusling, and Nora Treatbaby.

Workshop, *Movement-based Workshop with Adelita Husni Bey*, March 5, 2022, Brooklyn Army Terminal.

Performance, *Duvet*, March 6, 2022, Brooklyn Army Terminal.

With dancers Leslie Cuyjet, Weena Pauly, Eleanor Smith, David Thomson, Katie Workum, Anna Thérèse Witenberg, and Darrin Wright.

Study Group, *On Necessary Work with Imogen Beynon and Consuelo Vargas*, online with the Department of Drawing and Printmaking, Victorian College of the Arts.

With Adelita Husni Bey and Imogen Beynon, Deputy Director at the United Workers Union, and Consuelo Vargas, registered nurse and member of National Nurses United.

***Seminar 10: School of Tomorrow: From the Open Plan to the Tele-classroom*, March 14, 2022, online (postponed).**

With Video School (artist Gabo Camnitzer, curator Zoey Lubitz, and curator Candice Strongwater).

Study Group, *On Necessary Work*, March 17, 2022, Brooklyn Army Terminal and online with the Department of Drawing and Printmaking, Victorian College of the Arts.

With Adelita Husni Bey and writers Chiara Bottici and M. E. O'Brien.

Conversation, *Adelita Husni Bey in conversation with Eriola Pira*, March 19, 2022, Brooklyn Army Terminal.

With Adelita Husni Bey and Eriola Pira.

Conversation, *On Conditions and Conditionality: Ecological Injustices and the Biopolitics of Resistance*, April 2, 2022, Brooklyn Army Terminal with Contemporary Aesthetics Research Collaborative (CARC), Department of Arts and Arts Professions at NYU.

With Adelita Husni Bey, poet and essayist Kay Gabriel, and philosopher Romy Opperman, Assistant Professor of Philosophy, The New School.

Teach in, *Teach-In on Ukraine for Artists, Activists, and Arts Workers*, March 12, 2022, online with Creative Time.

With Mohammad Al Attar, playwright and essayist; Larissa Babji, writer and curator; Luba Cortes, Immigrant Defense Coordinator, Make the Road; Nadine Farid Johnson, Director, PEN America; Chelsi West Ohueri, University of Texas Austin Assistant Professor in the Department of Slavic and Eurasion Studies; Jessica Pisano, Associate Professor of Politics, The New School; and Mykola Ridnyi, artist.

***Seminar 11: Forces of Art: Protocols of Evaluation*, April 4, 2022, online.**

With Mbali Dhlamini and Phumulani Ntuli, members of the Johannesburg-based artist collective Pre-empt Group; curator Kabelo Malatsie; and artist and cultural producer Rocca Holly-Namb.

Exhibition, *Black Quantum Futurism: Time Zone Protocols*, April 4-18, 2022, Parsons School of Design, Anna-Maria and Stephen Kellen Gallery.

Catalogue, *Black Quantum Futurism: Time Zone Protocols*. Essay by Rasheedah Phillips. Designed by Partner & Partners. 2022.

Symposium, *Prime Meridian Unconference*, April 15-17, 2022, online and Parsons School of Design, Anna-Maria and Stephen Kellen Gallery.

Lecture, *Undesigning Systemic Time For Temporal Liberation And Reparations*, April 15, 2022, with artists Black Quantum Futurism (Rasheedah Philips and Camae Ayewa).

Screening, *Reticulation.1993.2019*, April 15, 2022. with scholar Katherine McKittrick, Professor and Canada Research Chair in Black Studies.

Workshop, *The Sun*, April 15, 2022, with artists Mendi + Keith Obadike.

Lecture, *Dead Line?: On Slowing Down in Black "Space-time,"* April 16, 2022. with Danielle Purifoy, Assistant Professor in the Department of Geography at The University of North Carolina at Chapel Hill (UNC).

Lecture, *Bending Space-Time with Botanicals*, April 16, 2022, with Asia Dorsey, herbalist and educator.

Lecture, *Cloud Time*, April 16, 2022, with V. Mitch McEwen, architect and Assistant Professor at Princeton University School of Architecture.

Lecture, *Occupying Vacancy: Looking at Detroit's Grassroot Activation of Vacant Land and Structures*, April 16, 2022, with Ujijji Davis

Williams, landscape architect, urban planner, and researcher.

Screening, *Prentice's Joy*, April 16, 2022, with Andrea Roberts.

Lecture, *Timecasting with Entropy & Lasers*, April 16, 2022, with Kendra Krueger, intersectional scientist and educator.

Lecture, *Epochs, Ages, and Yugas: Macro-Temporal Texture and the Expiration of White Power*, April 16, 2022, with Thomas Stanley (Bushmeat), artist, author, and activist.

Lecture, *CHRONOMORPHISM: A Conversation on the Black Speculative Science of Time Travel with Dwayne McDuffie*, April 17, 2022, with Walter D. Greason, chair of the Department of History at Macalester College.

Workshop, *Grief Reparations and Temporal Hush Harbors*, April 17, 2022, with Joy Tabernacle-KMT, miracle midwife and Alkhemist.

Lecture, *Black Fugitive Infrastructures and Cross-time Space Routines*, April 17, 2022, with Celeste Winston, Assistant Professor in Geography and Urban Studies at Temple University.

Lecture, *The Future of Time: The Metaverse and Black Health*, April 17, 2022, with Ingrid LaFleur, curator, design innovationist, pleasure activist.

Workshop, *Malleable Futures*, April 17, 2022, with Ingrid Raphaël, filmmaker.

Performance, *Land, Entangled Space, and Time* April 17, 2022, with musician Camae Ayewa.

Performance, *Super Massive Thunder Boom Ultimate Collection*, May 6, 2022, in partnership with Abrons Arts Center.

With 2022-2024 Borderlands Fellow Maria Hupfield and multidisciplinary artist and performer Ange Loft; performers The Dime Collective (Eruoma Awashish, Nahka Bertrand, Sarah Cleary, and Sarah Zakaib); artist and educator Dennis RedMoon Darkeem; and performance art band Jane Schoolcraft with writer Nicole Wallace.

Performance and Gathering, *La Siembra*, May 7, 2022, Union Settlement.

With Borderlands Fellow Carolina Caycedo, Arizona water protectors Nellie Jo David and Amber Ortega; Tatiana Roa Avendaño, environmentalist, educator, and researcher of Censat Agua Viva; and

Romy Opperman, Mellon Postdoctoral Fellow in Philosophy at The New School for Social Research.

Seminar 12: *Breaking Protocols: Desire Lines*, May 16, 2022, online.

With Joshua Lubin-Levy, Part-Time Lecturer, The New School; artist duo Rashaun Mitchell + Silas Riener; dance artist and audio describer Tess Dworman; architect Jing Liu; and performance curator and scholar Noémie Solomon.

Exhibition, *NEO-EXTRA-ACTVISM Protocols for Buen Vivir*, May 20, 2022, The Clemente Soto Vélez Cultural & Educational Center.

With the artist collective Boris Lurie Fellow Etcetéra.

Catalogue, *Etcétera: NEO-EXTRA-ACTIVISM-Protocols for Buen Vivir.* Essay by Tania Aparicio Morales. Designed by Buena Gráfica Social Studio (FKA Counterform).

Book, *Breaking Protocol*, co-published by Inventory Press and the Vera List Center for Art and Politics. Designed by IN-FO.CO. 2023.

With VLC Fellow Maria Hupfield and written contributions and artworks by Jackson 2bears, Pelenakeke Brown, Katherine Carl, Re'al Christian, Christen Clifford, TJ Cuthand, Raven Davis, Vanessa Dion Fletcher, Gabrielle L'Hirondelle Hill, Candice Hopkins, Akiko Ichikawa, Ursula Johnson, Kite, Charles Koroneho, Carin Kuoni, Tanya Lukin Linklater, Cathy Mattes, Peter Morin, Meagan Musseau, Wanda Nanibush, Archer Pechawis, Rosanna Raymond, Skeena Reece, Georgiana Uhlyarik, and Charlene Vickers, and reflections on Rebecca Belmore, Lori Blondeau, Dennis Redmoon Darkheem, Natalie Diaz, the Dime Collective, Cheryl L'Hirondelle, Jane Schoolcraft, and Laakkuluk Williamson Bathory.

Book launch, with Maria Hupfield and Thomas (T.) Jean Lax, October 8, 2023, Artbook @ MoMA PS1.

Book launch, *Off Script: Breaking Protocol and Aural Poetics*, March 2, 2024, University of British Columbia, with Morris and Helen Belkin Art Gallery with support from the Vancouver Art Book Fair.

With Re'al Christian, Maria Hupfield, Peter Morin, Michael Nardone, Patrick Nickleson, Skeena Reece, Dylan Robinson, Shelly Rosenblum, and Charlene Vickers with Claudia Fernandez.

PUBLISHING AS PROTOCOL: AN EPILOGUE

Beth Bouloukos and Carin Kuoni

As we consider the protocols shared within the pages of this book, the quest for accessibility looms large over our joint effort. As publishers at higher education institutions—the Vera List Center for Art and Politics is part of The New School, and Amherst College Press is a unit of Amherst College—the primary goal of all our activities is to better understand the world in order to contribute to more just communities and to share what we are learning in such abundance with you, the reader.

At the conclusion of the two-year transdisciplinary research initiative into protocols directed and curated by the Vera List Center, we turn to the task of knowledge distribution to ask ourselves about the protocols for making knowledge available. How do we accommodate interdisciplinary epistemologies and different ways of being in the world? Given that the technology of the printed book is over five hundred years old, what does the page still allow us to do that no other medium can? What other platforms are now available and what do they afford us? How can we accommodate different learners, and how do we cease perpetuating extractive conventions of knowledge production and distribution?

Looking into the mirror, so to speak, we engage here with some of these necessary questions.

As educational institutions, we set out to ensure that the research we support and generate is as accessible as possible, to think expansively about what accessibility means in both concrete mechanical and larger societal aspects related to access. This approach is central to Amherst College Press's mission, and partnering with Fulcrum, a community-based, open-source publishing platform, has allowed the press to keep accessibility as a core value and design component. At the VLC, as a research center, these core values translate to understanding individual learning experiences as shared, but also distinct, endeavors between faculty and students, artists and viewers, presenters and the public. This requires precise attention to the context in which such mutual learning occurs, in order to avail ourselves of the pedagogically essential immediacy it offers. Once we step outside the metaphorical classroom, we put protocols in motion in order to welcome everyone into these encounters: we work across platforms; we adjust language, design, content, technology; and we insert periods of reflection and time to accommodate different time spans and evolutions in thinking. For both ACP and the VLC, we deal with the inherent push and pull of protocols embedded within larger academic structures.

There are also unique protocols embedded into the co-editing/co-publishing process. In the arts and humanities, there is an emphasis on single authored books so that university administrators can quantify publications for tenure and promotion purposes. This discourages collaborative and relational research practices while marginalizing the important voices of activists and artists who remain underrepresented in scholarly discourse. Amherst College Press was proud to publish

The Border of Lights Reader: Bearing Witness to Genocide in the Dominican Republic in 2021, edited by Megan Jeanette Myers and Edward Paulino, which offers multimodal and multilingual contributions from activists, artists, and poets on the dominant narratives surrounding the Dominican–Haitian border as a space of perpetual violence. Similarly, *Seeds of Change* (published in 2023 by the VLC and ACP) documents a twenty-year project by artist Maria Thereza Alves that traces centuries of transatlantic trade of enslaved African people through the cultivation of ballast flora, culled from seeds found at port cities in Europe and the Americas. The resulting book—a mix of Alves's writing and photographs alongside those of other artists, scholars, and botanists—captured how the relationship between diasporic people and plants transcends borders, encapsulated in the budding beauty of these displaced flowers as well as the dust of the archive. Both projects were complicated and complex, and sometimes university presses can be wary of books that might seem too time consuming. Traditional university presses are nonprofit businesses but they are still businesses. They are market based and have had much of their financial support from their home institutions dwindle or disappear over the years, at a time when they need book sales more than ever to survive.

This is why models of institutionally supported open access publishing are so essential and challenge many aspects of late capitalism. We witness this in the restricted access to libraries more locally, or censorship of political critique worldwide. Although our organizations are housed within higher education institutions, we are not defined by the number of titles we publish or the projects we take on. Strictly market-based presses or art organizations often have to pass on projects, even if they are committed to the topics and/or methodology. As publishers, we are interested in publications that emerge from multilayered contexts. We have the possibility of assembling simultaneously a multiplicity of perspectives that are relevant to different readers.

This leads us to the question of peer review—what it is, and who it serves. The genesis of peer review has, at its core, a goal completely antithetical to accessibility: that of gatekeeping. It has served to keep the voices of marginalized groups out of the scholarly conversation. In choosing peer reviewers for *As for Protocols* we discussed issues related to representation and equity, trying to determine who the authors' peers really are and who might best be able to offer unbiased feedback that will improve the text. Historically, there have been unspoken standards in scholarly publishing that have encouraged the use of "expert" peer reviewers who are exclusively post-tenure at research-intensive institutions and top liberal arts colleges and have published at least one scholarly book in the field. This is changing, and we would like to think that, at ACP and the VLC, we have expanded our notions about who makes a desired peer reviewer and what the role of such a reader can be.

We complement this with feedback from peer reviewers within authors' fields so that they have a multiplicity of perspectives when undertaking a revision plan. We want peer review to really serve our authors and their projects and not just take on a role of credentialing.

Taking the topic of protocols at its most radical form of collective intervention, we had hoped to push the standards of peer review even further with this volume. We discussed undertaking a type of peer-to-peer review where the process would be captured in writing and excerpts would be included in the book itself. There are great models for this, especially in the fields of film and media studies. Such an approach reflects a commitment to enhance the range of voices and perspectives involved in a book's conceptualization and editing. Unfortunately, we simply didn't have the resources to do so for this volume, but we hope to see this type of collaborative peer review in the future, in our books as well as those of other publishers. An open peer review process would help us practice our goal of process transparency.

This book, ultimately, speaks to modes of communication, of reception and transmission, and technology is a fundamental part of this process. But we can't discuss technology without discussing accessibility. Design-heavy manuscripts have many elements that cannot be read by screen readers and cannot be made into EPUB files, which are the most accessible digital publication. For this book, we decided to produce two separate versions and make them available. One is a designed PDF fixed layout—a version that mirrors the printed book and foregrounds the design as a protocol-related feature—and the other is an EPUB file that does not have many of the design features, but it includes all the text of the book while still being extremely accessible to assisted reading devices.

Attention to the mechanical aspects of accessibility enables us to reach the widest possible audiences, a goal we share as a fully open access press and a nonprofit research center. Again, as with other aspects of our respective models, that can be more cumbersome, costly, and time consuming, but our mission is to provide a more equitable experience for everyone. This means that our standard is to provide intersemiotic translation whenever possible. This traversal between the written, the visual, the oral/aural, the gestural, or the kinesic frames our respective and joint practices as publishers.

As new modes of political engagement in art and society reveal themselves, publishing, too, is at a crossroad. As we continue building and navigating our own publishing protocols, we're apt to be able to share what we learn with more readers, in more ways, more consistently, and more unexpectedly. To develop such multipronged approaches within our own organizations and witness them among our peers is enormously exciting and affirming. What we've learned from this volume is that a protocol—a form embedded in the origins of publishing itself as a medium—can be unbound from any particular monovocal convention.

CONTRIBUTOR BIOGRAPHIES

Salome Asega is an artist and researcher exploring models for technology that are cooperative, distributed, and people-centered. She is the director of NEW INC, an art, design, and technology incubator program at the New Museum that offers artists professional development, mentorship, and shared workspace. She sits on the boards of Eyebeam, the National Performance Network, and the School for Poetic Computation. She has exhibited in numerous museums and shows, including the 11th Shanghai Biennale, the Museum of Modern Art, August Wilson Center, and the Munch Museum.

Carolina Caycedo is a Colombian multidisciplinary artist living in Los Angeles. Informed by Indigenous and feminist epistemologies, process and participation are central to Caycedo's practice as she contributes to the reconstruction of environmental and historical memory, a fundamental space for climate and social justice. Caycedo is a 2023–2024 Soros Arts Fellow and a 2023–2024 Getty Research Institute Artist in Residence. She was a 2020–2022 Borderlands Fellow at the Vera List Center for Art and Politics at The New School and the Center for Imagination in the Borderlands at Arizona State University.

Raven Chacon is a composer, performer, and installation artist born at Fort Defiance, Navajo Nation. A recording artist over the span of twenty-two years, Chacon has appeared on over eighty releases on national and international labels. He has exhibited, performed, or had works performed at LACMA, the Whitney Biennial, Borealis Festival, SITE Santa Fe, the Kennedy Center, and more. As an educator, Chacon is the senior composer mentor for the Native American Composer Apprentice Project (NACAP). In 2022, he was awarded the Pulitzer Prize in Music for his composition *Voiceless Mass*, and in 2023 was awarded the MacArthur Fellowship.

Re'al Christian is a writer and editor based in Queens, New York. She is the Assistant Director of Editorial Initiatives at the Vera List Center for Art and Politics, where she manages and edits the center's publishing projects, including anthologies, artist books, exhibition booklets, the digital publishing series *Post/doc,* and publishing related programs. She is the co-editor of Maria Hupfield's *Breaking Protocol*, published by the Vera List Center and Inventory Press. As a writer, her work has appeared in *Art in America*, *Artforum*, *BOMB Magazine*, *The Brooklyn Rail*, *Frieze*, and *ART PAPERS*, where she is a Contributing Editor. She has written texts for numerous catalogues and anthologies, including *Track Changes: A Handbook for Art Criticism* (Paper Monument 2023), among others. She received her MA in Art History from Hunter College. She holds a bachelor's degree from New York University, where she double majored in art history and media, culture, and communication.

Jesse Chun is an artist based between Seoul and New York City. Chun's immersive poetics in moving image, drawing, sculpture, and installation address language—invoking alternate semiotics and cosmologies of meaning, time, and the untranslatable. Chun's work has been presented in solo exhibitions at Commonwealth and Council, Los Angeles (2024) and the 12th Seoul Mediacity Biennale (2023). Group exhibitions include SculptureCenter, New York; The Drawing Center, New York; Ballroom Marfa, Texas (United States); Museum of Contemporary Art Toronto (Canada); the Nam June Paik Art Center (South Korea); Whitechapel Gallery, London (United Kingdom), among others. Chun's work is in the collections of Seoul Museum of Art (Korea); Museum of Modern Art Library, New York; Smithsonian Institution, Washington, DC; Metropolitan Museum of Art Library, New York; and KADIST (France/United States), among others.

Asia Dorsey is a bioregional herbalist in Denver, Colorado. Beyond her formal education in food studies, nutrition and global public health Asia has apprenticed with elders in India, Ghana, New Zealand, New York, and more to discern a practice of herbal medicine as a people's medicine. In 2020, she enlivened the traditional wisdom of her elders and founded Bones Bugs and Botany, a radical organization committed to seeding embodied liberation through food and herbal medicine education. Dorsey extends her work with physical bodies to heal the culture and body politics of organizations as an organizational consultant with Regenerate Change. Find her on the *Petty Herbalist* podcast helping her people to rise together in the power that is their birthright and at www.bonesbugsandbotany.com.

Taraneh Fazeli is an Iranian American curator, educator, and cultural organizer. Before becoming an independent curator, she worked at arts organizations such as *Artforum*, e-flux, Triple Canopy, and the New Museum. Her work is rooted at the intersection of the disability, diasporic, queer, and creative communities that she belongs to. She lectures extensively on time, accessibility, ableism, equity, and care, and has written on these topics for publications including *Artforum*, *Art in America*, *Hyperallergic*, and *Flash Art*. With Cannach MacBride, she is co-editing a field guide rooted in her recent peripatetic group exhibition series *Sick Time, Sleepy Time, Crip Time: Against Capitalism's Temporal Bullying*, which addressed the politics of disability, health, race, and care (2016–2020).

Pablo Helguera, a native of Mexico City, is a New York-based artist whose work spans from photography to drawing, performance to installation. His work has been extensively exhibited internationally and reviewed by the *New York Times*, *Art in America*, *Artforum*, *Flash Art*, *Tema*

Celeste, and *Art Nexus*, among others. Helguera has worked for over fifteen years in US museums. He has written four books: *Endingness*, *Las Brujas de Tepoztlán*, *The Pablo Helguera Manual of Contemporary Art Style*, and a novel, *The Boy Inside the Letter*. He is represented by Enrique Guerrero Gallery in Mexico City. He received a BFA from the School of Art Institute of Chicago.

Maria Hupfield merges performance art, design, and sculpture, drawing from Indigenous storytelling traditions through art, scholarship, and collaboration. The inaugural ArtworxTO Legacy Artist in Residency with the city of Toronto, Hupfield is a recipient of Hnatyshyn Mid-career Award for Outstanding Achievement and Toronto Friends of the Visual Arts Artist Prize, among others. Her work has been exhibited, performed, and collected across North America. Hupfield is an urban member of the Anishinaabe Nation belonging to Wasauksing First Nation, Ontario. She is the Canadian Research Chair of Transdisciplinary Indigenous Art and Assistant Professor at the University of Toronto Mississauga. She is the editor of *Breaking Protocol* (Inventory Press and the Vera List Center for Art and Politics) and was a 2020–2022 Borderlands Fellow at the Vera List Center and the Center for Imagination in the Borderlands.

Born and raised in Nigeria, **Emmanuel Iduma** is a writer whose work spans fiction, memoir, and criticism. He is the author of two acclaimed books of nonfiction, the travelogue *A Stranger's Pose* (2018) and the memoir *I Am Still with You* (2023). His honors include the Windham-Campbell Prize for Literature, C/O Berlin Prize for Theory, and the Irving Sandler Award for New Voices in Criticism by AICA-USA. In 2020, he was recognized in *Apollo International Art Magazine*'s "40 under 40 Africa" for the broad social impact of his work. He is based in Lagos, Nigeria, and Norwich, United Kingdom.

Nadir Jeevanjee studies the physics of clouds, radiation, and climate. He is currently a staff scientist at the Geophysical Fluid Dynamics Laboratory in Princeton, New Jersey, a climate modeling center. He holds a PhD in physics from UC Berkeley.

Carin Kuoni is a curator and writer whose work examines how contemporary artistic practices reflect and shape social, political, and cultural conditions. She is Senior Director/Chief Curator of the Vera List Center for Art and Politics at The New School and Assistant Professor of Visual Studies. She has curated numerous transdisciplinary exhibitions and is editor or co-editor of ten books, among them *Energy Plan for the Western Man: Joseph Beuys in America*; *Considering Forgiveness*; *Entry Points: The Vera List Center Field Guide on Art and Social Justice*; *Assuming Boycott: Resistance, Agency, and Cultural Production*. Most recently, she co-edited

Studies into Darkness: On the Perils and Promise of Freedom of Speech and *Maria Thereza Alves: Seeds of Change* for the Vera List Center and Amherst College Press. For the Prince Claus Fund, she was editorial director of *Forces of Art: Perspectives from a Changing World*.

Lupita Limón Corrales is a poet, educator, organizer, language justice interpreter, and karaoke DJ based in Los Angeles. Her poetry can be found in dozens of zines and handmade books; on Dublab and Lower Grand Radio; and in *Dryland*, *Protean Magazine*, *Longreads*, and *Huizache*. Her first book *ESTA BOCA ES MIA* was published by nueoi press in spring 2024.

Cannach MacBride is a white Scottish artist. Their PhD research at Creative Research into Sound Arts Practice, London, focuses on more-than-sonic listening awareness and regimes of intelligibility within listening practices. With Taraneh Fazeli, they are co-editing a book called *Sick Time, Sleepy Time, Crip Time: Against Capitalism's Temporal Bullying*, which shares practices for co-creating accessible worlds through art, culture, and organizing. Recent writing appears in *The Climate Justice Code* (Casco Art Institute 2023) and is forthcoming in *Bodies of Sound* edited by Irene Revell and Sarah Shin for Silver Press. They teach writing and research methodologies at Piet Zwart Institute, Rotterdam.

Mary Maggic is a Chinese American artist and researcher working within the fuzzy intersections of body politics and capitalist ecological alienations. Based in Vienna since 2017, Maggic frequently uses biohacking as a xeno-feminist practice of care that serves to demystify invisible lines of molecular biopower. After completing their masters at MIT Media Lab (Design Fiction) in 2017, their project *Open Source Estrogen* was awarded Honorary Mention at the Prix Ars Electronica in Hybrid Arts, and in 2019 they completed a ten-month Fulbright residency in Yogyakarta, Indonesia, on the relationship between Javanese mysticism and the plastic pollution crisis. Maggic is a recipient of the 2022 Knight Arts + Tech Fellowship, and they are a current member of the online network Hackteria: Open Source Biological Art and the Asian feminist collective Mai Ling Vienna.

Shannon Mattern is the Penn Presidential Compact Professor of Media Studies at the University of Pennsylvania. From 2004 to 2022, she served in the Department of Anthropology and the School of Media Studies at The New School in New York City. Her writing and teaching focus on media architectures and information infrastructures. She has written books about libraries, maps, and urban intelligence; she serves as president of the board of the Metropolitan New York Library Council;

and she contributes a column about urban data and mediated spaces to Places Journal. You can find her at www.wordsinspace.net.

V. Mitch McEwen leads the Harlem-based Atelier Office. McEwen also teaches at Princeton University's School of Architecture, where she directs the architecture and technology research group Black Box, exploring biomaterials and algorithmic processes in design and construction. She is one of ten co-founders of the Black Reconstruction Collective. McEwen's design work has been commissioned by the Museum of Modern Art and the Venice Architecture Biennale US Pavilion, as well as awarded grants from the Graham Foundation, Knight Foundation, and New York State Council on the Arts.

Rashaun Mitchell is a Guggenheim Fellow and recipient of the New York Dance and Performance ("Bessie") Award for "Outstanding Emerging Choreographer." He has received several Princess Grace Awards, a Foundation for Contemporary Art "Grant to Artist," and a Bessie Award for "Sustained achievement in the work of Merce Cunningham" (2004–2012). Mitchell's choreographic work with ongoing collaborator, Silas Riener, involves the building of collaborative worlds through improvisational techniques, digital technologies, and material construction. Since 2010 they have created over twenty-five multidisciplinary dance works in venues such as the Brooklyn Academy of Music, Barbican Centre, and the Walker Arts Center.

Romy Opperman is assistant professor of philosophy at the New School for Social Research, New York City, and is originally from London. Romy's research centers on feminist Africana, Indigenous, and decolonial thinkers to foreground their importance for liberated climate futures and considers issues of racism and colonialism in environmental and climate justice. Recent publications include: "Sylvia Wynter's Caribbean Critical Theory," in *Creolizing Critical Theory: New Voices in Caribbean Philosophy*, and "The Need for a Black Feminist Climate Justice: A Case of Haunting Ecology and Eco-Deconstruction," in *CR: The New Centennial Review*. Romy is writing a book tentatively titled "Groundings: Black Ecologies of Freedom."

Rasheedah Phillips is a queer housing advocate, parent, writer, interdisciplinary artist, and cultural producer whose work explores the construct of time, temporalities, and community futurisms through a Black futurist cultural lens and experience. Phillips's writing and artwork has appeared in *The Funambulist Magazine*, *e-flux Architecture*, *Flash Art Magazine*, *Philadelphia Inquirer*, *Recess Arts*, and more. Phillips is the founder of The AfroFuturist Affair, founding member of Metropolarity Queer Speculative Fiction Collective, co-founder of

Black Quantum Futurism, co-creator of the award-winning Community Futures Lab, and creator of the Black Women Temporal Portal and Black Time Belt projects. As part of BQF and as a solo artist, Phillips has been awarded an Arts at CERN Collide Artists Residency, Vera List Center Fellowship, Creative Capital Award, United States Artist, among others, and has exhibited, presented at, been in residence, and performed at Institute of Contemporary Art London, Philadelphia Museum of Art, Serpentine Gallery, Red Bull Arts, Chicago Architecture Biennial, Counterpublic, Manifesta 13 Biennale, documenta fifteen, and more.

Eriola Pira is a researcher and curator. She is the Curator and Director of Programs at the Vera List Center for Art and Politics at The New School, where she organizes and co-curates across the center's programs and initiatives. She works closely with artists to present new ideas and work on art and its politics, including exhibitions, performances, and publications. She's conceived and organized residency and fellowship programs, conferences, publications, and solo and group exhibitions at Art in General, NARS Foundation, and The Foundation for Culture and Society, where she held previous positions. She's contributed to and collaborated with institutions worldwide on exhibitions, symposia, and special projects. Her work has been published and featured in catalogues and publications such as the *New York Times*, *Hyperallergic*, *BOMB Magazine*, and *Artforum*. She has served as editor for *Guernica* and has guest edited issues of *Kosovo 2.0* magazine. A native of Albania, Pira has an MA in visual culture theory from New York University.

Silas Riener is a New York Dance and Performance ("Bessie") Award-winning performer and graduate of Princeton University, with an MFA from New York University's Tisch School of the Arts. A member of the Merce Cunningham Dance Company from 2007–2012, he continues to teach Cunningham Technique and stage new interventions with Cunningham choreography. Riener and his ongoing choreographic collaborator, Rashaun Mitchell, are 2023 Creative Capital Award recipients. Their physical practice synthesizes improvisation, formal dance training, athletic sports, and building and construction. They have been artists in residence at institutions such as Center for Ballet and the Arts, Lower Manhattan Cultural Council, the National Center for Choreography at the University of Akron, the Maggie Allesee National Center for Choreography, and Headlands Center for the Arts.

Robert Sember is an educator who has taught most recently at The New School's Eugene Lang College and with the Alabama Prison Arts and Education Program's Higher Education in Prison initiative, a college degree program for people incarcerated in two prisons in Alabama. As a member of the international sound art collective, Ultra-red, Robert received a 2009–2011 Vera List Center Fellowship. This provided him the opportunity to help establish Vogue'ology, a popular/political education initiative by and for members of New York City's multigenerational majority Black and Latinx queer House and Ballroom community.

Leanne Betasamosake Simpson is a Michi Saagiig Nishnaabeg writer, musician, intellectual, and member of Alderville First Nation. She is the author of eight books, including the novel *Noopiming: A Cure for White Ladies and Rehearsals for Living*, co-authored with Robyn Maynard.

Founded in 1994 by two AIDS activists, **Ultra-red** has expanded over the years to include activists and organizers from a variety of social movements in Los Angeles, New York City, and abroad. Members organize around concerns related to migrant rights, the HIV/AIDS crisis, housing justice, and anti-racism. The collective has partnered with numerous community-based organizations and movement groups, including Union de Vecinos in East Los Angeles and House Lives Matter in New York City. In art circles, Ultra-red is known for studying, developing, and testing procedures for collective listening that contribute directly to political struggles.

Underground Resistance, a techno music collective and label, was co-founded by Jeff Mills and "Mad" Mike Banks in the late 1980s. Currently led by Cornelius Harris, UR's work has always had a socially conscious message and "a militant, mysterious aesthetic" defined by the bandanas members wear while performing. Their project Submerge is a subterranean brick and mortar space that is part techno music history museum, part record store, and part site for workshops and classes. It pays homage to the rich history of Detroit techno, a specific genre of electronic dance music produced in the Motor City in the 1980s and 1990s.

VERA LIST CENTER FOR ART AND POLITICS

The Vera List Center for Art and Politics is an artist-focused research center and public forum for art, culture, and politics. It was established at The New School in 1992—a time of rousing debates about freedom of speech, identity politics, and society's investment in the arts. A leader in the field, the center is a nonprofit that catalyzes and supports politically engaged art, public scholarship, and research throughout the world. It fosters vibrant and diverse communities of artists, scholars, and policymakers who take creative, intellectual, and political risks to bring about positive change.

We champion the arts as expressions of the political moments from which they emerge and consider the intersection between art and politics the space where new forms of civic engagement must be developed. We are the only university-based institution committed exclusively to leading public research on this intersection. Through public programs and the VLC Seminars, the international Jane Lombard Prize for Art and Social Justice, artist and student fellowships, and publications and exhibitions that probe some of the pressing issues of our time, we curate and support new roles for the arts and artists in advancing social justice.

Every two years, the center identifies a research topic of particular urgency—our Focus Theme—that informs timely and expansive investigations and frames everything we do. In recent years, the Focus Themes have investigated such provocative concepts as *Homeland* when, in the aftermath of 9/11, the US Department of Homeland Security was founded. *Considering Forgiveness* illuminated transitional justice systems; *Thingness* examined the entanglement of living and nonliving matter; *Post-Democracy* confronted both the promises and disillusions of the condition of democracy, including the repercussions of *Citizens United v. Federal Election Commission*; and *If Art Is Politics* posited art as a political practice with its own opportunities of political validation, formulated in response to the radical contestation of the state of politics following the 2016 American presidential elections. At the time of this book's publication, the *Correction** Focus Theme explores the tension and discomfort found in the metaphorical, political, and social dimensions and implications of correction. *As for Protocols* was our 2020–2022 Focus Theme.

Vera List Center publications emerge from our Focus Themes. They respond to and nurture a thriving field of politically engaged art practices worldwide. With initiatives including anthologies, monographs, artist books, catalogues, and digital projects, our publishing work provides a space for writers, artists, designers, and scholars of all career stages who are committed to advancing the scholarly and creative dialogue on art and social justice through collaborative, creative, experimental, and urgent critical discourse.

As for Protocols is the ninth book published by the Vera List Center, following *Considering Forgiveness* (2009), *Speculation, Now*

(2015, co-published with Duke University Press), *Entry Points: The Vera List Center Field Guide on Art and Social Justice* (2015, co-published with Duke University Press), *Assuming Boycott: Resistance, Agency, and Cultural Production* (2017, co-published with OR Books), *ART, An Index to (see also POLITICS): 25 Years of Vera List Center Fellowships* (2018), *Studies into Darkness: The Perils and Promise of Freedom of Speech* (2022, co-published with Amherst College Press), *Maria Thereza Alves: Seeds of Change* (2023, co-published with Amherst College Press), and *Breaking Protocol* (2023, co-published with Inventory Press).

Part of a multiyear partnership, *As for Protocols* is the third title co-published by the Vera List Center and Amherst College Press. All titles under this imprint are available to purchase in print and are available for free digitally worldwide through the open access platform Fulcrum.

ACKNOWLEDGMENTS AND CREDITS

As for Protocols captures the reflections, artworks, analyses, scores, and ideas of twenty-four contributors, culled from two years of programming and artist fellows' commissions by the Vera List Center. The wealth of perspectives speaks to the Vera List Center's inquisitive nature but more so to the range of ideas on protocols and the recognition of their ubiquitous power and presence. Mining protocols during the COVID-19 pandemic became, by default, a preoccupation for many—this book offers opportunities to pursue some of the most liberatory and empowering protocols encountered.

Our most sincere thank you goes to the contributors to As for Protocols: Salome Asega, Carolina Caycedo, Raven Chacon, Jesse Chun, Asia Dorsey, Taraneh Fazeli and Cannach MacBride, Pablo Helguera, Emmanuel Iduma, Mary Maggic, Shannon Mattern, V. Mitch McEwen and Nadir Jeevanjee, Rashaun Mitchell and Silas Riener, Romy Opperman, Rasheedah Phillips, Leanne Betasamosake Simpson and Maria Hupfield, Ultra-red and Robert Sember, and Underground Resistance's Cornelius Harris and Nomadico (aka DJ Dex). Their uncompromising work is a lodestar for everything we do, and we are honored by their trust and collaboration and grateful for what we have learned on protocols at their sides.

Our publishing partnership with Amherst College Press has been a joy, made possible through the collaboration and insight of Director Beth Bouloukos and Acquisitions Editor Hannah Brooks-Motl. This book is indebted to our organizations' shared commitment to accessibility as a core value and practice in publishing and beyond. We would also like to acknowledge the support of Amherst's dedicated Editorial Board, the Chicago Distribution Center, Fulcrum, and Michigan Publishing Services, particularly digital publishing coordinator Katie Rokakis.

We are grateful to our designer Pacific, especially Founders Elizabeth Karp-Evans and Adam Turnball, and their team members, Alexander Lavertue and Ayline Le Sourd, for a book that captures the essence of protocols, in content and form. Thank you to our printer Grafiche Veneziane for translating this design to the printed page, and to the attentiveness of our copyeditor and proofreader Jenn Bennett-Genthner.

Partner organizations for *As for Protocols* programs include Abrons Arts Center, New York; BAK–basis voor actuele kunst, Utrecht, Belgium; Brooklyn Army Terminal, New York; Castello di Rivoli, Torino, Italy; CEC ArtsLink, New York; UnionDocs, New York; the Clemente Soto Vélez Cultural & Educational Center, New York; and Weeksville Heritage Center, New York. We are especially grateful for the partnership with the Center for Imagination in the Borderlands at Arizona State University, directed by Natalie Diaz, on the Borderlands Fellowship, which has allowed us to envision and practice new protocols for collaboration and reciprocity.

At the Vera List Center, we owe our utmost gratitude to our colleagues Tabor Banquer, Camila Palomino, and Adrienne Umeh for their unique and invaluable contributions. Each team member lent crucial support to the research and production of the *As for Protocols* programming cycle, and their dedication, wisdom, and collaboration has carried over into the pages of this book. We are grateful to our intrepid team of student workers, past and present, who supported the *As for Protocols* programs: Aryana Ghazi Hessami, Art and Social Justice Fellow, provided invaluable research, particularly to fellows Adelita Husni Bey and Rasheedah Phillips. Tania Aparicio Morales, Graduate Student Fellow, did the same for our inaugural Boris Lurie Fellow Etcétera, and 2019–2021 Curatorial Assistant Heran Abate was integral to the Jane Lombard Prize for Art and Social Justice selection process. Additionally, Paria Ahmadi, Maryna Arabei, Joshua van Biema, Marianne Hughes, Nelly Kobanenko, Ash Moniz, and Molly Ragan, along with CCS Bard Summer Curatorial Fellow Sofia D'Amico and Justice Capital Initiative Student Fellow Gabriela Ramos supported the *As for Protocols* programs and documentation. VLC Programs Intern Bella De Angelis provided the image descriptions that appear throughout the book. Public Engagement Fellows Jan Tancinco and Sabrina Tenteromano assisted in the manuscript preparation.

The New School and the Schools of Public Engagement are our intellectual home, and we salute Executive Dean Mary Watson and thank her for her thoughtful guidance and extraordinary support over many years. Our appreciation also goes to the entire team in the Executive Dean's Office, especially Dansha Cai. We would also like to recognize the members of the VLC Academic Advisory Council, Ujju Aggarwal, Andrea Geyer, Martha Naarendorp, Cresa Pugh, Joshua Scannell, Aisha Servia, Jeannine Tang, and Fay Victor.

The book and the Focus Theme *As for Protocols* have received the generous support of the Vera List Center Board as well as the American Chai Trust, The Andy Warhol Foundation for the Visual Arts, Boris Lurie Art Foundation/The Schaina and Josephina Lurje Memorial Foundation, the Dayton Foundation, Ford Foundation, Italian Council, Kettering Fund, Mellon Foundation, Native Arts and Cultures Foundation, New York State Council on the Arts with the support of the Office of the Governor and the New York State Legislature, Sigrid Rausing Trust, and The New School. We are especially grateful for support received from the VLC Producers Council and Vera's List.

As for Protocols
Co-edited by Re'al Christian, Carin Kuoni, and Eriola Pira

Designer
Pacific
www.pacificpacific.pub

Copy editor and proofreader
Jenn Bennett-Genthner

Printer
Grafiche Veneziane, Italy

Co-published by the Vera List Center for Art and Politics at The New School and Amherst College Press.

Distributed by the Chicago Distribution Center.

Open access e-book available via Fulcrum.

ISBN
978-1-943208-98-2 (print)
978-1-943208-99-9 (open access)

Library of Congress Control Number
2024942502

Vera List Center for Art
and Politics
The New School
66 West 12th Street, Rm. 604
New York, NY 10011
www.veralistcenter.org

Amherst College Press
Frost Library
61 Quadrangle
Amherst, MA 01002
www.acpress.amherst.edu

The publication of *As for Protocols* has been made possible by the Vera List Center Board and support from American Chai Trust, The Andy Warhol Foundation for the Visual Arts, the Boris Lurie Art Foundation/The Schaina and Josephina Lurje Memorial Foundation, the Dayton Foundation, the Kettering Fund, Mellon Foundation, Native Arts and Cultures Foundation, New York State Council on the Arts with the support of the Office of the Governor and the New York State Legislature, and The New School.